Security Threat Mitigation and Response
Understanding Cisco Security MARS

Dale Tesch and Greg Abelar

Cisco Press

Cisco Press
800 East 96th Street
Indianapolis, Indiana 46240 USA

D0898858

Security Threat Mitigation and Response: Understanding Cisco Security MARS

Dale Tesch and Greg Abelar

Copyright © 2007 Cisco Systems, Inc.

Cisco Press logo is a trademark of Cisco Systems, Inc.

Published by:
Cisco Press
800 East 96th Street
Indianapolis, IN 46240 USA

Printed in the United States of America 1 2 3 4 5 6 7 8 9 0

First Printing   September 2006

ISBN: 1-58705-260-1

Library of Congress Cataloging-in-Publication Number: 2005936230

Trademark Acknowledgments

Warning and Disclaimer

Corporate and Government Sales

Cisco Press offers excellent discounts on this book when ordered in quantity for bulk purchases or special sales.

For more information please contact: **U.S. Corporate and Government Sales**   1-800-382-3419
corpsales@pearsontechgroup.com

For sales outside the U.S. please contact: **International Sales**   international@pearsoned.com

Feedback Information

At Cisco Press, our goal is to create in-depth technical books of the highest quality and value. Each book is crafted with care and precision, undergoing rigorous development that involves the unique expertise of members from the professional technical community.

Readers' feedback is a natural continuation of this process. If you have any comments regarding how we could improve the quality of this book or otherwise alter it to better suit your needs, you can contact us through email at feedback@ciscopress.com. Please make sure to include the book title and ISBN in your message.

We greatly appreciate your assistance.

Publisher	Paul Boger
Cisco Representative	Anthony Wolfenden
Cisco Press Program Manager	Jeff Brady
Executive Editor	Brett Bartow
Managing Editor	Patrick Kanouse
Development Editor	Jennifer Foster
Project Editor	Betsy Harris
Copy Editor	Krista Hansing
Technical Editors	Larry Boggis
	Francesca Martucci
	Jeff Walzer
	Jerry Zepp
Publishing Coordinator	Vanessa Evans
Designer	Louisa Adair
Composition	Interactive Composition Corporation
Indexer	Tim Wright

CISCO SYSTEMS

Corporate Headquarters
Cisco Systems, Inc.
170 West Tasman Drive
San Jose, CA 95134-1706
USA
www.cisco.com
Tel: 408 526-4000
　　800 553-NETS (6387)
Fax: 408 526-4100

European Headquarters
Cisco Systems International BV
Haarlerbergpark
Haarlerbergweg 13-19
1101 CH Amsterdam
The Netherlands
www-europe.cisco.com
Tel: 31 0 20 357 1000
Fax: 31 0 20 357 1100

Americas Headquarters
Cisco Systems, Inc.
170 West Tasman Drive
San Jose, CA 95134-1706
USA
www.cisco.com
Tel: 408 526-7660
Fax: 408 527-0883

Asia Pacific Headquarters
Cisco Systems, Inc.
Capital Tower
168 Robinson Road
#22-01 to #29-01
Singapore 068912
www.cisco.com
Tel: +65 6317 7777
Fax: +65 6317 7799

Cisco Systems has more than 200 offices in the following countries and regions. Addresses, phone numbers, and fax numbers are listed on the
Cisco.com Web site at www.cisco.com/go/offices.

Argentina • Australia • Austria • Belgium • Brazil • Bulgaria • Canada • Chile • China PRC • Colombia • Costa Rica • Croatia • Czech Republic
Denmark • Dubai, UAE • Finland • France • Germany • Greece • Hong Kong SAR • Hungary • India • Indonesia • Ireland • Israel • Italy
Japan • Korea • Luxembourg • Malaysia • Mexico • The Netherlands • New Zealand • Norway • Peru • Philippines • Poland • Portugal
Puerto Rico • Romania • Russia • Saudi Arabia • Scotland • Singapore • Slovakia • Slovenia • South Africa • Spain • Sweden
Switzerland • Taiwan • Thailand • Turkey • Ukraine • United Kingdom • United States • Venezuela • Vietnam • Zimbabwe

About the Authors

Greg Abelar has been an employee of Cisco Systems, Inc., since December 1996. He was an original member of the Cisco Technical Assistance Security Team, helping to hire and train many of the engineers. He has held various positions in both the Security Architecture and Security Technical Marketing Engineering teams at Cisco. Greg is the primary founder and project manager of Cisco's Written CCIE Security exam. Before his employment at Cisco, Greg worked at Apple Computer, Inc., for eight years as a TCP/IP, IPX, and AppleTalk cross-platform escalation engineer. At Apple, he also served as a project leader in the technical platform deployment for the Apple worldwide network. From 1991 to 1996, Greg worked as both a systems programmer and an IT manager for Plantronics, Inc. From 1985 to 1991, Greg was employed by the County Bank of Santa Cruz, where he worked as an applications programmer. This book is Greg's second authorship of a technical publication; the first was a very successful and uniquely presented publication, also from Cisco Press, titled *Securing Your Business with Cisco ASA and PIX Firewalls* (2005). Besides authoring Cisco Press publications, he was a co-author of Version 2 of the premier Internet security architecture whitepaper, "SAFE: A Security Blueprint for Enterprise and Networks." His credentials also include technical editing of five security publications by Cisco Press. Greg lives with his wife, Ellen, and three children, Jesse, Ethan, and Ryan, in Aptos, California.

Dale Tesch is a product sales specialist for the CS-MARS product line for Cisco Systems' US AT Security Team. Dale came to Cisco Systems through the acquisition of Protego Networks in February 2005 and has held the primary responsibilities of training Cisco's Sales and Engineering team on SIMS and CS-MARS and providing advanced sales support to Cisco customers. While at Protego Networks, he was responsible for sales and engineering in parts of the United States, Canada, and Europe. Before Protego Networks, he was an AT security engineer for Cisco Systems' U.S. Channels Organization. Dale was the founding team leader of the U.S. Channels Security Technical Advisory Team and came to Cisco originally in 2000. Before Cisco, he was the senior systems engineer at Vitts Networks, a New England–based DSL provider. Previously, Dale spent ten years in the U.S. Navy Submarine Force and is a veteran of Desert Storm. He lives in Madbury, New Hampshire, with his fiancée, Janet, and their six children, Scott, Alex, Isabella, Douglas, Andrew, and Kristyn. Dale has published several articles on SIMs, security policy, and wireless security and has been a technical editor for Cisco Press. Dale also speaks as an industry expert and trainer for various technical seminars. He holds CCNP and CISSP certifications and is a graduate of Southern New Hampshire University.

About the Technical Reviewers

Larry Boggis, CCIE No. 4047, is a senior security consultant with Priveon, Inc., based in RTP, North Carolina. He has a strong and experienced background in host and network security design and implementation. At Priveon, a premier U.S. security consulting organization, Larry's focus is on security design, consulting, and research. Larry previously supported large enterprise security projects throughout the United States as a security consulting systems engineer for Cisco Systems for more than eight years. Larry has a CCIE in Routing and Switching and holds many network and security certifications, including CISSP. He is an avid cyclist and also enjoys camping, hiking, and fly-fishing in his downtime. Larry's greatest joy comes from his wife, Michelle, and their two children, Logan and Alex.

Francesca Martucci is the lead technical marketing engineer (TME) for CS-MARS. She played an instrumental role in the support of the product after its acquisition. Francesca has a strong background across all the different security technologies. She has been working at Cisco for more than six years within the Security Technology Group, covering different roles as test engineer first and TME later.

Jeff Walzer, CCDP, CCNP, CISSP, is a security administrator for a retail company.

Jerry Zepp, CISSP, works in information security for SEI Investments, in Oaks, Pennsylvania. He has managed incident detection/response and computer forensics practices for multiple organizations during his 16-year career in information security. His experience includes eight years with the National Security Agency and more than six years in the financial industry. His focus has been the development and management of multitool security solutions that provide beginning-to-end detection, analysis, response, and follow-up to all forms of system misuse and criminal behavior involving technical systems.

Dedications

This book is dedicated to the thousands of security analysts and security incident responders who have worked tirelessly over the years dedicating themselves to a single task, ensuring that attacks against their employers are recognized, mitigated, and cleaned up. Hopefully, you will be as excited as we are that there is a tool that can help you do your job exponentially faster and more accurately. Keep your heads up and know that there are people out there who are trying to make your job easier.

—Dale and Greg

Acknowledgments

The information contained in Appendix G was derived from data provided by Aji Joseph, manager of software development for CS-MARS.

From Greg Abelar: First of all, I would like to thank the two people who have been the most involved in making this book a reality: Brett Bartow from Cisco Press identified the market and motivated me to get involved in this project. Dale Tesch overcame substantial hurdles to help bring this book to press and provided the much-needed technical punch for this publication. Putting our personal strengths together provided an excellent formula to make this book happen. Dale, thanks for your time and effort.

Second, I would like to thank some folks inside the Cisco family for their support, encouragement, and technical input, helping to make this book successful. My manager, Larry Battle, supported my writing efforts from day one; my friend and colleague Ben Cruz provided me with the CS-MARS hardware used for testing and screenshots; and my friend and colleague Francesca Martucci provided much-needed support and technical information. I'd also like to thank Gary Halleen for his encouragement of and feedback to Dale and me during the development of this book.

Also, a very special thanks to the technical editors for helping us ensure the accuracy of this book: Larry Boggis, Francesca Martucci, Jeff Walzer, and Jerry Zepp. Without the unique contributions from these folks, this book could have easily become just another in the long line of depthless technical books saturating the market today.

And, of course, the biggest thanks once again goes out to my family, who put up with my spending countless hours late into the night and on weekends to complete this book. My wife, Ellen, and my boys, Jesse, Ethan, and Ryan, patiently waited for Daddy to finish his silly work so he could come home and play! Thanks, guys.

From Dale Tesch: First and foremost, I would like to thank my fiancée, Janet Bilodeau, for her patience and support through some very difficult times for me. Without her, I could not have accomplished what I have over the past several years. Janet, I love you endlessly and thank you very much for being there for me! A very special thanks to Greg Abelar for his wonderful support, guidance, and patience in writing this book and turning me into an author! Thank you, Greg—you have taught me so much. The technical editors deserve a big "thank you" for taking the time to review this book and offer some great suggestions and input. I appreciate your contributions sincerely.

Next, some very special people merit some much-deserved appreciation. If it were not for the dedicated developers who worked more than 12 hours a day in designing and coding this product, it would not be as successful as it is today. Way to go, guys! The success behind CS-MARS as a product is driven by the following individuals: Partha, Imin, Irene, Phil, Aji, George, Fred, Azlina, Paul, Greg, Steve, and, last but *not* least, Garfield! You guys are the best—keep up the drive and passion. Never forget the Protego days.

On a final note, I owe a profound "thank you" to my family. They tolerated countless hours of me in my office typing away at night while giving me so much without asking for anything in return. Thank you, Janet, for bringing me coffee to keep me awake, and to Andrew and Kristyn for waiting ten extra minutes for me to hook up the GameCube. I love you all very much and thank you again.

This Book Is Safari Enabled

The Safari® Enabled icon on the cover of your favorite technology book means the book is available through Safari Bookshelf. When you buy this book, you get free access to the online edition for 45 days.

Safari Bookshelf is an electronic reference library that lets you easily search thousands of technical books, find code samples, download chapters, and access technical information whenever and wherever you need it.

To gain 45-day Safari Enabled access to this book:

- Go to http://www.ciscopress.com/safarienabled
- Complete the brief registration form
- Enter the coupon code 63C3-JVCD-WKMC-WNDB-ZU5K

If you have difficulty registering on Safari Bookshelf or accessing the online edition, please e-mail customer-service@safaribooksonline.com.

Contents at a Glance

Table of Contents

Foreword

Today's biggest challenge in computer security is dealing with the huge amounts of data that pour in from disparate and distributed sources. Gigabytes of firewall logs, intrusion detection system logs, and user activity logs are more than any human can expect to cope with or analyze; we need software layers to help sort through the mass of data and turn it into useful, actionable information. The notion of "actionable" information, in this context, is especially important. It's no longer enough to inform a security administrator, "Something suspicious happened on this host at 11:54 p.m." The threats are too complex and fast-moving for a human to be effective inside the response cycle. We need software that wraps the data analysis with a knowledge base of what are reasonable reactions to take to certain classes of events, so that an administrator is presented not merely with a problem diagnosis but also a resolution recommendation. That's what Cisco's MARS is all about—turning data into actionable information and recommendations.

Typically a technical book's foreword is a chance for someone who has read the book to ramble for a couple pages about some high-level topic, then end with a ringing exhortation to "buy and read this book!" For most of us, that adds nothing (except for two or three pages you can flip past), so I thought I'd approach this foreword a bit differently. To me, one of the things lacking in most technical books is a feeling for the authors themselves. Who are these guys? What motivated them to write this book? Besides, you probably didn't pick up this book because you wanted to read *my* pontifications—you wanted to see what Dale and Greg have to say!

Instead of my opinions, I thought I'd use this space to interview the authors about some of the things you *won't* find elsewhere in the book. Dear reader, let me introduce Dale Tesch, Jr, and Greg Abelar:

Marcus: *So CS-MARS is obviously a system in which you have a lot of time and energy invested. How did you first get involved with it, and what got you excited about it?*

Dale: I was first introduced to MARS while I was a security engineer for Cisco working with Channel Partners. I had a partner approach me looking for a solution that could help them deploy a security managed service to their customers. They had customers with all kinds of products and looked to Cisco to help them find a solution. Cisco did not have a product that could help them, so I started looking outside the Cisco product set. I turned to my fellow engineers in Cisco and discovered one of them left Cisco to start up Protego Networks. They had a product that may do what my Cisco Partners needed. I contacted him and fell in love with the product. As a security engineer I was very passionate about security technology that promised what it delivered, and MARS delivered what I needed and more. It filled a gap in the security market that no company was fulfilling. I knew it was going to take off! Protego MARS was so simple to operate yet very strong in SIM and behavioral analysis. It was making me so successful with our key security partners that I decided to leave Cisco and join Protego.

Greg: I first experienced CS-MARS when it was still part of a company called Protego. I was deeply involved in network intrusion prevention systems (IPS) at the time. IPSs have their strengths, but their value is diminished by the huge volume of noise and false positive alerts they generate. A friend of mine called me asking about a company called Protego that had a device that could supposedly reduce false positive alerts. Intrigued, I set out to find out a little bit about this technology. As luck would have it, the next day I saw some engineers testing a Protego box in the lab, so I hung out to see what the big deal was. Big deal, indeed. I saw a demo where they ran an attack that triggered a group of IPS alerts, but CS-MARS consolidated those alerts to a single event and also recommended a command to mitigate the attack. It did multidevice event consolidation and event correlation. It was easy to use and also made and deployed mitigation recommendations. The rest is history. I was hooked. Cisco acquired Protego, and the daily nightmare that security responders faced dealing with several thousand alerts was significantly reduced. They suddenly had a tool that improved their efficiency to a level that was staggering.

Marcus: *You're talking about a technology that sits right in the middle of the entire computer/network security problem—it's a lot to get a handle on! How did you figure out where to start?*

Greg: On the surface CS-MARS appears to be a tame animal. You launch the GUI, configure it, then off you go, right? Well, right but also wrong. Your question indicates there is much more to it than that, and you are correct. You can configure CS-MARS with a basic configuration and get some valuable data that will help you respond to threats. But to get the most out of your CS-MARS appliance, you need to have a good understanding of your network topology, your security devices, and how attacks work. Then you need to understand the capabilities of the CS-MARS product.

This book answers exactly this question. It not only addresses how to start working with CS-MARS, but it also addresses where you go after you have started. Looking at the book from a high level, we take the reader from the basics of security reporting and mitigation, explain any new terminology and technology used by CS-MARS, explain basic configurations, and then explain how to interpret incidents as they are reported. To simplify the learning experience for the reader, the book includes plenty of step-by-step guidelines as well as clearly explained technical tidbits to give you an excellent jumpstart into this technology.

Dale: Good old trial and error worked for me! You can take all kinds of advice, training courses, or pointers from the pro's, but until you get your feet wet in real operational networks with the technology, you can never get the insight and experience on how to solve business problems with it.

Marcus: *Dale, you say it's important to experiment. Do you remember any "AHA!" moments that you've had that really made things click for you? I've found with many of the products I've worked, sometimes you use it in a way that nobody expects, and it works great. It's always fun when you talk to the designers and say, "It's great for doing blah blah blah," and they respond, "Really!!? We never thought of that!"*

Dale: When I first joined Protego and really started working with MARS, I discovered the product was schizophrenic. Meaning, it had many personalities. The appliance was built for security threat detection, analysis, and mitigation, yet it could play many other roles in a network. Shortly before the acquisition by Cisco, I was in a VARS SOC. I was rather impressed by the facility they had and how automated it was. They were bragging about how they could manage it remotely from anywhere via the web. Their HVAC system, physical security system, and lighting systems were all automated and sent log data via SNMP. Just for show and tell and a little experiment, we configured the systems to report to MARS and built rules outlining normal behavior of temperatures, lighting, and physical access control. We began to design rules and alarms to go off when temps went out of range, visitors checked in but not out, and even when certain lights were turned on during odd hours. The VAR then took this to the company that sold them the building systems and they bought one for themselves. They are now positioning it as a monitoring solution for their building automation products. They recently installed one for an airport in Canada with three terminals and use it solely for building monitoring. Rather odd application, but it works great!

Marcus: *The idea of a piece of software recommending how to respond to an attack is interesting! I'm sure we can all imagine ways that could go horribly wrong—or be very comforting. What's your experience with that?*

Greg: This is a very important question that should be asked by every single customer before moving forward on a CS-MARS deployment. Obviously Cisco has a very high confidence that the quality of the decisions made by this software is accurate. The quality assurance cycle to ensure the software operates as advertised is immense. Probably the most comforting part of the way the software makes critical decisions is the fact that it correlates messages from several different security and network sources. The more sources correlated is directly related to more accurate and decisive decisions. True, a customer could find themselves in a position where very little information is being correlated, which could lead CS-MARS software to report false positives. To reduce the impact of this problem, CS-MARS engineers either will not make a mitigation recommendation or elect to only suggest mitigation commands and give the customer the final decision on whether to actually deploy the mitigation command. Regardless of these safeguards, my personal experience has been that the mitigation recommendations even in a minimally configured CS-MARS appliance have been extremely accurate.

Marcus: *One of the things I've heard a lot of authors say is that they learn much more in the process of writing a book than they ever expected. What's the biggest/most important lesson you've come away with from this experience?*

Dale: Marcus, this is so true and I never would have fully realized it unless I experienced it. Since I worked with the product since its infancy, I really thought I knew most of it. Writing this book opened my eyes to how much I didn't know. I have always been comfortable with explaining the technology to people and how they can use it. What I really didn't know is what made this thing really tick (the "secret sauce") and what it took to do it. Additionally, I learned what this could not do and how not to use it.

Greg: This is the second book I've authored. The lesson I learned in the first book held true while writing this book also. As a technical author I need to write about something that I believe in, and something that I feel will bring real value to people who read the book. CS-MARS is such a critical technology and can add so much value to security responders that it was very easy for me to stay motivated and bring this project to closure. I'm not fooling myself into believing that this book will be a best-seller and Dale and I will become famous because of it. However, I do feel confident that whoever reads this book will learn about CS-MARS and will be able to use it and add value to any security deployment.

Marcus: *So what's your favorite part of this book? What did you enjoy writing the most? If you could tell a reader, "Hey, whatever you do, make sure you read the part about XYZ!" what would it be?*

Dale: It would be Chapter 9. I had lots of flexibility on how to write the customer stories and no technical guidelines. So I was a bit more free in my approach to writing this chapter. What was fun was that I personally experienced every single story in this chapter, and they were amazing to experience. I really enjoyed telling about them. The disappointing part is that I had so many "cool" stories to tell about the success of the product but could only pick a few. I had a hard time deciding which ones to use. I would recommend everyone read this chapter, because it gives real-life examples of how this product really worked for all different kinds of customers. Readers can really understand the benefits of this product simply by identifying the stories to their own experiences.

Marcus: *Final word: What's the most important thing in security?*

Dale: Good qualified people with a plan! O.K. that is kind of two things, but they need to be together. No matter how you look at security (either network or physical security), the purposes of both are practically pointless unless you have motivated, well-trained people executing a well-written plan. I have consulted for very large firms who have some very sophisticated network security systems with no written security policy or business continuity plan. They spent millions of dollars on great product and people. They have talented individuals who could do just about anything, but no plan on how to use them or what to do if something goes wrong. I find that a lot of organizations, from governments to commercial business, implement security because they are being told to do so. When an organization is out to satisfy some piece of legislation that is poorly written to begin with, their focus tends to be on not getting in trouble instead of how to continue operations if something does go wrong. Security is hard to justify, and organizations need to look at it like insurance to protect their business instead of an operations expense chewing away at their revenues. Once they adopt this reasoning, they'll understand they need a POLICY to implement the insurance to protect their operations and a PLAN to make a claim on that POLICY for business continuity. Bottom line: no plan, no security.

Marcus: *Gentlemen, thank you! And thank you for taking the time to write this book.*

So there you have it, dear reader. Perhaps this little chat has given you a chance to get to know Dale and Greg a little bit. I've certainly enjoyed meeting them and reading this book, and I hope you will, too.

Marcus J. Ranum

July 26, 2006

Bellwether Farm, Morrisdale PA

Introduction

In today's network security environment, an epidemic of sorts exists. Many corporations understand that they need security devices to protect them from network-based attacks. The problem is, because security devices have been deployed, corporations blindly trust that they are doing their job and that threats are being stopped. This is the biggest fallacy in the network security world today. Hackers, of course, know this and design attacks to subvert existing security appliances by using valid protocols and valid network packets.

Enterprises and corporations now realize that to really provide effective protection for their networks, they need to take the next step and closely examine network infrastructure, host, application, and security events to determine whether an attack has exploited devices on their network.

The Cisco Security Monitoring, Analysis, and Response System (CS-MARS) is a network appliance that takes security deployment to the next tier and provides automated threat recognition and mitigation to the existing security and network deployment. In nearly every case, enterprises will realize substantial cost savings and drastically change the effectiveness of their security responders by electing to deploy CS-MARS.

CS-MARS consolidates and correlates security events and syslogs from the following Cisco and third-party hardware and software devices:

- Cisco and third-party network switches
- Cisco routers
- Cisco and third-party firewalls
- Cisco and third-party security appliances
- Cisco and third-party software-based security applications
- Industry-leading web servers
- Industry-leading application servers
- Windows and UNIX-style host operating systems
- Windows and UNIX-style network operating systems

The result of this consolidation and correlation is that CS-MARS accurately determines valid network and hosts attacks and then adds substantial value to that information by making recommendations on where you can mitigate these attacks on your network.

Goals and Methods

The primary objective of this book is to provide you with all the information that you need to understand, configure, and deploy your CS-MARS security appliance. The book also provides the following information:

- The risks involved with using the Internet to do business
- The advantages of transitioning from a security-reporting system to an all-inclusive security and network threat recognition and mitigation system
- How CS-MARS works from a technical and procedural standpoint

- How to configure and deploy CS-MARS in your network
- The potential return on investment resulting from a successful CS-MARS deployment

Who Should Read This Book?

This book will be of interest to the following sets of professionals:

- Security engineers
- Security analysts
- Security incident responders
- Managers responsible for evaluating corporate risk
- Network administrators
- Network engineers
- Operating systems administrators
- Application developers
- IT, network, and development managers

Even if you are an experienced security or network engineer, you will find value in this book because it encompasses leading-edge threat recognition and response technology not yet seen in today's security and network industry.

How This Book Is Organized

The book is divided into five distinct parts. Part I, "The Security Threat Identification and Response Challenge," is dedicated to helping you understand different technologies available for event consolidation and security reporting. This part of the book then explains the advantages of taking reporting a step farther and including threat recognition and response. Part II, "CS-MARS Theory and Configuration," guides you through the underlying technologies that enable CS-MARS to do its event consolidation, correlation, and threat recognition and response. Also included in this part is information on how to configure and deploy your CS-MARS device. Part III, "CS-MARS Operation," is a practical guide on how to operate CS-MARS and how to investigate and respond to detected threats. Part IV, "CS-MARS in Action," brings everything together. It provides real-life examples of how CS-MARS is deployed in different environments and how it is used to reduce or eliminate the impact of a threat. Following the main parts of the book is a comprehensive set of appendixes that provide general information about the product and also provide some Internet-based security references.

This book is intended to be read cover to cover, but it is flexible enough that you can choose to read an individual chapter and first understand that CS-MARS topic before moving on to employ the information found within as you see fit.

The book is organized as follows:

- **Part I, "The Security Threat Identification and Response Challenge"**—Establishes a knowledge of existing reporting systems and calls out the advantages of an all-inclusive threat recognition and response system such as CS-MARS. This part also includes return-on-investment information that you can realize by deploying CS-MARS in your network. Part I includes the following chapters:

— **Chapter 1, "Understanding SIM and STM"**—Explains the differences between a security information management (SIM) system and a security threat mitigation (STM) system. An STM is called out as a superior architecture because it includes information consolidated between security devices and your network infrastructure that can be used to help determine threats and to mitigate threats.

— **Chapter 2, "Role of CS-MARS in Your Network"**—Provides an overview of how to protect your network with a concept called defense-in-depth and explains how an STM system such as CS-MARS can extend that protection.

— **Chapter 3, "Deriving TCO and ROI"**—Uses some real-life examples to help you determine the cost of an attack if CS-MARS is deployed during a network attack versus the cost if CS-MARS is not deployed.

- **Part II, "CS-MARS Theory and Configuration"**—Explains the underlying technology that enables CS-MARS. It also provides a comprehensive step-by-step guide on how to deploy and configure CS-MARS in your network. Part II includes the following chapters:

— **Chapter 4, "CS-MARS Technologies and Theory"**—Explains the theory and technology that lives under the covers in a CS-MARS device.

— **Chapter 5, "CS-MARS Appliance Setup and Configuration"**—Offers a step-by-step guide explaining how to set up and configure a CS-MARS device out of the box and how to customize it for your environment.

— **Chapter 6, "Reporting and Mitigative Device Configuration"**—Acts as a step-by-step deployment guide explaining how to configure CS-MARS to communicate with your existing hosts, servers, network devices, security appliances, and other devices in your network. This includes not only configuration information for Cisco devices, but also configuration information for supported third-party devices.

- **Part III, "CS-MARS Operation"**—Explains how to use CS-MARS to investigate reported threats. Part III includes the following chapters:

— **Chapter 7, "CS-MARS Basic Operation"**—Explains how you use the CS-MARS device to investigate threats that are reported and how to use canned reports and queries to get additional information about events and devices in your network

— **Chapter 8, "Advanced Operation and Security Analysis"**—Explains how to use custom reports and custom queries to generate almost any useful combination of device and event information possible about your network and security events

- **Part IV, "CS-MARS in Action"**—Shares success stories from existing CS-MARS customers. Part IV includes the following chapter:

— **Chapter 9, "CS-MARS Uncovered"**—Shares stories from customers regarding how CS-MARS added value to their networks and, in one case, how CS-MARS even paid for itself "before" it was officially deployed on a customer network

- **Part V, "Appendixes"**—Provides valuable information that didn't fit within the context of the chapters of the book. Part V includes the following appendixes:

  — **Appendix A, "Useful Security Websites"**—Lists some of the authors' favorite websites that include information about attacks, attack tools, attack research, and general security information

  — **Appendix B, "CS-MARS Quick Data Sheets"**—Provides consolidated data sheets containing useful technical information about the CS-MARS product

  — **Appendix C, "CS-MARS Supplements"**—Includes worksheets that provide information useful for configuring and deploying CS-MARS

  — **Appendix D, "Command-Line Interface"**—Provides information about the commands that are available through the CS-MARS command-line interface

  — **Appendix E, "CS-MARS Reporting"**—Lists information about the canned reports available in CS-MARS 4.1

  — **Appendix F, "CS-MARS Console Access"**—Explains how to use a PC to connect to the CS-MARS serial console to access the CS-MARS command-line interface

  — **Appendix G, "CS-MARS Check Point Configuration"**—Provides critical information explaining how to configure your Check Point security appliance to communicate with your CS-MARS device

## PART I

The Security Threat Identification and Response Challenge

This chapter covers the following topics:

- Understanding Security Information Management (SIM) Legacy Threat Response
- Understanding the Unified Security Platform

## CHAPTER 1

Understanding SIM and STM

For a CxO, Security Manager, or Network Security Professional involved in today's industry, there is a growing need to understand the security information management (SIM) and security threat mitigation (STM) technologies. To most readers, it is apparent why security networking equipment is needed, but it is not obvious how to manage the vast amounts of data they produce.

In this chapter, you are introduced to SIM and STM technologies. STM technology is relatively new and is a subset of SIM. You will discover how both of these technologies help you manage networking security data, what their role is in your network, and why a proactive event-management solution is the most important element in completing a successful security framework. This chapter then examines the challenges of finding the right solution for your network and how Cisco Security Monitoring, Analysis, and Response System (CS-MARS) can aid in achieving your security objectives.

Understanding Security Information Management Legacy Threat Response

Security information management technologies strive to offer unification of network-, security-, and host-related data into a single tool. The technology was developed to ease the burden of network security personnel in filtering through massive amounts of log data so they can easily identify a security-related incident on the network and take action.

SIMs are designed to automate the collection of event data and help security personnel make sense of it. SIMs achieve this by applying the data received to correlation algorithms and normalizing the data from all different sources for a uniform appearance.

The SIM concept is explained in three different sections:

- Understanding Security Information Management
- Meeting the Needs of Industry Regulations
- Understanding the Unified Security Platform

Understanding Security Information Management

Most SIM offerings are software based and designed to operate on standard hardware platforms; however, recently a wave of optimized appliances tuned for performance has entered the market. SIMs have five core functions:

- Collect event data from reporting sources
- Store data for analysis, reporting, and archiving
- Correlate the data to show relationships
- Present the data for analysis
- Report on, alarm on, and/or notify about the data

These five functions are the core features of a SIM. Some manufacturers have developed the SIM into a very robust tool that incorporates many features and functions, although every aspect is categorized in the core functions listed.

The major differentiator among SIMs is architecture. The architecture of the SIM dictates how the five core functions are delivered. It is important for you to understand how a SIM delivers these functions so that you can fully grasp the complexity and the challenges faced with delivering and deploying the SIM technology.

This list describes each of the core functions:

- **Collection of event data**—Event data is collected from a source through either a "push" or a "pull" of the data. Pushing the data means that the source of the data sends it to the collection device. Pulling the data means that the collection device has the means of requesting the data from the source. Both of these methods of data collection can be accomplished through native functionality of the reporting device or with a software agent installed on the reporting device. It is important to mention that another method for event collection is data capture. This involves placing a packet-capture device inline to the data or through port mirroring. Regardless of the method, a device must transmit its event data for the collection to work.

- **Storage of event data**—For the SIM to process and retrieve the data as needed, it is necessary to store the event data for the SIM. The storage method depends on the philosophy used by the SIM manufacturer to accommodate long-term and short-term storage. Depending on which methods of storage are used, SIMs vary in how they approach event data storage. The most common method is to use a database because of the functionality databases offer a SIM in speed, high availability, and capacity. Other methods used are ASCII files, CSV files, or proprietary methods.

- **Correlation of event data**—Correlation of the event data is often referred to as the heart of the SIM. *The American Heritage Dictionary* defines *correlation* as the "relationship between two variables during a period of time, especially one that shows a close match between the variables' movements." Taking this context into consideration with event data, correlation exists when two pieces of data have a functional relationship with each other over time. This relationship can be defined by common fields contained in event data, such as Source IP, Port, or Destination. Thus, the true power of a SIM lies in its capability to correlate information to form a perspective that easily presents itself to an end user.

- **Presentation of event data**—This is typically achieved through user interfaces. SIMs vary in their approach to the presentation of the data through management console software, web UIs, and command-line interfaces. Regardless of the technique used, SIMs must enable an end user to look at the data and manipulate the data into different views for analysis. User interfaces often enable the user to command and control the SIM in addition to viewing the event data.

- **Reporting, alarming, and notification**—This is typically achieved through standard network-management techniques. Current reporting methods are conducted through text summarization of the data indexed on one of its variables or in a graphical format such as a pie chart or bar chart. Reports can be generated on a summary of occurrences over time, detailed raw event data, or near-real-time analysis of event data based upon a variable. Alarming is the capability to notify the end user of a specific value based upon a preset condition. Notification can be done through an audible alarm, a graphical indicator, an e-mail message, a text page, or an API developed to trigger a response by a specific device or application. It is important to note that as technology evolves, new methods of notifications will become available.

Now that you have discovered the core functions of a SIM, it is important for you to learn how a SIM delivers these functions. Figure 1-1 shows a model of the SIM and its functions.

Figure 1-1   *SIM Flow Model*

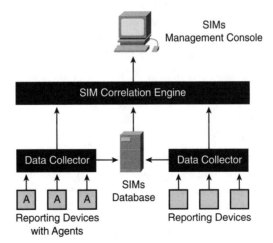

These components are part of most popular SIMs:

- **Event-reporting tools**—These are software programs installed on devices to transmit event data to a collector. In some implementations, a SIM can run on a standalone device, and a tool to support remote collectors might not be necessary.

- **Data collectors**—These are devices throughout your network where event data is sent for collection and parsing. To facilitate end-to-end communications and storage, the data must be sent to these storage media in a specific format.

- **Storage warehouse (database servers)**—These servers are typically commercially available databases that can store the vast amounts of data that have been collected and parsed.

- **Correlation engines**—These are software engines that correlate the data and manipulate it as directed through the management station or built-in algorithms. Correlation functions normally perform tasks such as grouping events based on various criteria such as time or similar events. When it is correlated, the information is easier to view for decision-making purposes.

- **Management station**—This is a software command center that provides a user interface to control the SIM and read, evaluate, and report its data.

A SIM deployment can consist of all these components as separate entities or a mixture of individual and combined entities on your network. Deployment scenarios in organizations that use SIM technologies vary widely, depending on factors such as budget, network design, manpower, and possibly security policy.

Meeting the Needs of Industry Regulations

Times have changed: The days of insecure networks or networks that don't have fully deployed threat-response systems are over. The government now holds organizations accountable for the privacy and protection of information they maintain, especially companies that store information such as the following:

- Personal information (identity), such as social security numbers, birth dates, addresses, phone numbers, and account information

- Health information

- Financial data

Government regulations have defined rules and laws for all enterprises, government branches, medical institutions, and financial organizations when critical personal data is stored. These companies must undergo audits on their information, handling policies, change control, and physical and network security measures to protect such information.

This section briefly examines the major industry regulations and how SIM technologies help companies meet their respective legislative requirements.

Regulatory compliance is dictated by many entities other than government entities, so it is difficult to address all forms of legislation; this book addresses the most popular U.S. federal regulations. These are some examples of regulatory entities other than U.S. federal regulations:

- European Data Protection Regime
- ISO/IEC17799 and BS7799
- Payment Card Industry (PCI)
- 28 U.S. states (more pending)

The following are the three most commonly recognized and enforced government security-related regulation acts:

- Sarbanes-Oxley Act (SOX)
- Gramm-Leach-Bliley Act (GLBA)
- Health Insurance Portability and Accountability Act (HIPAA)

The Sarbanes-Oxley Act

The Sarbanes-Oxley Act of 2002 changed rules for corporations in the United States regarding financial reporting and auditing for publicly traded companies. Before SOX, there was little accountability for companies that maintained financial records. The Sarbanes-Oxley Act now regulates a company's financial record systems and outlines accountability for infractions.

The challenge for security personnel is how to change the corporate network to become compliant with SOX. SOX calls for companies to account for and report on all information technology (IT) processes that touch system operations, change control, and access to financial applications. Achieving this level of compliance is a monumental task for even the best-organized companies in the United States.

SIMs aid corporations in meeting the accounting and reporting requirements required by SOX and provide them with the means of providing "proof" of security policies, processes, and accountability mechanisms. Additionally, SIMs aid organizations in meeting SOX requirements that companies establish procedures for the receipt, retention, and treatment of complaints regarding accounting, internal accounting controls, and auditing matters by providing accountability data and "proof" that they are addressing legitimate complaints and are being proactive in countering electronic "white collar" crime.

SOX means different things to different companies. But as you will see when we talk about STMs, it's important to remember that not a single system will completely meet your needs; a healthy mix of products is required, based upon every organization's respective needs.

Gramm-Leach-Bliley Act

The Gramm-Leach-Bliley Act of 1999 was established to protect the privacy of financial data during disclosure of that data to authorized parties. GLBA regulations are applicable only for financial institutions engaged in banking, insurance, and financial services.

To meet the requirements of GLBA, IT organizations must implement risk-assessment and auditing controls and develop safeguards and operations to respond to and mitigate identified risks to protected data.

Health Insurance Portability and Accountability Act

The Health Insurance Portability and Accountability Act of 1996 is an extremely complex piece of legislation that has numerous requirements. HIPAA was released with specific target dates for compliance, with a final date of April 21, 2006. To view these compliance timetables, visit http://www.hipaacomply.com and click **Timeline**.

According to http://www.hipaa-101.com, "HIPAA helps ensure that all medical records, medical billing, and patient accounts meet certain consistent standards with regard to documentation, handling, and privacy."

SIM technology applies to HIPAA because it requires administrative, physical, and electronic protection mechanisms to be in place to protect unauthorized disclosure of personal medical information. SIM focuses on the administrative mechanism, while STM focuses on the administrative and electronic aspects.

Most important, though, HIPAA specifically states that an "information system activity review" must be conducted. Traditionally, this is called an audit, and this is achievable using the functions that a SIM provides.

Understanding the Unified Security Platform

Have you ever heard of the adage "garbage in, garbage out"? Let's put a new spin on it and apply it to security response. Information or events from several different sources can be "garbage" unless they are put together in a useful way. Otherwise, the usefulness of the data is limited and no cohesive response can be derived from the information.

When you consider the different data that must be put into a usable format and add the ill-defined government regulations, you have a real mountain to climb.

Fortunately, this is the problem that SIM strives to answer. SIMs are marketed as "unified security platforms." Their purpose is to integrate security hardware event data into a single solution. Most SIMs are successful in event correlation alone, but they do not provide any meaningful link back to the network itself.

In reality, a true unified security platform is a single-product solution with the capability to centrally manage event data from all sources, including network hosts, servers, and security devices. It takes the entire network infrastructure into consideration and adds a complete level of insight, integration, and control.

Implementing a unified security platform brings these benefits:

- Ease of management and operation
- Lower manpower requirements, including staff size and training
- Time and resource savings
- Efficiency in security incident management
- Efficiency in log consolidation
- Ease of forensics through normalization
- Centralized log retention

In reality, there is little chance that you will be able to deploy a true unified security platform. Although there are some very obvious advantages to having a single vendor as your complete network and security provider, it doesn't happen often enough. The complexities, costs, and competitive nature of vendors rarely allow a single platform to exist. Because of this, many companies are faced with selecting a "best of breed" product that encompasses the vast majority of solutions installed on their networks. Imagine if you had the luxury of choosing your network-management and security-management solutions first. This would be the only way to guarantee complete compatibility. But in the real world, this isn't how infrastructure purchases play out.

This section covers the following:

- Introduction to security threat mitigation
- Leveraging your existing environment

Introduction to Security Threat Mitigation

The role of the SIM has been diminished by the speed at which network attacks can spread, thus greatly increasing the vulnerability of networks. It often takes just a single computer that might not have been properly used or updated to cause a worm or virus to spread through an organization's network within minutes. Even if such attacks do not destroy or steal data, they often cause storms of excess traffic and seriously impact the capability of an organization to do business. This results in downtime and lost revenues.

Therefore, companies are no longer deploying security devices and applications on their networks simply to control access and identify possible problems. Their primary goal is to keep their networks and applications up and running optimally. They are finding that existing SIMs cannot act quickly enough to stop attacks and keep their networks healthy.

Beyond SIM, the next step is to add thorough network awareness and speed of analysis to identify real network attacks and react to those attacks in near–real time. This capability is called security threat management (STM). STM automates much of the legwork currently done by security analysts, reducing their burden and freeing them to concentrate on real threats, future policy, and strategy.

This section covers the following subjects related to STM:

- Benefits of moving from SIM to STM
- Understanding a mitigation, analysis, and response system
- Advantages of a proactive security framework

Benefits of Moving from SIM to STM

STM appliances are real-time devices that enable proactive countermeasures to be applied to defend the network through timely mitigation. Traditional SIMs still do not address these needs. They are reactive monitoring devices that require trained security analysts to interpret the data and reports and then recommend mitigative responses. With SIMs, the level of analysis available is not deep enough or timely enough to stop a network attack in its tracks. SIMs provide tools to determine that a network was attacked, that certain elements of the network were compromised, and that certain devices in the network were involved in that compromise.

STM is considered a form of a SIM. STM appliances have all the core technologies that a SIM offers, but they monitor the multiple types of logging and reporting mechanisms available from the diverse host, security, and network products that make up networks. Innovative algorithms are used to reduce the flood of network event information and provide network operators with relevant information for the incident the analyst is investigating.

STM technology begins by receiving network events from both security devices and network components. It combines event information with its network awareness to identify "hot spots" where network attack activity is concentrated. It also illustrates the path the attack took through the network. It then pinpoints the specific network or security device where an operator can mitigate attacks, providing appropriate device-configuration information to stop dangerous traffic.

To truly understand the power of STM is to look at it as an efficient, high-performance system used to analyze event data, identify network traffic patterns, and do forensic analysis of network attacks.

The real value of an STM over a SIM is achieved through the following:

- **Data reduction**—An STM appliance with deep awareness of network topology and addressing can reduce millions of security events to hundreds of actual network incidents.

- **Timely attack mitigation**—An STM has both the performance and the built-in intelligence to recognize and recommend mitigation for attacks before they bring down an entire network.

- **End-to-end network awareness**—An STM uses the full configurations of all types of network devices and end systems, with the capability to process NAT and MAC address information to identify attackers, targets, and network hot spots in graphical form for quick action.

- **Integrated vulnerability assessment**—An STM determines whether a possible network attack is genuine or a false positive, further reducing the number of alarms and the time needed to take action.

- **Session correlation**—Intersession correlation, combined with its very flexible rules framework, enables timely analysis and mitigation of incidents.

Understanding a Mitigation, Analysis, and Response System

The Cisco Systems Mitigation, Analysis, and Response System is one that enhances deployed network and security devices by combining network intelligence, Context Correlation, SureVector analysis, and AutoMitigate capabilities. CS-MARS as an STM technology gives companies the flexibility and power to readily identify, manage, and eliminate network attacks and maintain compliance.

CS-MARS goes beyond typical SIMs by more efficiently consolidating and sessionizing massive amounts of network and security data. By being network aware, CS-MARS effectively identifies network and application threats through patented event-correlation and threat-validation processes. With CS-MARS, verified attacks are visualized through a topology map to assist in incident investigation. Upon incident discovery, the operator can prevent an attack in near–real time by pushing mitigation commands to network devices in the path of the attack. The system supports custom rule creation, incident notification, and event forensics.

As indicated earlier, CS-MARS uses three innovative, patented processes:

- Context Correlation
- SureVector analysis
- AutoMitigate

These three processes are discussed in more detail in Chapter 4, "CS-MARS Technologies and Theory."

Advantages of a Proactive Security Framework

CS-MARS is the catalyst in turning heterogeneous networks into proactive security frameworks.

An infrastructure that provides a set of security elements that work together in a dynamic approach to behave actively in the prevention of security threats or policy violations is considered to have a proactive security framework.

The key to this framework is the network's capability to behave actively. This does not necessarily mean to take action itself, but to automatically collect data from numerous sources and come to a decision. This decision is often a mitigative or remedial recommendation offered to a system operator or analyst. Modern IPS solutions and some firewalls take automatic action; however, they do not collaborate with other devices in the network to validate the offending traffic as legitimate. This noncollaborative approach breaks the framework, thus eliminating it as such. Taking it one step farther, certain industries are forced into adopting these uncorrelated and often false positive–plagued systems to take automatic action because technologies such as CS-MARS have not been available until now.

This framework is becoming crucial in maintaining business operations. With the flood of new network technologies designed to make our workforce more efficient, coupled with the vulnerabilities these systems and applications have, it becomes difficult to determine what is valid traffic. Additionally, existing platforms on the network are full of exploits that we are not aware of. Combine this with social engineering, and you have a recipe for disaster.

Regardless of whether automitigation is used in CS-MARS, the information available to the network/security analyst is above and beyond that currently offered by SIMs. In an instant, CS-MARS can tell the analyst the type of attack, the source, the target and where it is located in the environment, what devices can be used to mitigate the attack, and what policy or configuration changes can be applied to stop the attack.

Several operations give a proactive security framework its strength:

- Collaboration of security events
- False-positive reduction
- Incident notification
- Attack mitigation or remediation

Collaboration of Security Events

The results of normalization and correlation combined are collaborated security events. The capability to make events from all different types of systems appear uniform and conform to a standard is the key to collaboration in heterogeneous networks. Correlation of the normalized data based upon some form of relationship gives the data relativity. Thus, the incident being reported is the result of data from multiple systems.

False-Positive Reduction

False positives are a common problem in network security appliances that monitor packet data. They occur quite often because these systems look into only a portion of the payload data or do not consider the data content expected by certain networks or applications. Reducing false positives has become an important process because it gives the alarm data more legitimacy. False-positive reduction is the result of desensitizing data that doesn't possess an attribute that triggers an incident. This process must be accurate for it can cause a system to make incorrect recommendations for mitigation.

Two types of false positives arise:

- A device classifies data as a possible intrusion or policy violation, although it is legitimate data.

- A device classifies data as a possible intrusion or policy violation, although the data will not be successful in its intent.

While understanding the two types of false positives, it is important to mention that these definitions can vary slightly. Although a legitimate attack might not be successful and is classified as a false positive, the data should still be reported because this could be a purposeful attack. This data should not be mixed with the confirmed-positive data and should be reported in a separate view for a more methodic review. CS-MARS meets these needs by separating false-positive data into different views and giving a user the means of investigating and acknowledging these false-positive alarms.

This brings us to the question, "How does a system determine accurately whether data is a false positive?" CS-MARS uses several methods to determine the validity of event data:

- Verifies the data path on the network by cross-checking the capability of the data traversing the network topology (network awareness—system determined)

- Verifies the destination system's susceptibility to the data by using vulnerability assessment information, fingerprinting, or manual entry of host vulnerabilities (system determined)

- Weighs the data against system- or user-defined rules that define the data as a false positive (user determined)

Incident Notification

Incident notification is simply the capability of the framework to notify external entities of its actions or incident data. For example, when an inline IPS device blocks certain traffic, it sends an SNMP packet to a network-monitoring system. With the CS-MARS in your framework, one example is that, when the IPS takes its action, the IPS device sends the SNMP trap to the MARS, and then the MARS sends an e-mail message to a user or group of users.

The advantage of having CS-MARS in the notification schema instead of using direct notifications from the reporting devices themselves is that the notification being sent from CS-MARS is the direct result of the correlation and false-positive reduction, thus reducing the number of the notifications and concentrating verified notifications on legitimate, well-baked incident-related information.

Two methods of notification exist: in-band and out-of-band. A proactive security framework uses both.

The in-band notification method informs security personnel via the data network. These are some examples of in-band methods used:

- SNMP
- SMTP (e-mail)
- Syslog

The out-of-band notification method uses analog and digital (non–TCP/UDP) devices such as modems or serial-connected devices via RS232 adapters to inform security personnel. These are some examples of out-of-band notifications:

- ASCII text messages
- SMS text messages
- Audible alarms

Attack Mitigation or Remediation

Attack mitigation or remediation empowers the STM framework by recommending or taking evasive action to stop or prevent a threat. These are some common mitigative responses:

- Sending out TCP resets
- Issuing shuns
- Recommending or applying access lists
- Recommending or pushing security policies
- Turning off Layer 2 ports
- Isolating VLANs

CS-MARS makes mitigative recommendations with the manageable device closest to the source of the violation as the "recommended" mitigative device. All other devices in the path of the attack are displayed as "alternatives." The analyst can select either, and several methods then are displayed.

Currently, CS-MARS can only push a Layer 2 command to a mitigative switch or enable a Cisco DTM IPS signature on an IOS IPS-enabled router. All other mitigative commands are recommendations and cannot be pushed to the mitigative device.

Most STMs today only make mitigative recommendations; however, with the introduction of the Cisco Network Access Control Phase II (NAC), automated action will become more common in the network. To learn more about the Cisco NAC and the different phases, please visit http://www.cisco.com/go/nac.

Leveraging Your Existing Environment

One of the key goals of SIM/STM technology is to use the existing infrastructure in accomplishing its task. This proves to be difficult with a myriad of network vendors and the technologies they offer; thus, the challenge becomes what vendor can offer you the most coverage of your network. With SIM, certain security products and host logs leave gaps in their offerings. STM increases your coverage by giving you integration into network devices as well as security and host products.

As a security or network professional, you have been trained and programmed to analyze data from your security devices to discover what is going on. Vendors build specific applications to interpret their data and rarely allow other forms of data to be combined with their own. Thus, the need for SIM arises.

However, the most powerful security devices on your network are ignored. Your switches and routers provide your host and server behaviors, data patterns, MAC address (CAM) and routing tables, and their changes. The problem is, there have never been any tools to interpret this information and then place it into a security perspective. STM takes you there; it combines this data with your security device data to give you a complete and robust tool for network security.

CS-MARS capabilities are uniform, regardless of the size of your network. However, the need for this technology can be considerably different. The following section helps you identify the needs for different types of networks:

- Small to medium business (SMB) networks
- Enterprise networks
- Multivendor networks

Small-to-Medium Business Networks

Not too long ago, organizations with small to medium-size networks were isolated from SIM technology. Traditional SIMs are still too complicated and expensive for the technology to be implemented. Unfortunately, the need for a SIM still exists in these networks. Now that STM technology is available, these organizations can take action above and beyond SIM to enable their networks to be proactive security frameworks for an affordable price.

SMB networks have several challenges. They typically incorporate integrated networking and security equipment and have small staffs that operate and administer them. The major challenges SMB networks face are listed here:

- Protection of assets and investment
- Limited manpower and time
- Inefficiency in operation
- Product selection

Solving these challenges can be quite difficult. In deciding what solution to implement, one must consider the following several points:

- Affordability
- Compatibility with integrated devices
- Simplicity to manage and operate
- Capability to leverage existing network investment
- Scalability for future growth
- Reduction of total cost of ownership (TCO)
- Improvements to security responsiveness

SIM technologies solve only one or a few of these points; CS-MARS answers them all. An SMB organization that implements a CS-MARS STM deployment can be assured that it will get a solution that offers more insight, integration, and control into the network.

CS-MARS can do this by offering a small standalone platform that can be placed on the network and be self-sustaining.

A typical CS-MARS deployment for SMB requires one standalone hardware platform to meet the needs of the SMB market. After being installed and configured, CS-MARS can sit on the network and monitor the network's activity without constant supervision. When something abnormal or in violation of policy occurs, CS-MARS notifies the appropriate personnel and offers recommendations on how to mitigate the offending traffic. Additionally, the CS-MARS deployment is scalable and can grow to a distributed architecture if the organization grows to the extent that requires this. This protects the company's investment. If the SMB organization is required to conform to legislative requirements, CS-MARS further meets this need by giving the company a centralized logging, reporting, and auditing tool that aids in compliance.

Enterprise Networks

Most enterprise networks have had the luxury of being able to afford and operate a SIM. Those that did not are faced with making the decision today because of increased consumer demand for security and/or legislative requirements. The SIM deployed was typically operated by security department personnel and did not reach out to other departments. Most enterprises have very large networking and security departments with very specific roles and responsibilities; thus, until now, when an incident occurred these departments had to be reactive and work together to resolve the issue. Because of internal politics and procedures, the damage had already occurred, and the results of their actions were more postmortem.

Enterprise organizations are now searching for a solution that can meet the needs of many different departments in their company and unify interdepartmental communication and operation, to become seamless in protecting their infrastructures. This, then, would make them proactive rather than reactive.

STM technology in a distributed architecture enables companies to use their existing infrastructure to solve their problems. To fully understand how CS-MARS can accomplish this, you must first be familiar with the challenges of implementing this technology. The following is a list of the most common challenges enterprise class networks face today:

- **High volumes of data**—Presents many problems for the enterprise. Companies require terabytes of storage to maintain their syslog and device logs. Additionally, this data must be stored in its raw format, unchanged, to meet log integrity purposes. This data needs to be stored for long periods of time, often exceeding 5 to 7 years.

- **Lack of application awareness**—Creates issues with visibility into who is accessing what applications, from where, what changes have been applied, and how the application is behaving with the changes.

- **Device support diversity**—Required because, in the enterprise, many different products make up the entire network solution. Most of the time, every department has its own budget and purchasing requirements and rarely takes other departments' equipment into consideration. A single solution that can interoperate within a heterogeneous network is quite attractive.

- **High availability**—Is a must because downtime means lost revenue. Additionally, because of legislative accountability, downtime could cause an enterprise to be in violation of its respective legislation. High availability applies not only to the STM devices themselves, but to the data stored within them.

- **Distributed network topology**—Taking log data from WAN links and VPN tunnels can cause bandwidth congestion and impede business operations. Having a solution in place that can take full advantage of multiple WAN technologies while respecting the integrity of the link is imperative.

- **Centralized and localized management**—Is necessary when enterprise customers have a distributed network with remote support faculties who are accountable for themselves. Centralized management and localized management have specific needs separately, but having a unified solution that allows both is a more attractive feature for the enterprise network. This allows multiple support facilities and departments to work seamlessly with the same solution to achieve a common goal while maintaining their own responsibilities when necessary.

- **Software-based SIM solutions**—Are complex and require multiple departments within an enterprise organization to become involved. This adds complexity to the solution because organizations are faced with purchasing, supporting, and maintaining hardware for the software-based SIM to operate. TCO is increased as licensing becomes complex and support man-hours are increased.

When a solution that resolves these issues is implemented, it's a matter of updating internal procedures to accommodate the different organizations to use the shared technology.

Now that you understand these issues, the question that needs to be answered is, "How does an STM leverage the existing infrastructure to meet the needs of the enterprise?"

An STM goes above and beyond the traditional SIM, providing a flexible framework that accommodates a two-tier distribution method of collecting and analyzing data throughout all points on your network. It gives an IT organization the capability to look deep into the network at all three layers: Access, Core, and Distribution, respectively. Using your existing network components STM addresses the challenges of the enterprise network by giving IT organizations the following advantages:

- STM technology distributes storage across multiple platforms. *High volumes of data* are stored in each respective device using a self-sustaining database. Storage per device can be up to 1000 GB of RAID (Redundant Array of Independent Disks) storage.

- *Device support diversity* is accomplished through supporting a mixture of standards-based reporting protocols, proprietary protocols, and the creation of custom parsers. A custom parser is provided to allow the system to normalize and summarize the data that it is receiving when inherent support is not provided. This allows for support of internally developed applications and systems that the STM does not natively support.

- STM technology achieves *high availability* with redundancy through distributed collection points, distributed archiving, distributed storage using RAID arrays, and distributed management. There is no single point of failure in the design.

- Communication between elements is secure and thin client in architecture, which supports a large *distributed network topology*. Data is never transmitted over a WAN link unless requested by a user; however, the summarized incidents are sent to the Global Controller, where it can be viewed and analyzed.

- Having the capability to manage all devices globally yet maintain localized authority for each respective device gives the enterprise *centralized and localized management* of the solution. It is important to note that this is the top level of management. A valuable STM system allows for any combination of management structures needed to meet an organization's specific needs.

The Multivendor Approach and Associated Challenges

A technology that supports many different manufacturers' systems or custom applications has its challenges. It is very difficult for one vendor to be the "end all" for every technology. The proper approach for SIM manufacturers in creating a multivendor solution should be to focus on the priorities and the needs of the customer. The SIM manufacturer should design its solution to be customizable, to allow unique or nonmarket-leading solutions to be implemented into its product.

The largest obstacle, which will never be overcome, is business—or, simply put, money. Each manufacturer develops its solutions to communicate to its tools in a manner that will maintain and protect its business. However, the manufacturer does realize that third-party products give considerable value to their solutions, so most of them have developed open APIs or software-development kits to allow third-party communication. Although this practice is extremely helpful, it has caveats. Manufacturers limit the capability of the integration and, therefore, restrict the usefulness of the solution in an attempt to force organizations to have both their solution and the third-party tool. Others take a different approach. They allow their data to be exported or sent to third-party devices via a standards-based reporting protocol.

It must be mentioned that manufacturers do have certification programs for third-party vendors. They require certification of the third-party application by themselves, to prevent a security compromise or damage to their solution. It is common for competitive vendors to belong to each other's programs; you will just not find their logo advertised on their website!

Some common programs in which manufacturers have developed third-party integration are listed here:

- Cisco's Architecture for Voice, Video, and Integrated Data (AVVID) partner program
- Check Point's Open Platform for Security (OPSEC) partner program

Another challenge needs to be mentioned: Product updates, bug fixes, signature updates, and device support all require a multivendor-supported application to modify or update its systems to support them. An example of this challenge is supporting IDS signature updates. When an IDS manufacturer updates its signature sets, SIM and STM vendors alike must prioritize which signature sets they will support so that they can prioritize development time to their software-development teams. The timeline in which these releases become available depends on the relationship the vendors have with each other. In competitive situations, the multivendor company must await the public release of the signature set.

The only solution to this problem today is a combination of self-customization tools (custom parsers) and patience. But with the deployment of CS-MARS, although you don't completely eliminate the need for product updates, because of its zero-day protection capabilities, you maintain a good level of security until critical patches can be deployed on your systems.

Summary

This chapter was a primer explaining the basics of security information management (SIM) and security threat mitigation (STM) systems. As a result of the lack of functionality SIMs offered, STM picked up where SIM left off. STM delivers unification of network, host, and security components by taking a myriad of data sources into consideration for its analysis.

Security information management typically includes five core functions:

- Collecting event data from reporting sources
- Storing data for analysis, reporting, and archiving
- Correlating the data to show relationships
- Presenting the data for analysis
- Generating reports, alarms, and/or notifications on the data

While these functions may look good on paper and have helped security responders limp through many emergencies in the past, SIMs have some inherent weaknesses when it comes to helping threat responders quickly recognize and respond to active or recently identified threats.

Security threat mitigation (STM) systems add value to SIMs by adding some key technology features. Those features include the following:

- Thorough data reduction
- Timely attack mitigation
- End-to-end network awareness
- Integrated vulnerability assessment
- Unification of network and security devices

When you add the five core features of SIMs to the advanced capabilities of STMs, you get a security system that can truly be used by threat responders to accurately and quickly respond to threats against your network and network assets.

When you add CS-MARS to the solution set, you take STM one step farther by turning your network into a proactive security framework.

In the following chapters, you will see that CS-MARS provides the additive features of both the threat response and the mitigation technologies described in this chapter.

This chapter helps you to understand important information related to the functions and deployment of CS-MARS in your network. You learn the following:

- The Self-Defending Network and the Expanding Role of CS-MARS
- CS-MARS as an STM Solution

## CHAPTER 2

Role of CS-MARS in Your Network

CS-MARS plays two major roles in your network's security solution. The first is as a critical component that enhances the self-defending network (SDN). The SDN increases the level of protection in your network by enabling additional communication between devices. The second role of CS-MARS is as a security threat mitigation (STM) system that enables substantially quicker and more accurate information for threat response. In addition to these roles, CS-MARS reporting is a valuable tool that can meet legislative and reporting requirements.

After examining the features that CS-MARS provides, you will see how the appliances can be deployed to achieve enhanced security and response.

The Self-Defending Network and the Expanding Role of CS-MARS

The self-defending network is a security deployment methodology that many of the nation's top security engineers recommend and support.

The basic concept of the self-defending network is that there are many layers of defenses to recognize and protect against malicious activity, and the devices in these layers can communicate with other layers to further enhance your network and device security. For example, if a device recognizes an attack in the core of your network, that device could notify the perimeter devices of the offending traffic, and the perimeter device could put protection in place to stop the attack from reinfecting the core or spreading to other parts of your network. As an added bonus, the core device would still have the capability to recognize the attack, so you could stop the attack at multiple layers.

In this section, in addition to getting a more detailed description of the self-defending network, you will learn how CS-MARS can help you take that defense to a new level. CS-MARS does this by correlating alerts from many different security devices manufactured by multiple security vendors and then recognizing and responding to attacks. CS-MARS identifies attacks accurately and quickly to help security responders mitigate attacks and contain malicious activity.

The following topics are discussed in this section:

- **Understanding the Self-Defending Network**—This section helps you to understand how the self-defending network expands on the defense-in-depth concept and works to mitigate attacks against networks, network devices, and PCs in your enterprise.

- **Enhancing the Self-Defending Network**—This section explains the missing links in the self-defending network. With these missing links addressed, the capability of the network to protect itself, critical assets, and critical applications; the capability of network engineers to achieve fast and accurate forensics; and the capability for fast, accurate mitigation of attacks are greatly enhanced.

- **CS-MARS: Filling the Gaps in the Self-Defending Network**—This section highlights how the CS-MARS product enhances not just the capability of the network to defend itself, but also the capability of security response teams to recognize an attack in progress and to accurately respond to that attack.

Understanding the Self-Defending Network

To understand the self-defending network, you must look at the foundation of the SDN, which is known as defense-in-depth, and explain how the self-defending mechanism helps automate and expand the security posture of your network.

Defense-in-Depth and the Self-Defending Network

Defense-in-depth is a multilayer model that defines layers of protection for your network. Each layer has network- and host-defense features and is capable of stopping a network or host attack. In addition to the layers of defense that build up the basic foundation of your security, the self-defending aspects automatically and intelligently learn about threats and communicate with other network devices to change their configurations and build a stronger network defense.

When you put these layers together, they not only have the specific functions for stopping an attack, but they also provide multiple chokepoints to contain malicious activity and keep it from spreading throughout your network.

At a high level, defense-in-depth defines four main layers of protection for your network and an abstract layer that encompasses security best practices. These layers are as follows:

- Authentication layer
- Perimeter layer
- Network intrusion-prevention layer
- Host intrusion-prevention layer
- Security best practices

We start with a discussion on these layers of protection and then discuss how the self-defending network is used to augment defense-in-depth.

Authentication Layer

The basic description of authentication is that it employs user or device credentials before allowing access to your network or to devices in your network.

Authentication is possible only if a protocol or application is designed to accept and track usernames, passwords, or certificates.

Commonly used protocols that allow authentication include the following:

- **IPSec**—For remote network and remote management access
- **SSH**—For remote management access
- **HTTPS**—For remote management access
- **HTTP**—For inbound and outbound web connections
- **SMTP, IMAP, and POP**—For e-mail access
- **FTP**—For file transfers
- **802.1x**—For device and user authentication

IPSec, HTTPS, and SSH encrypt traffic and use certificates and passwords to authenticate devices. This encryption mitigates against attackers who might be sniffing your network to glean these important bits of information.

You should always use authentication before allowing access to critical devices in your network. This includes hosts, servers, routers' switches, firewalls, load-balancers, infrastructure servers such as DNS and DHCP, and IP telephony equipment. To deploy centralized authentication on your network, you normally use a product such as the Cisco Secure Access Control Server (Cisco Secure ACS), which provides a common authentication database and works in conjunction with most devices that use the protocols listed earlier. In addition to providing authentication to local usernames and passwords, Cisco ACS can forward authentication requests to domain databases, LDAP databases, and UNIX and Microsoft password databases.

In many cases, you want to allow anyone on the Internet to access data on your web server, such as product and marketing information. Because of this, most transactions from the Internet to the web server are not authenticated, meaning that anyone can get to your web server to access public information.

Take note that although allowing anyone into a web server on your network is the correct thing for your business, it opens the door for hackers who use this access to exploit vulnerabilities in your web server, access your network, and launch other attacks or view critical information. Because of this, you must be sure to deploy the additional layers of the defense-in-depth model in your network.

In the Cisco world, network admission control (NAC) is used in conjunction with network-access devices such as these:

- Routers
- Switches
- VPN concentrators
- Wireless access point

These devices act similarly to authentication proxies and authorization proxies. They forward security posture information about your device to authentication servers to see if it has security software installed that meets your network-access security policies before giving you access to the network. Based on what is learned during the NAC process, your network devices either grant access, grant limited access, or deny access to the device.

The intelligence is also built into NAC so that if a device changes its security posture after it has authenticated, NAC will discover this and take appropriate action, such as denying the device network access.

The dynamic nature of NAC and its capability to learn and respond classify it as a self-defending technology.

Some network experts believe that NAC falls into either the defense-in-depth category of host security or authentication, as we have defined it in this book. It really has aspects of both of these layers of defense, and where it should be defined depends on an individual's viewpoint.

Perimeter-Layer Defenses

After users or devices have been authenticated (or not authenticated, as is the case for most web traffic), the next step is to determine what these users can or cannot do after they access the network. This level of access is applied at the perimeter layer.

The perimeter layer has two main functions:

- Traffic filtering
- Network perimeter-attack protection

The first function of perimeter protection, traffic filtering, enforces rules that define what traffic is allowed into the network. This traffic is defined by your security policy. Traffic filtering is deployed to ensure that outside users have access to only devices and services that you have defined.

These are common types of Internet traffic that enterprises allow in their networks:

- Clear-text web traffic (HTTP), for viewing noncritical data.
- Encrypted and authenticated web traffic (HTTPS/SSL), for secure transactions and viewing critical data.

- Domain Name Services (DNS), to handle Internet requests to translate domain names that you own to IP addresses.

- Simple Mail Transport Protocol (SMTP), for sending and receiving mail traffic to and from Internet users to your internal users.

- File Transfer Protocol (FTP), for transferring files between Internet hosts and file servers on your network. Although it is not as prevalent as it was in the early days of the Internet, FTP is still used enough to warrant mentioning.

The second function of network perimeter-attack protection is to defend against attacks on the perimeter of your network. These are examples of the most popular of those attacks:

- Denial-of-service attacks

- Unauthorized perimeter device access

- Application attacks

- Worm and virus propagation

These types of attacks are usually recognized and mitigated using various security devices, protocols, and techniques.

Denial-of-service attacks (DoS or DDoS) are generally recognized and mitigated by devices such as firewalls, routers, and specialized devices such as Cisco Guard. These various security and network devices use a combination of techniques to defend against denial-of-service attacks:

- Anomaly-based traffic recognition

- Algorithms that look at excessive flows

- Signature-based systems that recognize an excess of traffic conditions that indicate a DoS attack in progress

- Trigger points that recognize more traffic than normal passing onto the network

Denial-of-service attacks are mitigated by various device actions. Routers use rate-limiting, a technology that limits the flow of data that has been classified as malicious. Firewalls examine their state tables and tear down flows that are deemed malicious. Cisco Guard devices use a combination of rate-limiting and filtering technology to determine valid traffic and stop malicious traffic. IPS uses signatures and anomaly algorithms to determine whether an attack is underway and can report or drop the traffic.

Defending against DoS attacks is a good example of how defense-in-depth can be improved, as discussed in the section "Enhancing the Self-Defending Network." In many cases, these devices need to be manually configured and can't change dynamically. If you have a true self-defending network that can recognize behavior and share information to stop bad behavior, the solutions just mentioned become much more attractive and cost-effective.

Unauthorized perimeter device access is an attack that becomes possible mainly when firewalls are not correctly configured. For example, during the Slammer attack, a buffer overflow was caused by sending a crafted packet to exploit a vulnerability using TCP port 1434. Under normal circumstances, perimeter devices would block that port, but as it ended up, several thousand perimeters were opened to that port, allowing hundreds of thousands of hosts and servers to be exploited by the Slammer worm. That being said, one of the main purposes of perimeter protection is to ensure that only traffic that matches an enterprise's access security policy should be let into the enterprise network.

Note that the two types of protection provided by the perimeter layer of defense-in-depth will potentially stop thousands of attacks. But if a hacker is launching an attack that uses valid data and there is no mechanism to stop the attack, perimeter security won't stop the attack; the attack will make it to your next level of security defense.

Application attacks are attempts by hackers to use existing application protocols and pass attacks through perimeter devices. Most firewalls and perimeter security devices now have application-inspection protection engines. These devices look for violations of well-known applications such as HTTP, FTP, or SMTP. If a violation is detected, the device can stop or report the attack before it passes into the network.

It's important to recognize that the attacks we've discussed in this section are not always sourced from Internet attackers. Other sources include the following:

- Employees who have accidentally (or not accidentally) had malicious software installed on their machine

- Employees who are connected to your campus network and have picked up malicious traffic from Internet download, spyware, or e-mail

- Disgruntled employees who launch attacks from inside your network

- Misconfiguration of hosts or network devices

- Trusted networks such as VPN termination points

The following are descriptions of devices that provide protection at the perimeter:

Appliances that defend against DDoS attacks are good examples of devices that adapt to a learned threat and then change their posture to more accurately protect against that threat. For example, Cisco Guard works in conjunction with Cisco Traffic Anomaly Detectors to learn what the normal flow of traffic looks like. If that traffic varies a certain amount from the norm, Cisco Guard will analyze that traffic and then take defensive action against the threat by modifying its own tables to recognize the valid traffic and let only that traffic into your network. You can learn more about Cisco Guard from Cisco's website at http://www.cisco.com/go/guard.

Firewalls are the most common of perimeter devices. Traditionally, firewalls don't learn that a threat is active and change their configuration; they do, however, have the capability to accept commands from IPS devices called shuns. As of IPS v5.1, Cisco IPS devices also have the capability to recognize DoS and DDoS traffic and send commands to a router to rate-limit that traffic; this helps to reduce or eliminate the denial-of-service attack. IPS v5.1 also can accept signatures from the Cisco Incident Control Server to stop new Internet threat outbreaks.

Although Cisco Incident Control Server (ICS) is more of a manual process, it is another excellent example of a security service that sends learned threat information to devices to strengthen their security posture if a threat is recognized. The process for ICS starts manually. When a new threat is detected on the Internet, the ICS server is populated and sends access-control lists and signatures that are crafted to stop the new threat. The ICS server can send data to Cisco routers, firewalls, and IPS devices.

Network Intrusion Prevention

Up to this point, with the first two layers (authentication and perimeter) of defense-in-depth, you have effectively done the following:

- Granted access only to desired users
- Enforced rules specifying what traffic will traverse your network
- Provided protection against many perimeter attacks
- Verified device security posture before allowing network access
- And in many cases, changed (strengthened) your security posture based on learned threats

All this protection probably sounds good. But the problem you run into is that hackers are adjusting their exploit methods to use valid traffic and follow valid protocol standards. Because of this, you need the next layer of defense-in-depth, called network intrusion prevention.

The purpose of this layer is to look inside the traffic that you have allowed after you have applied all the previous defenses to your traffic.

This level of protection is normally achieved with one or more Cisco security devices:

- Cisco Intrusion Prevention (IPS) appliances
- Cisco Intrusion Prevention Catalyst Service Modules
- Cisco ASA appliances with Security Service Modules running IPS software
- Cisco integrated security routers

These devices recognize attacks using various different technologies:

- **Signature matching**—The traffic is matched against attack signatures. If the device finds an attack, it takes whatever protective action you have defined for that signature.

- **Anomaly detection**—Using this technology, a device establishes a baseline for normal traffic. If traffic starts to flow outside that baseline, the device takes whatever protective action you have defined for this type of alert. Anomaly protection is an effective technology to stop mutating and scanning day-zero worms.

- **Application inspection**—This is the same security feature described for the perimeter layer. IPS devices and perimeter devices are capable of stopping traffic that violates a well-known protocol. It is often desirable to do this protection in the IPS layer and free up CPU cycles on the perimeter to filter traffic and protect against high-bandwidth attacks such as DoS and DDoS.

If one of the devices mentioned earlier identifies an attack, you have the option to configure the device to either drop or drop and report the traffic. Users who elect to drop the packet must make sure that they are not dropping valid packets; therefore, the signatures shipped with the security appliance are well-known attacks and leave very little chance of valid traffic being dropped.

The main problem with signature-based network intrusion prevention is that it's only as good as the last attack. That means that signatures can stop only known attacks. Day-zero attacks, or new attacks, pose the greatest threat to network and host security. Because of this, host intrusion prevention, which protects against bad behavior prevalent in day-zero attacks, is the next layer of defense-in-depth that should be deployed.

Host Intrusion-Prevention Layer

Even though you have deployed the first three layers of defense-in-depth, the possibility exists that attack traffic that does not match these signatures or behaviors can pass through to the inside of your network. Host intrusion prevention (HIPS), the last layer of defense-in-depth, is designed to stop the remainder of attacks.

Host intrusion prevention is designed to stop the following:

- Any attack that doesn't traverse the perimeter security appliances as described in the previous layers of defense-in-depth. An example is an attack sourced by users located inside the perimeter.

- Any attack that was sourced from the outside of the security appliance but wasn't stopped by the security appliance filters or the application firewall. An example is traffic that follows network or application protocol but has an exploit built into the payload.

HIPS can stop these attacks that have bypassed signature and anomaly detection because it looks for behavior on a host and stops behavior that it recognizes as being malicious. Malicious behavior includes the following:

- Browsers acting as servers listening for incoming connections from the Internet
- Browsers trying to write data to a disk besides log, cookie, or history files

- Browsers trying to install software

- Processes trying to execute code that has been written to a system or application data stack following a buffer overflow

- Unauthorized processes or applications attempting to install software, write to the system directory, or modify the system registry

At the HIPS layer, Cisco Security Agent (CSA) is an excellent example of a self-defending technology. Not only does it protect against unknown attacks based on the behavior that it observes at the endpoint, but it also dynamically builds rules when it recognizes malicious behavior on a host and then downloads those rules to other hosts running Cisco Security Agent software. In addition, it can recognize scans against hosts and build rules to prevent those scans on other hosts.

This presence on the endpoint and the accuracy of the alerts make CSA a unique and valuable source of data to provide information to other network devices and enhance the self-defending network to a new level.

If NAC is used in conjunction with network-access devices, it can ensure that this critical layer of protection (HIPS) is activated in your network.

Security Best Practices

Even if defense-in-depth has been applied in your network as described in the previous sections of this chapter, you should follow certain network, host, and server security best practices to ensure additional protection.

Examples of those best practices include the following:

- Network device security posture hardening

- Host and server security posture hardening

- Layer 2 security posture hardening

- Management best practices (Chapter 1, "Understanding SIM and STM," offers more information on management and response best practices.)

- Security response best practices

- Password management best practices

Security best practices are essential to having a secure network. Consider what potential damage can be done if you deploy a firewall as a perimeter device to allow only desired traffic into your network and then allow management access from the outside with a username and password of Cisco and Cisco. It would take about five minutes for someone to hack your firewall and completely compromise the perimeter of your network. Of course, this example describes an unlikely omission of procedure, but at every level of defense-in-depth, you need to consider best practices on how to deploy that layer to reduce the chance of a similar error.

For a detailed discussion on security best practices, refer to the "SAFE Enterprise Architecture" whitepaper on the Cisco website at http://www.cisco.com/go/safe.

Enhancing the Self-Defending Network

The defense-in-depth paradigm has worked quite well for several years to defend against worms and mutating viruses, in addition to attacks launched by inexperienced script kiddies.

But there are still some missing links to the self-defending network:

- **Automated log correlation**—Provides a single source for log correlation

- **Automated threat response**—Automatically learns your network topology, analyzes security alerts, and notifies security responders with up-to-date accurate threat information

- **Automated mitigation**—Automatically evaluates threats and recommends a mitigation action to your security responders that will stop or contain the attack in your network

These items are mostly in the area of automated threat response. Automated threat response is simple in concept but very complicated in delivery. The concept is simply that when an attack occurs, it needs to be automatically recognized and verified by your security devices; then a response action needs to be taken to mitigate or contain that threat.

This area of the self-defending network has been relatively ignored until recently by most security vendors and customers alike. From a customer perspective, there has always been a mentality that security equipment should be installed and then just work. Unfortunately, new threats and vulnerabilities occur on a daily basis. Because of this lightning-fast changing environment, security gear needs to be capable of responding in kind. Log correlation, threat response, threat mitigation, and threat containment need to happen automatically as much as possible. The remainder of this chapter is dedicated to those concepts and also to how CS-MARS works to help automate these tasks.

Automated Log Correlation

Customers commonly have several different vendors' equipment in their networks to perform specific best-of-breed operations. Although this sometimes provides enhanced security, it commonly causes problems related to logging security events and alerts such as correlating logs between different systems. Most customers end up not reading or even keeping logs unless they need to because of legislative requirements.

For those customers who do check their logs, security-response engineers manually look at this data and decide whether an attack actually has occurred. If they determine that it has, they begin the manual prevention process.

Automated log integration is a function that allows devices to collect and correlate logs from almost any security device, network device, host, server, or key software system on your network. Automated log integration needs to encompass not only support for Cisco devices, but also popular third-party devices.

If a device isn't supported by a logging server, it should have the flexibility to define custom log parsing for any device that generates syslog or SNMP data.

The logging integration server should have the capability to not only collect, normalize, and correlate all logs, but also to classify and analyze each log that it receives.

This functionality is the first step in giving security responders the tools they need to increase the accuracy and speed at which they respond to threats.

Automated Threat Response

Another significant hurdle to the self-defending network is the capability to automatically recognize a threat and provide as much data as possible about that threat. An example is a system that would report to security responders that a successful attempt was made to exploit your web server at address 10.1.1.1, that the threat was sourced from address 192.169.1.10, that the source device is located in your network data center, and that the path the attack took was through the Internet firewall to the core and finally to the data center.

If a security responder had all this information and the confidence that the alerts were not false positives, it would add substantial value to the self-defending network.

Automated Mitigation

If events and logs from all systems have been correlated and analyzed and threat information is found, providing guidance or recommendations for mitigation is the next logical step.

If you know the type of attack, the source, the destination, the location of the exploited device in your network, and the path the attack traversed, what's standing in the way of either mitigating the attack or making a mitigation recommendation? As you will see in the remainder of this book, CS-MARS mitigates attacks or makes a recommendation for you. Automated mitigation is not yet achievable because many security devices still put out false-positive alerts, but CS-MARS makes a recommendation for mitigation and offers security responders a single click to deploy commands on devices that will stop offending traffic after the responder has analyzed the attack data.

CS-MARS: Filling the Gaps in the Self-Defending Network

Many network security experts feel that the self-defending network is a powerful methodology for mitigating network-based attacks. If you add to that existing SDN model log correlation, automated threat response, and automated threat mitigation, you have a stronger, more maintainable, and more robust security solution. This solution now provides not just defense in-depth and the capability to learn and respond but it also enables your security-response engineers to streamline the process of recognizing and responding to attacks. That recognition and response is exactly the purpose of the CS-MARS STM appliance.

CS-MARS Log Integration

CS-MARS is capable of collecting, correlating, analyzing, and storing data from thousands of different systems. This includes not only security systems, but also network devices, hosts, servers, and applications.

The following is a list of the hardware devices and software applications that have reporting capabilities and are supported natively by CS-MARS. Notice the supported devices aren't only security devices; the list includes operating systems, databases, web servers, web caches, antivirus servers, vulnerability scanners, authentication servers, and SNMP servers.

- Cisco routers
- Cisco switches (IOS and CATOS)
- Extreme switches
- Generic routers
- Cisco PIX
- Cisco Adaptive Security Appliance (ASA)
- Cisco Firewall Services Module (FWSM)
- Cisco IOS Firewall Feature Set
- Juniper NetScreen
- Check Point OPSEC NG/AI and Provider-1
- Nokia Firewall (running Check Point)
- Cisco VPN concentrator
- Cisco network IDS and IDSM
- Cisco intrusion-prevention system (IPS), Network IPS v5.0
- Cisco IPS ASA Security Services Module
- Cisco IOS IPS module
- McAfee Intrushield
- Juniper NetScreen IDP
- Symantec ManHunt
- ISS RealSecure

- Snort
- Enterasys Dragon
- Cisco Security Agent
- McAfee Entercept
- ISS RealSecure Host Sensor
- Symantec AntiVirus
- Cisco Incident Control System
- Network Associates VirusScan
- McAfee ePolicy Orchestrator
- eEye REM
- Qualys QualysGuard
- Foundstone Foundscan
- Windows NT, 2000, XP, 2003
- Solaris
- Red Hat Linux
- Microsoft Internet Information Server
- Sun iPlanet
- Apache
- NetApp NetCache
- Oracle
- AAA Server
- Cisco Secure Access Control Sever (ACS)
- SNMP and syslog servers
- Generic syslog server

In addition to these systems, CS-MARS has a function that enables you to write a custom parser for devices that don't appear on this list.

NOTE   Custom parsing for appliance or software event data supports syslog or SNMP logs only.

Each of the event data from these different systems is sessionized with other events to formulate information about possible attacks. The sessionized data is then weighed against vulnerability-assessment information to determine whether the attack is possible or likely. The CS-MARS device then can accurately determine the probability of an attack.

After collecting the alerts and log data, CS-MARS displays it in nicely formatted graphs or reports. Strictly from a reporting standpoint, CS-MARS has taken you from legacy syslogs and IPS alerts (see Figures 2-1 and 2-2) to automated log integration and correlation (see the CS-MARS Device Summary screen shown in Figure 2-3).

Figure 2-1 *Legacy IPS Alerts*

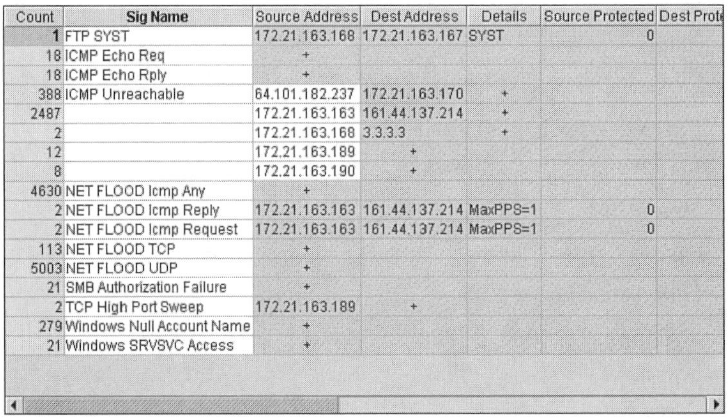

Count	Sig Name	Source Address	Dest Address	Details	Source Protected	Dest Prot
1	FTP SYST	172.21.163.168	172.21.163.167	SYST	0	
18	ICMP Echo Req	+				
18	ICMP Echo Rply	+				
388	ICMP Unreachable	64.101.182.237	172.21.163.170	+		
2487		172.21.163.163	161.44.137.214	+		
2		172.21.163.168	3.3.3.3	+		
12		172.21.163.189	+			
8		172.21.163.190	+			
4630	NET FLOOD Icmp Any	+				
2	NET FLOOD Icmp Reply	172.21.163.163	161.44.137.214	MaxPPS=1	0	
2	NET FLOOD Icmp Request	172.21.163.163	161.44.137.214	MaxPPS=1	0	
113	NET FLOOD TCP	+				
5003	NET FLOOD UDP	+				
21	SMB Authorization Failure	+				
2	TCP High Port Sweep	172.21.163.189	+			
279	Windows Null Account Name	+				
21	Windows SRVSVC Access	+				

Figure 2-2 *Legacy Syslog Alerts*

Figure 2-3   *CS-MARS Device Summary Display*

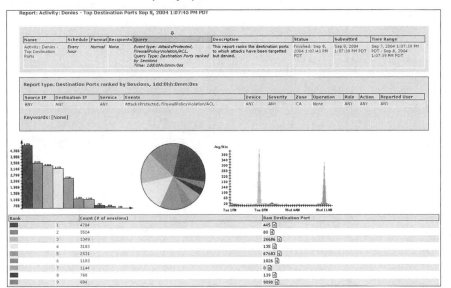

CS-MARS Automated Threat Response

In parallel with the data collection by the logging integration processes, CS-MARS is also querying network device routing tables, configurations, ARP tables, CAM tables, system probes, and other processes to determine the topology of your network and the location of each device.

After the log data is collected and the alert information is analyzed, it is cross-referenced with this topology information to determine the validity and calculate the attack path. CS-MARS has accurate topology and attack information, and can display this to security responders in both report and topology illustrated format.

Now, in addition to a strong security defense, you have accurate and powerful data that your responders can use for threat response.

Figure 2-4 is an example of a map generated by CS-MARS to show the topology of an attack.

Figure 2-4 *CS-MARS Attack Path Topology Map*

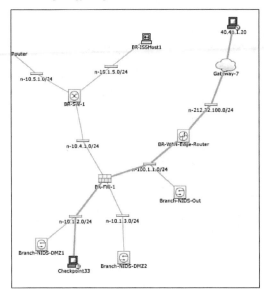

CS-MARS Automated Mitigation

CS-MARS has collected data and presented you with the information about the threat. It is now ready to take threat response a step further. Because CS-MARS has topology information and accurate threat information, it can easily determine the source of the attack and the destination of that attack. Because it has routing information, it also can determine the path that the attack took. With all this information, it's just a matter of CPU cycles to present the attack path to your security responders and to identify a network or security device that should be configured to mitigate or contain the attack. To isolate an attack and keep it from spreading, normally the network or security device closest to the source of the attack is selected for mitigation; the remainder of the components in the path of the attack are suggested as alternatives.

CS-MARS uses either SNMP, Telnet, or SSH to look at the configuration of the device it has chosen to mitigate the attack. It uses its analysis of the attack data and the device configuration to determine the commands that need to be entered to stop the attack. This mitigation suggestion shows up on the mitigation screen of the CS-MARS device. The security responder would look at the incident report, view the attack analysis, click the Mitigation icon, and select the suggested configuration changes. If the responder chose to mitigate, he or she then would click the red Push button, instructing CS-MARS to issue the suggested command to stop the attack.

Figure 2-5 is an example of a screen recommending a configuration that will mitigate an attack detected by CS-MARS.

Figure 2-5 *CS-MARS Mitigation Window*

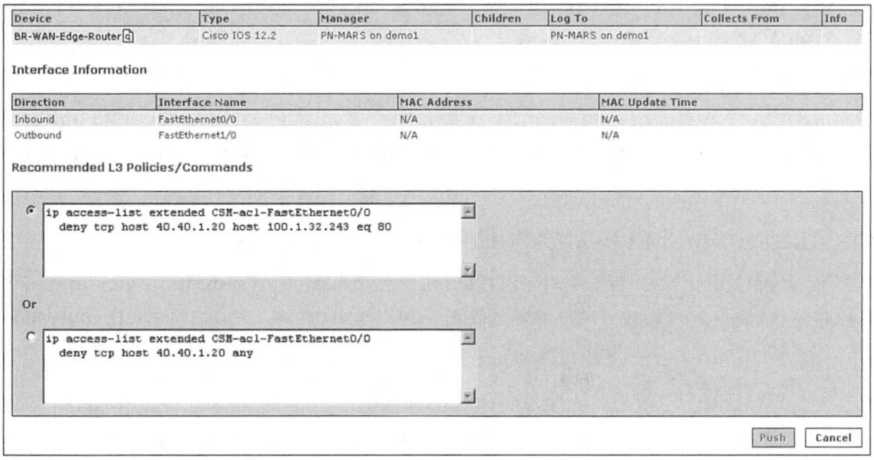

Device	Type	Manager	Children	Log To	Collects From	Info
BR-WAN-Edge-Router🔍	Cisco IOS 12.2	PN-MARS on demo1		PN-MARS on demo1		

Interface Information

Direction	Interface Name	MAC Address	MAC Update Time
Inbound	FastEthernet0/0	N/A	N/A
Outbound	FastEthernet1/0	N/A	N/A

Recommended L3 Policies/Commands

```
ip access-list extended CSM-acl-FastEthernet0/0
    deny tcp host 40.40.1.20 host 100.1.32.243 eq 80
```

Or

```
ip access-list extended CSM-acl-FastEthernet0/0
    deny tcp host 40.40.1.20 any
```

Push Cancel

CS-MARS as an STM Solution

This section explains the advantages CS-MARS provides beyond interaction with network and security devices. As discussed in Chapter 1, CS-MARS is a powerful solution that provides the necessary features of STM.

Reasons for an STM

In Chapter 1, you learned the benefits of moving from SIM to STM technology. Now let's look at a few of the specific advantages of an STM and take that first step to a proactive security framework. The following are some true examples of how STM gives you the advantage. The company names are fictitious, but the details of the stories are true.

Day-Zero Attacks, Viruses, and Worms

Think about Sasser, one of the more recent, notorious, fast-moving day-zero worms, before it had its name. What it did and what was affected were not apparent until the damage was already done.

You probably didn't even know it existed because there was not a known vulnerability for it to exploit. Network infrastructures were pummeled by the malicious code overnight, and 24 hours later, the worm was given a name. Now picture a system that informed you that a host on your network was behaving abnormally and opening hundreds of connections to other hosts. That system then allowed you to shut down the port that the offending host was connected to, giving you the switch name and specific interface. Because this is not normal behavior for a host on your network, you pushed the "red button" and stopped it. 24 hours later, an AV or HIPS signature was released, and news about the new worm spread. Now it's time to update those hosts with patches, and you're not scrambling around trying to do damage control.

CS-MARS stopped Sasser exactly as described. It recognized the attack using its anomaly algorithms and provided security responders with a timely and accurate mitigation suggestion, saving customers hundreds of thousands of dollars in tangible recovery costs.

Monitoring and Enforcing Security Policy

Widgets, Inc., just approved an addendum to its existing security policy and mapped out a new VLAN for its wireless access network. According to policy, users must authenticate to a Cisco VPN concentrator and tunnel into the LAN to use wireless. If a user does not have a Cisco VPN client, all it gets is a default gateway to the Internet. The policy calls for periodic audits of user access to the wireless segment. Security personnel are overwhelmed as it is with day-to-day responsibilities; however, because they have CS-MARS installed on their network, they just have reports automatically generated according to policy and sent via e-mail to the auditors.

Since the security department has configured the CS-MARS for the automated report, it has not had to spend any time on the new addendum. This has freed up the security engineering resources to work on security-related problems.

Insight, Integration, and Control of Your Network

At approximately 3:00 p.m., ABC University's help desk started to get trouble calls about failed access to servers on its network. The help desk immediately notified the network engineer on staff; she was at her desk eating lunch. When she received the call, she attempted to access the servers in question and confirmed that they could not be reached. She then attempted to access other devices from her machine and had no issues. She opened her web browser and decided to log in to her new CS-MARS appliance. She noticed a spike in port 53 activity and immediately began investigating. She discovered that her secondary DNS server on the private university network was going haywire. She made the decision to use the CS-MARS to shut it down. When the DNS server was offline, access to the other servers in the same segment was restored.

It took her 3 minutes to get it under control and 5 minutes to find out what was going on. She used CS-MARS to discover that several crafty students had hacked into the DNS server and placed a homemade Doom relay application using port 53 to circumvent the firewall policy that prevented Internet Doom contests. The students were identified and reprimanded.

The network engineer finished her lunch without getting up from her desk, and the university saved thousands of dollars in post-attack research and other potential recovery activities.

Auditing Controls

Investment firm Y is a public company and, therefore, must conform to SOX auditing. The third-party auditing firm requested access logs from its Microsoft servers, COBIT DS 9.4—Configuration Control, and Successful Object Modification logs from their Oracle database servers. The auditing company requested that the reports be prepared for review on the third day of the audit. The day the auditors arrived on the premises they were greeted, introduced to the staff, and handed the reports in a nice three-ring binder. At the end of the audit, the auditors commented on how well prepared the investment firm was and praised them on their efficiency.

It took the security department one hour to run, print, and bind the reports. This left them free to focus on security-related activities.

Monitoring Access Control

Bob is an employee of Company X and finished his project a little early on Friday. He had time on his hands before the end of the day. Bob decided to click his My Networks icon on his desktop and look around. He ran across an HR file server and clicked the icon.

Eric, the IT admin for HR, had a long day yesterday. The director for HR was having issues with getting access to the file server, and Eric just couldn't get permissions to work. To save time and embarrassment, he just set permissions to All.

Bob ran across a file marked "John D. offer letter." John D. is Bob's new teammate, and it was too irresistible not to open the file. He opened the document and, to his amazement, discovered that John earns $10,000 more per year than him and negotiated an extra week of paid vacation.

This is a good example of an intangible cost of bad security. Bob was upset and might have acted inappropriately based on what he saw, not to mention that he could have searched for other, more interesting data on the HR server. Because he was granted access to the server, there might be no audit trail, and Bob becomes a potential problem. With CS-MARS deployed appropriately, a single report showing access to the HR database would have been a great forensics tool for threat responders to use to recognize unauthorized access.

Using CS-MARS to Justify Security Investment

Eric was a one-man security shop for his company. He was again tasked with helping his ISO/IT director create the security budget for next fiscal year. Eric had his challenges last year asking for money to purchase IPS. He was given a small portion of his requested budget and told that, from a financial perspective and with the lack of security breeches on the network, they could not justify purchasing IPS. With a little investigation and help from a security analysis firm, he was advised to look at STM. Eric convinced his ISO to use the budget money to purchase CS-MARS and a server so he could use free-ware Snort on the demilitarized zone (DMZ) where clients access their extranet. With the CS-MARS in place, Eric used the existing network to send NetFlow data to the CS-MARS and correlate with the basic Snort event data from the extranet. He was able to identify numerous security threats to the network and customers' information in a matter of only one week.

Coincidently, Eric now manages three IPS sensors, two CS-MARS 100s, and a CS-MARS Global Controller. It's still the same budget year, and the company's sales media now coin a catchy security phrase identifying strong security as a reason people should do business with the company.

The STM Deployment

Chapter 1 defined the requirements for an ideal STM as a reporting and mitigation system that reduced the time and increased the accuracy of threat mitigation, threat containment, and threat reporting.

STM can be deployed many ways in your network; the choice is determined by the requirements of your organization. For example, if your organization has several remote locations and lower-bandwidth access portals, you might choose to locate a CS-MARS box in a remote location, to reduce the amount of traffic on that slow link and ensure that the network link is available for your company's revenue-based tasks.

How you deploy the CS-MARS in your network is critical to the success of achieving your organization's goals. With the CS-MARS product, there are two types of deployment scenarios: global and standalone.

To fully understand these deployment scenarios, you must first be familiar with the CS-MARS product line. At the time of this writing, Cisco offers two types of products in the CS-MARS portfolio:

- **Global Controller**—A master unit that allows for global management of one or more Local Controllers.

- **Local Controller**—A single appliance, ranging from a CS-MARS M20 to CS-MARS M200

Table 2-1 explains the Cisco offerings for the CS-MARS product family.

Table 2-1   *CS-MARS Product Portfolio*

CS-MARS	EPS	NetFlow per Sec	Storage
M20	500	15000	120 GB*
M50	1000	25000	120 GB
M100e	3000	75000	750 GB
M100	5000	150000	750 GB
M200	10000	300000	1000 GB
MARS GC	—	—	1000 GB
MARS GCm	—	—	1000 GB

*The CS-MARS 20 does not have RAID storage.

NOTE	Note that there are two GC offerings. The MARS GC has an unlimited license that allows any number of CS-MARS Local Controllers to communicate with it. The MARS GCm allows only five Local Controllers, mixed between CS-MARS M20s and M50s, to communicate with it.

A global deployment simply means that one or more Local Controllers are reporting to the CS-MARS Global Controller. In this deployment, Local Controllers report summarized event and session data to the Global Controller in both text and graphical format over an HTTPS session. Additionally, all operations in the Local Controller now become globally manageable. A Global Controller does not do global correlation—that is, the data from each Local Controller is not correlated. You need a global CS-MARS deployment for several reasons:

- To conserve WAN bandwidth
- To log data security
- To facilitate distributed processing of event data
- To facilitate distributed management and reporting
- For high availability and to archive log retention

In a standalone deployment, all event-reporting devices send their respective log data to a single CS-MARS device. All capabilities discussed in this text are the function of the Local Controller, unless specifically indicated otherwise. This deployment is the most common for small to medium-size businesses. These are some reasons for deploying a single Local Controller:

- Cost
- Isolated (non-WAN) or local network with Internet or VPN
- Minimal number of reporting devices

Summary

This chapter explained defense-in-depth combined with the self-defending network.

The layers of the self-defending network are the following:

- Authentication layer
- Perimeter layer
- Network intrusion-prevention layer
- Host intrusion-prevention layer
- Security best practices

Table 2-2 outlines some the different network devices and their capability to self-defend inside your network.

Table 2-2   *Network Devices and Self-Defending Capabilities*

Cisco firewalls and ASA appliances	Accept and apply commands called shuns that stop traffic flows that Cisco IPS devices have identified.
	Accept and apply access control lists that Cisco Incident Control servers have generated, to block new network outbreaks such as high-priority worms and viruses.
	Send syslog files to CS-MARS for correlation and analysis to be used with syslogs and events from other security servers. CS-MARS uses this data to determine threat conditions and to formulate the correct response to that threat.
	Send SNMP data to CS-MARS to report high CPU utilization conditions, enabling CS-MARS to take defensive action to protect the CPU that might be getting attacked.
	Send critical data to CS-MARS to allow for network topology discovery.
IPS appliances, IPS Service Modules, ASA Security Services Modules, and integrated security routers running IPS	Send Security Device Event Exchange (SDEE) alerts to CS-MARS for correlation and analysis to be used with syslogs and events from other security servers. CS-MARS uses this data to determine threat conditions and to formulate the correct response to that threat.
	Recognize attacks and send shuns to firewall and Cisco IOS devices, to protect against malicious flows.
	Recognize attacks and send commands to rate-limit malicious traffic.
	Recognize attacks and drop traffic in-line to protect network assets of both hosts and network devices.
	Analyze destination hosts to determine the probability of an attack succeeding.
	Send critical data to CS-MARS to allow for network topology discovery.

Table 2-2   *Network Devices and Self-Defending Capabilities (Continued)*

Host intrusion-prevention technology (CSA)	Recognizes and stops bad behavior on a host or server.
	Updates itself with globally correlated data and then automatically creates and deploys resulting rules that will stop security outbreaks, network scans, and hacker reconnaissance activity.
	Kills applications that are behaving badly.
	Sends alerts to CS-MARS for correlation and analysis to be used with syslogs and events from other security servers. CS-MARS uses this data to determine threat conditions and to formulate the correct response to that threat.
Cisco Network Admission Control	Works with routers, access points, VPN concentrators, and switches to stop hosts from accessing your network if those hosts do not have the proper security posture.
	Takes protective action and can shut down a Layer 2 port if it's determined that a host is behaving badly.
	Sends alerts to CS-MARS for correlation and analysis to be used with syslogs and events from other security servers. CS-MARS uses this data to determine threat conditions and to formulate the correct response to that threat.

CS-MARS extends the self-defending network by providing a much-needed layer of automated threat identification and response.

The following features of CS-MARS were discussed:

- **Automated log integration**—Provides a single source for log aggregation
- **Automated threat response**—Automatically learns the network topology, analyzes security alerts, and provides up-to-date accurate threat information.
- **Automated mitigation**—Automatically evaluates existing threats and recommends a mitigation action to security responders that will stop or contain the threat in the network.

Now that you understand the role that CS-MARS plays in your network from a technical or engineering standpoint, you examine in the next chapter how this technology can result in cost savings.

This chapter helps you understand the real threats in relation to Internet security. It addresses the following topics:

- Fact, FUD, and Fiction
- Real Threats to Enterprises
- Attack Impact
- Total Cost of Ownership
- Using CS-MARS to Ensure ROI and Protect Your Assets

## CHAPTER 3

Deriving TCO and ROI

The first thing you need to do when deciding what security equipment to put into place to secure your network and enterprise assets is to understand the threats that can affect these assets. This can be a difficult task because there is so much fear, uncertainty, and doubt (FUD) and fiction that is communicated through television news shows, vendors, newspapers, and websites. This chapter helps you understand what the real threats are in relation to Internet security. You'll step through a little bit of FUD and perceived threats so that you understand that they do exist and how you can deal with them. In addition to established threats, you'll read about emerging threats that represent risk moving forward.

The difference between tangible and intangible costs is explained and presented in a scenario illustrating how much cost you can expect to absorb during a new Internet attack. This helps you understand the total cost of ownership (TCO) to build, maintain, and protect your network.

The chapter then looks at how much cost you can expect to absorb during the same attack with CS-MARS deployed in your network. It explains how using CS-MARS can ensure a worthwhile return on investment (ROI) and protect your information.

Fact, FUD, and Fiction

You've heard it all before: "Buyer beware." You're fighting an opponent who is invisible and who has powers you can't assess. To complicate matters even more, you are being exploited by people for their own personal gain. Oh, and by the way, your own employees could be among the people trying to hurt you. Can there be much more working against you?

Are you scared yet? No one could blame you if you are. The art of understanding what's real in relation to Internet security threats is a deep and complicated subject. In this section, you see a few examples of how different people use this information and sometimes exaggerate the threats and impact of threats to scare you for their own purposes. For example, the person spreading this fear, this FUD, could be trying to sell you something. This person also could be giving you a worst-case scenario because somehow it means political or personal gain to him or her.

FUD vs. Reality

Probably the first thing that you need to understand is that when you hear or read about the dangers lurking in the Internet, you need to do a bit of follow-up to find out what's true, what's not, and how it affects you.

The following are two very public examples of the cybercrime confusion. These examples exemplify how Internet dangers are communicated differently, thereby causing confusion in the marketplace.

Example 1: The 2005 FBI Cybercrime Reports

The yearly *FBI Crime Report,* a reputable source, reported in early 2006 that $67 billion in damage was incurred in 2005 as a result of cybercrime. The article, titled "U.S. Cyber-Crime Damage Pegged at $67bn," can be found on the www.vnunet.com website.

Around the same time, *Forbes* magazine wrote an article that cited an FBI source stating that only $32 million in damage was incurred in 2005 as a result of cybercrime. This article, titled "Mueller's FBI Puts Computer Crime Losses At $32M," can be found on the www.forbes.com website.

With one article reporting $67 billion in losses and a second reporting only $32 million, that reflects a disparity of 2093 times. Where do you even begin to glean the reality? The facts are likely somewhere in between these numbers. When it comes down to it, each of these stories has little information to justify the numbers that were reported. The popular thought from security experts is that, although it's not specifically stated, the *Forbes* article most likely reported information from a limited survey, and the FBI report might have established an average cost per attack and simply multiplied that by the number of attacks reported in 2005. So likely, a different sampling of data caused a wide disparity in reported damage.

This leaves a really big question: Who do and should you believe? The answer: nobody. Consult many sources to get an understanding of Internet threats and costs before you try to use the information to make decisions about protecting your enterprise network and assets.

Example 2: The U.S. Critical Infrastructure Is Vulnerable

For your next scare, you don't need to look much farther than any newspaper or TV news station. Many declarations have been made in the last few years about the security of the United States' critical infrastructure locations. It has been said several times that dams, nuclear power plants, and critical infrastructure in the United States are wide open and completely vulnerable to Internet attacks. It might be comforting to know that, in speaking with consultants responsible for network infrastructure architecture in more than 100 dams and nuclear power plants, fewer than 5 percent of these infrastructure network architectures even have a connection to the Internet.

These consultants also went on to say that, of the 5 percent that have Internet connectivity, all of them are very cognizant of placing fully operational and audited security mechanisms and threat-response features in the network. This doesn't mean that national infrastructure locations are completely safe from cybercrimes, but it does indicate that perhaps they're not quite as vulnerable as what is sometimes reported.

Real Threats to Enterprises

The bottom line here is that, yes, the Internet can be the source of financial and operational hardships for your enterprise because of cyberattacks. However, it might not be as horrific as you sometimes read in magazines and newspapers or see on TV. All of this being said, make no mistake: Because threats do exist, it is in your best interests to have the proper infrastructure in place to mitigate these threats. If you are attacked, depending on the impact, the cost could be substantial to your enterprise.

Keep in mind that nobody can accurately determine what the risk is of your company being attacked. However, the fact is that you can significantly reduce that risk by deploying a strong security architecture and strong threat identification and mitigation responses. In addition, you should have a strong security policy that is actively enforced by both your security infrastructure and the people running that infrastructure. With a security posture such as this in place, your risk will be substantially reduced and the cost of an attack will be significantly decreased; the few attacks that are successful can be identified and stopped quickly, thereby reducing the probability of resulting catastrophic expenses.

In this section, we discuss the common Internet threats that cost enterprises millions of dollars per year (or billions, depending on which report you believe). These are the leading threats:

- Viruses
- Worms
- Viruses/worms
- Spyware
- Rootkits
- Trojans
- DoS/DDoS attacks
- Spam
- Zombies/bots
- Phishing attacks

All these threats are generally easy to inject into your network. The amount of damage that can be done depends on how well you have deployed security devices, how quickly you can recognize attacks, how quickly you can stop attacks, how critical your assets are to your company, and how well prepared you are for attack recovery.

We cover the total cost of security deployment and recovery in the upcoming section "Total Cost of Ownership," but first let's look at the common Internet threats your security infrastructure needs to defend itself against.

- **Viruses**—These threats are most commonly delivered to your network via e-mail. Viruses are usually triggered when a user clicks an attachment, unaware that the attachment is malicious software that will cause damage to files and possibly seek out other network devices to infect or damage. Viruses are generally stopped by host antivirus software, host intrusion-prevention software, or network antivirus appliances. Viruses gained the distinction of causing more damage than any other type of computer attack in 2005.

- **Worms**—A worm is usually a malicious piece of software that seeks out vulnerable machines, installs itself on those machines, and then repeats the cycle, exponentially spreading across the Internet and your network. A worm can do any number of malicious activities to a machine, including deleting files, stealing information, crashing it, and launching DDoS attacks on specific sites (such as the Slammer worm did to www.whitehouse.gov). Historically, worms such as Slammer, Sasser, and Blaster did the most damage once unleashed on a network, but, as mentioned already, viruses earned the distinction of causing the most damage in 2005. Worms are usually stopped by properly configured firewalls, IPS devices, and host intrusion-prevention software.

- **Viruses/worms**—This is a category of malware that starts out as a virus, usually attached to an e-mail. When the attachment is clicked, the software acts like a worm and spreads itself to other machines on both the local network and the Internet, causing extensive damage. Viruses/worms are usually stopped by properly configured firewalls, IPS devices, network antivirus appliances, antivirus software, and host intrusion-prevention software.

- **Spyware**—Spyware installs itself several different ways, and several hundred different variants of spyware exist. The actions that many of them have in common are that they exploit a browser, collect various types of data from your machine, and then send the information to servers on the Internet. This all takes place without any user interaction whatsoever. Spyware is generally stopped by antispyware software, antivirus software, IPS devices, antivirus network appliances, and host intrusion-prevention software.

- **Rootkits**—This is a set of software utilities often used by a hacker after gaining access to a system. These utilities are usually used to cover the intruder's footprints, elevate privileges, install back doors for future access, and glean data from the local network. Rootkits are often stopped by IPS devices, host intrusion-prevention software, and specialized software designed specifically to protect the integrity of system files.

- **Trojans**—This form of Internet threat is a malicious piece of software that looks like a valid operating system file or utility. For example, a hacker might write a utility called ping, which is found on almost every system and simply checks connectivity to another network device. That hacker's version of ping, from a user's perspective, will act exactly like the standard application. However, each time it is launched, it might also scan other devices on your network for vulnerabilities and send that information to a server on the Internet where the attacker has access. Trojans are often stopped by IPS devices, host intrusion-prevention software, and specialized software designed specifically to protect the integrity of system files.

- **DoS/DDoS attacks**—Denial-of-service (DoS) and distributed denial-of-service (DDoS) attacks are malicious software applications that simply try to put more traffic on the network or send more traffic to a server than either can handle. Many times, these attacks are destined for a specific server, either as revenge against a company or to extort money. A DDoS attack effectively stops any users trying to access network resources and cripples any servers that are under attack. DDoS attacks are DoS attacks that are coordinated among many hundreds or thousands of machines, usually all destined to attack the same server. Denial-of-service attacks are often stopped by black-hole routing, IPS devices, and devices specialized to stop the DoS attacks, such as the Cisco Guard appliance.

- **Spam**—Spam affects all of us but is generally seen as merely an annoyance. In reality, spam is very costly. Although it is not addressed in this book, according to reports from websites that track such statistics, spam eats up as much as 40 percent of a company's bandwidth. How much do you spend on your network infrastructure—and how much less would you spend if spam weren't an issue?

- **Zombies/bots**—As the name indicates, this malicious software is both stealthy and robotic. Worms, viruses, Trojans, and spyware are known to install small stealth applications called bots on machines. The user is completely unaware of the software installation. A bot often uses a protocol called Internet Relay Chat. It simply waits until it receives a command from a server or another bot telling it to do something, such as download a worm to itself or send a DoS attack to a specific server. A DoS attack is just an example; in theory, a bot can download or execute any malicious code. Bots are generally stopped by host intrusion-prevention software. The malicious code they spread is stopped by intrusion-prevention software and firewalls.

You can see from this that there is no shortage of threats or methods that a hacker can use to distribute attacks throughout the Internet. Your ability to recognize and respond to these threats is paramount to how much cost you will absorb if one of these threats is successful in penetrating your network.

Attack Impact

In the Internet Age, everything seems to move at the speed of light. Because of modern technology, the cost of business is going down, competition is fiercer than ever, and margins have shrunk to all-time lows in an attempt to sell goods at the lowest possible cost. In a nutshell, many enterprises are walking a very fine line between achieving profitability and risking additional costs from recovering from an Internet attack, which could be financially devastating. This section helps you understand the cost impact of a security incident and how you might reduce that risk.

The impact of an enterprise being attacked includes both tangible costs (the loss of revenue and the cost of cleaning up after an attack) and intangible costs (the hidden implications and considerations).

Tangible Costs

Table 3-1 lists tangible costs if an attack is successful. The upcoming section, "Total Cost of Ownership," addresses the costs associated with security software, security hardware, and licenses, such as antivirus software and Cisco SmartNet.

Table 3-1 correlates the threats listed in the previous section to the tangible costs of being attacked. Because a successful attack often means that critical servers need to go offline, loss of revenue is listed as a tangible cost in this table. This cost can vary dramatically between enterprises, so a value is not assigned to it when going through loss calculations in this chapter.

The following is an example of threat-recovery tasks resulting in measurable, tangible operational costs incurred during a computer attack:

- Personnel to analyze the threat and take action against a threat
- Equipment needed to prevent the threat from recurring
- Operating system and application reinstallations to ensure that the threat has been removed from the systems
- Patch installations to protect against future threats
- Data recovery to ensure that the systems have an accurate, uncompromised data area
- Hardware replacement, in case any hardware was damaged during an attack

An informal survey at executive briefings indicates that security managers and administrators believe it takes an average of two to five man-hours per incident per host to recover from an attack. If an attack is successful on a server, it generally takes more than five hours to recover because most enterprises do extensive testing before putting the server back online. Keep in mind that if automated procedures exist to do some of this work remotely, the time it takes to recover could be considerably less, thereby resulting in a lower cost to recover from a security incident.

Table 3-1 describes the detailed relationship among recovery tests, tangible costs, and threat types.

Table 3-1   *Costs of Threats*

Successful Threat	Hours Per Host	Tangible Costs
Virus	3	Identify infected hosts
		Remove virus
		Scan system
		Update local virus files
		Possibly restore operating system and applications
		Possibly apply vendor security patches
		Loss of revenue
Worm	3	Identify infected hosts
		Remove worm
		Possibly restore operating system and applications
		Install vendor security patches
		Upgrade HIPS if not behavior based, like CSA
		Loss of revenue
Virus/worm	3	Identify infected hosts
		Eradicate virus/worm
		Scan system
		Update local virus files
		Possibly restore operating system and applications
		Possibly apply vendor security patches
		Loss of revenue
Spyware	2	Identify infected hosts
		Remove spyware
		Scan system
		Update local virus files and spyware scanners
		Loss of revenue
Rootkits	2	Identify infected hosts
		Remove rootkits
		Scan system
		Possibly apply vendor security patches
		Loss of revenue

continues

Table 3-1   *Costs of Threats (Continued)*

Successful Threat	Hours Per Host	Tangible Costs
Trojans	3	Identify infected hosts
		Update local virus files
		Restore operating system and applications
		Loss of revenue
DoS/DDoS attacks	Unknown	Identify and filter DoS sources
		Work with your service provider to identify and stop DoS source IPs
		Configure a network device to protect against DoS attacks
		Identify any local systems participating in the attack
		Configure outbound security devices to filter attacks if they are sourced on your network
		Remove malicious "DoSing" software, usually a worm or bot
		Possibly restore operating system and applications
		Possibly apply vendor security patches
		Loss of revenue
Spam	Unknown	Can't be easily calculated but affects every single enterprise that runs an e-mail server
Zombie/bot	1	Identify infected hosts
		Eradicate virus
		Scan system
		Update local virus files
		Possibly restore operating system and applications
		Possibly apply vendor security patches
		Loss of revenue

Using the data from this table as a guideline, you can approximate the loss you will incur responding to specific threats. For example, it will cost you a maximum of about 3 hours per host to respond to a successful virus attack. To extrapolate that, if you pay your security responders or administrators $20 per hour and you have 500 hosts in your network, the average cost of this single incident will be approximately 3 (hours) × 500 (hosts) × 20 (salary) = $30,000.

Here's some additional fodder for thought when trying to understand the costs of a cyberattack:

- The average wage per hour for most security responders and administrators is more than $20 per hour, depending on wages in your geographical market and the current economic demands.

- Most enterprises have several incidents per year, so you would need to multiply out the $30,000 cost for each new incident.

- Intangible costs, which we talk about in the next section, could substantially increase the financial risk of an attack.

Figure 3-1 is a graph extracted from the 2005 Computer Security Institute/Federal Bureau of Investigation (CSI/FBI) Crime Report. This graph summarizes the cost of recovering from certain types of attacks for the 639 enterprises that responded to the survey. Although you might not be able to correlate these costs directly to your enterprise, the graph clearly shows that the tangible costs of a cyberattack can indeed be significant.

Figure 3-1   *CSI/FBI Cost of Cybercrime Graph*

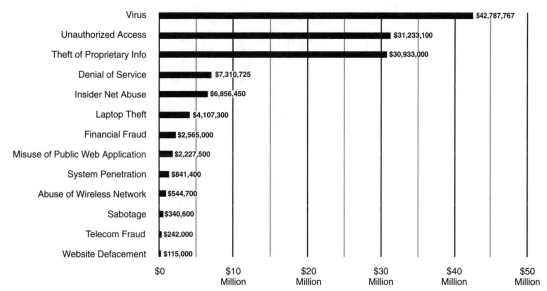

CSI/FBI 2005 Computer Crime and Security Survey   **Total losses for 2005 were $130,104,542.**   2005: 639 Respondents
Source: Computer Security Institute

Intangible Costs

Intangible costs are costs that cannot readily be entered as an expense on a financial ledger. They represent the long-term effects of an attack and need to be considered when deciding whether you need to add automated threat response to your network. These costs represent a very real risk to enterprises and are the types of risks that keep chief executive officers (CEOs), chief security officers (CSOs), vice presidents (VPs), board members, major shareholders, and directors awake at night.

Intangible costs include but are not limited to the following:

- The credibility of your company as viewed by customers, end users, and the market. No one wants to do business with a company that can't secure customer, user, and partner information.

- Possible liability if an attack is launched against another business from inside your network.

- Possible liability if an attack is successful against your network and sensitive data belonging to partners, end users, or customers is compromised.

- The cost of lost business when your network and hosts are down.

- Loss of shareholder confidence.

- Negative publicity for competitors to use against a company.

- Legal liability if you are a health-care provider or have customer financial data on your network that is lost because of a network attack.

- Legal liability if you are a health-care provider and your network is compromised and patient data is stolen or, worse yet, modified.

We don't go into detail on the amount of most intangible costs listed because it's so difficult to analyze exactly how much it could cost an enterprise. But consider this example: Suppose somebody on your internal network accidentally launched an e-mail virus. That virus acts like a worm and starts attacking other devices on your network. One or several of the devices on your network might go out over the Internet and infect a device on someone else's network. (This doesn't have to be a competitor it infects, although that would be really bad.) The infected party sustains financial losses because of this attack and gets forensic consultants and law enforcement involved. Law enforcement tracks the source of the attack back to your network. The cost of this attack could now skyrocket.

The best you can hope for in this situation is that you have what the court views as adequate security in place and that you need to pay for only your lawyers and any damage caused to your network by the cyberattack.

However, the worst-case scenario is that the court determines that you did not have adequate security in place at the time. Therefore, you are required to pay for your lawyers, the plaintiff's lawyers, court costs, the plaintiff's investigative costs, the damage caused to your network, the damage caused to the plaintiff's network, and the public-relations cost to repair the reputation of your company. Finally, you must consider the cost of purchasing equipment and hiring staff to bring your security posture to a level at which a court will never again decide that you do not have adequate security in place.

This is just a guess of what this worst-case scenario could cost you. Again, you can calculate the total costs with the following assumptions:

- Your company had 500 desktops infected.
- The company you inadvertently attacked had 500 desktops infected.
- The cost of cleanup was $20 per hour.
- The lawyer fees on each side ran $100,000 each. (Granted, this is a random estimation and could be more or less, depending on the depth the lawyers needed to get into on this case.)
- The investigative fees ran approximately $10,000. (This cost is close, based on conversations with consultants who do this type of work.)

Based on these assumptions, we can make the following calculation:

```
3(hrs) × 500 (hosts) × 20 (salary) × 2 (for both companies) = $60,000.
$100,000 × 2 = $200,000 in lawyer fees.
$10,000 to cover the forensics costs of the other company.
$5,000 in public-relations consultants.
Total costs = $275,000.
```

The bottom line is that, without proper security in place, this incident could have cost you a minimum of $275,000.

This calculation doesn't even consider the other tangible costs listed at the beginning of this chapter. Of course, in the unlikely case that you inadvertently attacked a competitor, the costs and your problems could be compounded.

Based on this simple example, it's clearly in your best interests to have security in place to protect against Internet and network threats. In addition, it is in your best interests to have an infrastructure in place to recognize and mitigate network threats and to stop them from spreading within your own organization and beyond the boundaries of your network.

Emerging Threats

Other threats that have become very real in 2005 and are expected to get even worse in the future include a combination of cyberextortion, new exploits available for purchase, and Internet robots for rent (botnets).

These new threats need to be taken seriously because they can be difficult to stop and are much more costly than traditional threats. Usually, the threat is sourced through another country or trafficked through several jump hosts, thereby making it difficult for criminalists and investigators to find the source of the attacks. To you as an enterprise, this means that if you don't have adequate defenses and responses built into your network, you will likely either have to pay to not be exploited or suffer the costs of the network attack.

Extortion

The year 2005 saw several instances of cybercrime-related extortion. Extortion attacks take on a couple different flavors, but the foundation of the attacks is usually one of the following:

- Attackers let victims know that something valuable has been stolen and that, unless money is paid, they'll exploit the value of what they have.

- Attackers show victims that they can attack at will. Unless the victims pay money, the attackers threaten something like a DoS attack that will severely impact the victims' revenues.

What you are seeing here is basically cyberblackmail.

Most attacks are associated with a substantial ransom or payoff. The amount of the ransom is generally less than the damage the attacker can inflict, so you might think the ransom is an attractive offer. The problem with paying this money is that if the attacker successfully blackmails you once, that person is more likely to do it again. If you find yourself facing an extortion attack, you need to take action and put the correct resources in place to ensure that it can't happen a second time.

These extortion attacks are well documented on the Internet. Here are some random examples gleaned from a Google search of the keywords "cybercrime ransom." To get an understanding of the costs associated with extortion, look at some of the following links.

An American credit card company received an extortion letter for an undisclosed amount of money, the extortion wasn't paid, and DDoS attacks were launched against the company. To its credit, www.authorized.net immediately purchased the required security gear to mitigate the attacks. The attack appeared to be sourced from outside the United States, so the chances of bringing the criminals to justice are slim. Information about this attack can be found in an article titled "Authorize.Net Battles Extortion Attempts," on the www.eweek.com website.

In May 2005, CNN and *Computerworld* reported that extortionists were breaking into computers, encrypting critical data, and then demanding $200 for the decryption key so companies could read their own data again. This type of extortion has been given the catchy title of "ransomware." Information about this attack can be found in an article titled

"New Computer Scam Holds Your Info for Ransom," at www.cnn.com, and an article titled "Trojan Writers Coding for Money—Freezes PC for Ransom," at www.darknet.org.

Just these few examples should give you a good idea of how real, how costly, and how prevalent extortion threats are today. Although every hit in Google is not a unique extortion threat, the query used for this research generated 202,000 website hits.

Zero-Day Exploits for Sale

Next on the list of emerging threats that enterprises need to consider is that zero-day exploits can now be purchased on the web.

Although this might sound benign at first, it's a disturbing trend. First, you should understand that a zero-day exploit is an attack for which no signature is available to stop it. Previously, only elite hackers had access to zero-day attacks. Now that these attacks are for sale, anybody with a grudge and $4,000 to spend can buy an exploit and attack your Internet site. The following URLs are examples of hackers selling zero-day exploits.

The article "WMF Exploit Sold Underground for $4,000" at www.eweek.com talks about the sale of an exploit that was traced back to Russia. Again, notice that this was from a country where the FBI doesn't have jurisdiction and that the criminal will likely never be caught.

The boldest attempt to sell exploits was done on the world's most popular auction site, eBay. The article "Zero-Day Excel Flaw for Sale on eBay" at www.smh.com describes an eBay user selling a zero-day Excel exploit for only $40! Of course, eBay pulled the ad as soon as it became aware of what was going on.

The boldness of selling exploits on the web is relatively new. Although it seems to have just started in December 2005, cybercrime experts are worried that a trend is being established and that we will see much more of this in the near future.

Botnets and Botnet Rental

News flash: The hacking industry is no longer a friendly bunch of well-intentioned, huggable, brilliant engineers exploiting systems for the betterment of the Internet. Some of that charming mentality still exists, but the hacking industry has gone commercial with one-stop shopping. The only thing missing is technical support. Not only do they sell anyone exploit code and extort money from you if you don't do as they wish, but they also rent unscrupulous characters hundreds and thousands of computers (called botnets) that can be used to attack you. I guess things weren't complicated enough! I'll bet you can't wait to see what the coming year has to offer.

A botnet is a group of hundreds—in some cases, thousands—of computers that have been exploited by hackers, just waiting for a hacker to send a command to tell them what to do. After a hacker builds a botnet, the hacker rents the network to people who run malicious software, usually for criminal or profitable purposes. Rest assured that botnets are never used for any purpose that is helpful to you.

Here is a list of articles that have been found by Google, this time using the keywords "botnet rental." The following are random, interesting articles returned by the search:

- The article "Botnet Operator Pleads Guilty" at www.eweek.com highlights an individual who compromised 400,000 machines that were used for illegal purposes. This article does not indicate that his bots were used as rentals but does show that botnets exist and need to be taken seriously. If 400,000 machines are all programmed to send data to your site at the same time, this could cause very serious problems for your website.

- The article "Phishers Dodge Shutdowns by Striking via 'Botnets'" at www.eweek.com describes how botnets have been used as a source of phishing attacks.

- The research paper "Large Botnets and Distributed Denial of Service Attacks" at www-inst.eecs.berkeley.edu is the result of research done at University of California–Berkeley. It describes botnets, how they are used, and how rental rates are determined.

- If you are interested in finding out more about botnets and how they are created, the *Washington Post* has an excellent interactive website that describes how botnets are created. This interactive website, called "Building a Botnet," is at www.washingtonpost.com.

Impact of Attacks and Probability of Reoccurrence

The bottom line is that Internet attacks are a reality of doing business on the World Wide Web. It doesn't matter that you're only doing e-mail or browsing the web and don't have a web server; your network devices can still suffer infections. These infections can spread to the rest of your network and to other companies on the Internet. As discussed already, this exposes you to both tangible and intangible risks, increasing your cost of doing business.

In this chapter, you've looked at what you need to consider when you assess the risk of an Internet attack. This includes the tangible costs, the intangible costs, and the emerging threats that could put your enterprise at future risk. The one thing we haven't yet talked about is the probability of attack reoccurrence and the cost associated with getting hit by the same attack more than once. An informal survey involving 20 security professionals (engineers, managers, and consultants) revealed that reoccurences incurred at least 80 percent of the original cost. This assumes that, based on the lessons learned from the first attack, they figured out how to more quickly identify and respond if they got hit again.

How probable is it that, if you have been successfully compromised once, the same attack will happen again? Very probable. After a successful attack, the chances are good that the hackers have let other hackers know about their success and might even sell this information to other attackers along with how to exploit your network. The one thing that is a given is that, if you have been attacked, you need to take action to ensure that it doesn't happen again. In most cases, this means that you need to either configure your network or security devices to block the attack, or, if you did not have the right hardware and software in place, you must put it in place. But even more important, you must ensure that processes and equipment are in place to recognize and mitigate your attacks quickly and accurately. The faster an attack is mitigated, the less risk your enterprise faces. The statement "Time is money" has never been so true; the longer it takes you to recognize and mitigate an attack, the more it will cost you in the end.

Total Cost of Ownership

Now that you've looked at the cost of recovering from an Internet attack, let's take a quick look at the total cost of ownership (TCO) of your network.

You must take several things into consideration when looking at your TCO from a security perspective:

- **Hardware**—The original purchase cost of the hardware needed to protect you from Internet threats is important to note. This equipment includes firewalls, DDoS mitigation appliances, intrusion-prevention systems, VPN concentrators, web proxies, routers, switches, and network access control devices.

- **Software**—The original purchase cost of the installed software needed to protect your network from Internet threats is also significant. This software includes host intrusion prevention, network access control, host firewalls, tripwire applications, vulnerability scanners, antivirus software, antispyware software, access-control servers, authentication servers, and software web proxies.

- **Licensing**—The cost of recurring licensing for both hardware and software includes licensing for all of the hardware and software listed earlier. Licensing costs from all best-of-breed security companies now include signature updates for IPS, HIPS, and antivirus. Previously, these costs were not passed on to you, but now that signatures need to be created and tested for so many new attacks, companies are spending millions of dollars keeping up with these threats. Most security companies cannot stay in business without charging fees to support this ongoing threat-defense effort.

- **Ongoing costs of security devices**—The initial and sometimes recurring cost it takes to install, train, and manage your security devices includes setup tasks for all the hardware and software listed earlier.

- **Ongoing costs of software**—The recurring cost of the time it takes to install, train, manage, and patch your applications, intrusion-prevention software, host intrusion-prevention software, antivirus software, and operating systems includes core operating systems and applications such as Microsoft Windows, Linux, Mac OS, Apache web server, Internet Information Server, database servers, and core business applications.

From this brief list, it is apparent that most enterprises have a substantial investment in building a network and security infrastructure. The amount of time it takes to recognize and respond to an Internet attack directly impacts your cost of ownership for this infrastructure. The longer it takes you to recognize and mitigate an attack, the more damage will be done to the systems. For example, if you can recognize and mitigate an attack in 10 minutes, you might have to patch only from 1 to 20 network devices. But if it takes you several hours to recognize and mitigate an attack, several hundred (or thousand) devices might be affected, and recovery costs will be exponentially higher.

The next section explains how CS-MARS reduces the costs you incur from an Internet attack, which reduces your total cost of ownership.

Using CS-MARS to Ensure ROI and Protect Your Assets

The traditional approach to addressing security concerns involves installing devices and software that block attacks and stop attacks from recurring. This is a viable approach to basic network security, but with this traditional approach, a high cost is still associated with the recognition and mitigation of an attack; the process of recovering operating systems, applications, and data after an attack involves additional cost.

In this section, we talk about how CS-MARS can be used to reduce the cost of recovering from an Internet attack.

As discussed in Chapter 1, "Understanding SIM and STM," STM processes and correlates information from the entire network, not just security devices. The result of this technology is automated, quick, and accurate threat identification and response that saves you money on every single successful attack on your network.

Cost of Recovery Without CS-MARS

In the earlier section, "Tangible Costs," Table 3-1 estimates how much time it takes to recognize and recover from specific threats. This is followed by a calculation showing that responding to a virus that damaged 500 desktops could cost you as much as $30,000 from the recognition phase to recovery. Let's follow that example from the threat-recognition phase to recovery when this process is done manually.

Without CS-MARS, you must perform the following tasks, which represent tangible costs during cleanup:

- Identify the 500 infected hosts.

- Remove the virus from 500 hosts.

- Scan the system on 500 hosts to ensure that there is no other damage on the host. (For some enterprises, this step is optional if they reinstall the operating system; however, viruses do not always infect the operating system.)

- Update local virus files on 500 hosts. This is done only after the AV vendor has released a virus signature, but this process is automated in most enterprises.

- Possibly restore the operating system and applications on 500 hosts.

- Possibly apply vendor security patches on 500 hosts.

When you evaluate tangible, measurable cleanup costs, you also have to add in the loss of revenue incurred while hosts and servers are out of commission. Earlier in the chapter, this cleanup was estimated to cost $30,000. I think you can glean from the way the calculation was done that, in many circumstances, this is probably a low estimate.

Cost of Recovery Using CS-MARS

Now let's put CS-MARS in the mix during this same virus attack and see how the equation changes based on the information and functionality that CS-MARS puts into the recognition and response phase.

1 The virus starts trying to infect other hosts.

2 Depending on how the virus behaves (how fast and what port numbers are used) and how the network is designed, a certain number of hosts are infected before CS-MARS triggers an event notifying security responders of abnormal flows in the network. It's impossible to calculate the exact number of infected hosts because of the different ways that virus and worm attacks behave. In the best case, the virus tries to spread itself via e-mail or acts like some worms and tries to infect random IP addresses. In this case, it's possible that no additional hosts are infected. In the worst case, an entire subnet could be infected, which would be about 200 hosts. Although it is just as likely that fewer than 200 hosts will be infected, let's go with the worst case in this scenario.

3 An e-mail page is sent to a security responder 24 hours a day, 7 days a week, as soon as CS-MARS triggers the anomalous event.

4 The security responder gets the page and logs into CS-MARS to view the event. A topology map of the network is displayed showing the sources and destinations of the attack. Additionally, a mitigation recommendation tells the responder what command will stop the attack and to what device the command should be applied.

5   In most cases, the security responder can click the mitigation button and keep the attack from spreading beyond that point.

6   The attack is contained at this point, and because we used the worst-case scenario, 200 hosts need to be cleaned up but not identified; CS-MARS already did that for you.

Now that your attack has been contained, let's run the same equation and see how your cost of recognition and recovery has been affected simply by adding CS-MARS to your network.

The simple calculation tells you that this time 200 hosts were infected instead of 500, so your cost of cleaning up is 40 percent of $30,000, which comes out to $12,000—that's a cost reduction of 60 percent. But if you dig deeper, you will find that your cost savings are higher:

- Zero costs were involved in identifying infected hosts because CS-MARS did this for you.

- There is no chance that the attack will spread to the Internet because CS-MARS stopped the attack before it propagated, which, as previously illustrated, could have a high associated cost.

- The attack was mitigated in a specific subnet. Therefore, there was no lost revenue associated with Internet connectivity.

- This represents only a single attack; if you multiply this by the number of attacks your responders need to address per year, the savings are exponential.

Figure 3-1, shown earlier, reveals that in 2005, 639 companies incurred tangible losses of about $157,000 related to viruses, intrusions, and information loss. Assuming that CS-MARS could have saved these companies 60 percent of their measurable losses, these companies would have spent $62,800 instead of $157,000. Take a look at the 2005 *CSI/FBI Cybercrime Report* to get a better idea of the profiles of these companies; it will help you calculate what your potential losses from cybercrime could be, and you can apply the 60 percent CS-MARS rule to see how much money you could have saved.

Summary

The main purpose of this chapter is to help you understand that cyberattacks can be very costly.

While examining the actual costs of responding to a security threat, you focused on tangible, measurable costs. It is important, however, to also consider intangible costs, such as legal liability and lost business. Even though intangible costs are difficult to measure, you were presented with these costs because you need to be aware of them when analyzing risk and making informed decisions before purchasing security equipment and hiring security responders.

If manual response is the method you use to recognize, respond to, mitigate, and recover from an attack, you will undoubtedly incur a high cost of recovery. Using CS-MARS as an automated response and mitigation system, you can substantially reduce your costs of recovery. When you take advantage of the automated features of CS-MARS during the recognition and response cycle, the cost savings are approximately 60 percent.

Now that you understand the basic features of CS-MARS, how CS-MARS fits into your self-defending network, and the cost advantages of deploying CS-MARS, the following chapter introduces you to the inner workings of CS-MARS.

PART II

CS-MARS Theory and Configuration

This chapter introduces you to the CS-MARS hardware appliances and shows you how CS-MARS operates and processes its information. Topics in this chapter include the following:

- Technical Introduction to the CS-MARS Appliance
- Database Storage and Utilization
- Network Topology Used for Forensic Analysis
- NetFlow in CS-MARS
- Positive Alert Verification and Dynamic Vulnerability Scanning
- Methodology of Communication

## CHAPTER 4

CS-MARS Technologies and Theory

In this chapter, you are introduced to the CS-MARS appliance and discover what it is really about. Part I, "The Security Threat Identification and Response Challenge," introduced you to the SIM and STM industry and covered why networks need to become proactive security frameworks. CS-MARS was mentioned briefly as the solution to complete that security framework; now you discover why.

This chapter discusses in detail hardware specifications, database operations, terminology, and the patented technologies. You also learn how the CS-MARS Oracle database is used inside CS-MARS. The chapter then describes how CS-MARS learns your network topology, how you can use and understand the diagrams and vectoring tools, and what information you can derive from using the topology maps. Following that is a discussion of how CS-MARS uses NetFlow information and develops network baselining and behavioral profiling.

The final two sections of the chapter cover false positives and introduce you to the built-in vulnerability tool and the support of third-party vulnerability assessment (VA) tools. Finally, you learn how CS-MARS communicates with reporting devices, archives its database, and handles incident notification.

Technical Introduction to the CS-MARS Appliance

As you already know, CS-MARS is a unique platform that is categorized as an STM technology. In learning about SIM and STM technologies, you discovered that every solution has its own uniqueness to accomplish the task at hand. CS-MARS is no exception: It takes a very different approach in what data it collects, how it uses that data, and how that data is presented.

To better understand how CS-MARS accomplishes its mission, you must be familiar with its core technical attributes. The following sections discuss in detail the attributes you need to know to successfully deploy and operate the CS-MARS platform:

- CS-MARS at a Glance
- CS-MARS Product Portfolio and Hardware Specifications
- CS-MARS Terminology
- CS-MARS Technologies

CS-MARS at a Glance

CS-MARS is a family of high-performance appliances that, when placed in your network, provide unified threat management, data monitoring, and mitigation. This then helps you to make more effective use of your network and its operational and security data. CS-MARS can operate in standalone deployment or in a distributed deployment reporting to a master management unit, enabling you to scale the solution to support your existing network architecture.

CS-MARS is simply not a piece of software installed on "off-the-shelf" hardware. The hardware has been designed to work specifically with the software processes, enabling the product to be extremely fast in operation and self-sustaining, for low maintenance. The CS-MARS operating system operates off a modified Linux kernel that has been protected using the necessary services CS-MARS requires; additionally, it uses ip-table firewall rules on the appliance so that ports used by internal services can safely receive data without compromise. The Oracle database(s) used to store the data operates in a "sandboxed" environment, in which the only access to the database is through the operating environment contained in the web GUI. To further protect CS-MARS, each appliance has two Ethernet interfaces, one of which can be used in an out-of-band network for secure management. Therefore, it is not vulnerable to any outside compromise or attack. Access to the appliance is through Hypertext Transfer Protocol–Secure (HTTPS) or Secure Shell (SSH) for operation and administrative functions, respectively. Administrative operation through SSH is not root-level access to the kernel but a structured and protected shell that enables an administrator to configure the variables discussed in Chapter 5, "CS-MARS Appliance Setup and Configuration," and Appendix D, "Command-Line Interface."

CS-MARS can be a passive device on your network unless it is configured to actively communicate with certain devices. Pushing data from reporting devices to CS-MARS does not require CS-MARS to communicate with anything. Two-way communications might be necessary, depending on the devices you configure to work with CS-MARS or if you want to enable mitigation. CS-MARS can become chatty on the network when SNMP discovery is enabled; however, this is a one-time process or a scheduled evolution. When using dynamic vulnerability scanning, CS-MARS uses its built-in Nessus scanner in a targeted fashion to determine whether a host is susceptible to a specific threat; therefore, if you enable this function, CS-MARS actively scans hosts.

One of the most unique features of the CS-MARS appliance is one that is not technical but that is still important to mention. The CS-MARS appliance has only an unrestricted license. That is, there are no licensing limits to the number of sessions and users that can connect to or administer/operate the device. Additionally, Cisco places no restrictions on the physical number of devices that can communicate to the appliance. Each appliance has different storage and processing capabilities that define how much data can be sent to the appliance.

CS-MARS Product Portfolio and Hardware Specifications

CS-MARS is a family of appliances that vary in size and function. Currently, two types of appliances exist:

- Local Controllers
- Global Controllers

Local Controller (LC)   This appliance features everything we have been discussing and discuss shortly. Every type of LC has the same software features available to it; the only differences are hardware capabilities, speeds, and throughput. In short, this is the CS-MARS.

Global Controller (GC)   This is an appliance that communicates with one or more LCs and allows centralized operation and management of LCs in a CS-MARS distributed deployment. It is important to note that the GC does not conduct global correlation of all LC data.

Communication between the LC and the GC occurs through HTTPS. The CS-MARS LC sends summarized snapshots of the data to the GC. Therefore, all raw data remains on the LC. When you click the data in the GC, a new HTTPS session is opened to the LC; you then actually view the data on the LC. All management or administrative commands sent from the GC to the LC are done so through HTTPS communications.

This book discusses the LCs in detail, with brief mention of the GCs. For detailed information about GC operation and deployment, see *Security Monitoring with CS-MARS* (ISBN 1587052709), which will be released by Cisco Press in 2007.

Table 4-1 lists the different LCs and their hardware and throughput specifications.

Table 4-1   *Local Controller Hardware Specifications*

LC Type	CPU	Storage	Flow per Second	Events per Second	RAID Level
M20	P4 3.0 GHz	120 GB	15,000	500	None
M50	P4 3.0 GHz	240 GB	25,000	1000	Level 0
M100e	(2)Xeon 2.8 GHz	750 GB	75,000	3000	Level 10
M100	(2)Xeon 2.8 GHz	750 GB	150,000	5000	Level 10
M200	(2)Xeon 3.0 GHz	1 TB	300,000	10,000	Level 10

NOTE   At the time of writing, Cisco Systems released the M20r, which is a restricted version of the M20. The M20r has the same specifications, except that it handles 50 events per second (EPS). Additionally, the related heading in Table 4-1 refers to the NetFlow flows per second that CS-MARS receives.

Table 4-2 lists the different GCs available and their corresponding hardware and throughput specifications.

Table 4-2 *Global Controller Specifications*

GC Type	No. LC Supported	Storage	RAID Level
GCm	5 (M20 and M50 only)	1 TB	Level 10
GC	Unlimited	1 TB	Level 10

NOTE	All CS-MARS GCs use the same hardware as an M200 LC.

CS-MARS has built-in redundancy features to maintain high availability. All models of CS-MARS except the SMB models have the following redundant features:

- Hot-swappable RAID 10 hard drives
- Multiple processors
- Multiple removable fans
- Redundant power supplies
- System software watchdogs (all models)

As with all Cisco products, technical support is available every day of the year: 24 hours a day, 7 days a week. Table 4-3 outlines the part numbers and SmartNet levels for each CS-MARS product.

Table 4-3 *CS-MARS Part Numbers*

Product Type	Cisco Part Number	Cisco SmartNet Part Number
M20	CS-MARS-20-K9	CON-SNT-MARS20
M50	CS-MARS-50-K9	CON-SNT-MARS50
M100e	CS-MARS-100e-K9	CON-SNT-MARS100E
M100	CS-MARS-100-K9	CON-SNT-MARS100
M200	CS-MARS-200-K9	CON-SNT-MARS200
GCm	CS-MARS-GCM-K9	CON-SNT-MARSGCM
GC	CS-MARS-GC-K9	CON-SNT-MARSGC

CS-MARS is a turnkey hardware appliance. In building the appliance, the hardware was specifically selected to support real-time correlation, sessionization, and mitigation. These components make up the CS-MARS appliance:

- Steel chassis, 19-inch rack-mountable
- Motherboard

- Intel Pentium or Xeon processor(s)
- DRAM memory
- Hot-swappable RAID 10 IDE drives (most models)
- Network interface card 10/100/1000
- DVD-ROM drive
- KVM ports (USB and serial)
- Serial-management port
- Toggle switches (reboot and power on/off)
- 120 V AC, single 300 W or dual 500 W power supply
- Rack-mounting brackets
- User guides (printed Quick Start, PDF user guide)
- Proprietary software
- Oracle database (no additional licensing required)
- Linux kernel v4.1.2
- OpenSSL library
- Tomcat Web Server

Each appliance is UL approved and has two Ethernet interfaces. The higher-end models—M100e, M100, M200—and both GCs have dual-redundant 500 W power supplies. All hardware provided is covered for 90 days or according to its respective SmartNet agreement.

CS-MARS Terminology

In the world of CS-MARS, you need to be familiar with certain terms and understand their meanings as they relate to SIM and STM. CS-MARS uses these terms to label certain data. Most are SIM specific; however, CS-MARS might use them differently. The following are definitions of each of these terms as used for the CS-MARS:

- Event
- Parser
- Session
- Incident
- Rule

Event   This is a system message generated by a reporting device that records an occurrence. An example of an event is a syslog message generated by a router or an IDS alarm. In CS-MARS, each event has a unique ID assigned to it that it displays, as shown in Figure 4-1.

Figure 4-1 *CS-MARS Normalized Sessions*

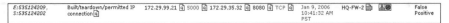

Parser This is a set of static or dynamic parameters that map the fields of an event to an identification and labeling process. This is the first phase of normalization. In CS-MARS, devices that are supported have built-in parsers. For devices that are not inherently supported, parsers can be customized using the built-in custom parser tool.

Session This is a group of events that have been grouped together because of their relationship, regardless of the reporting device. This is the result of a quintuple match in the event records using source IP, destination IP, port(s), and protocol. When a quintuple match occurs, it is correlated with the time stamps. In CS-MARS, each session has a unique ID assigned to it and is displayed on the appropriate reporting screens and CS-MARS panels, as shown in Figure 4-2.

Figure 4-2 *CS-MARS Session Information*

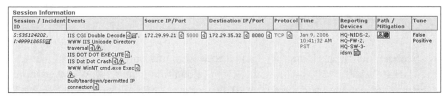

Incident An incident is created when a session or sessions match a rule condition within the specified parameters. In CS-MARS, each incident has a unique ID assigned to it and is displayed on the appropriate reporting screens and CS-MARS panels. Simply click the incident ID to get to the detailed forensic data, as shown in Figure 4-3.

Figure 4-3 *CS-MARS Incident Summary*

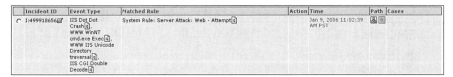

Rule A rule is a set of parameters that must be met to take an action. An incident is automatically generated when a rule is triggered. Rules can be defined by behaviors, specific event messages, certain fields in messages, or occurrences over time. In CS-MARS, two types of rules exist: inspection rules and drop rules.

Inspection rules are rules that define parameters that event and session data must meet to produce an incident and take a specific action.

With drop rules, when their conditions are met, CS-MARS refrains from creating an incident from the event and either drops the data from the database entirely or just logs the data to the database. Drop rules don't have the same structure as system rules; they cannot have a sequence of events to trigger them.

Each type of rule has two states: active and inactive.

Active rules are rules that CS-MARS currently processes using the received data. Inactive rules are rules the system ignores when processing received data.

CS-MARS does not allow the deletion of a rule, just a change in state. This was done intentionally. Additionally, these inactive rules do not take up system resources because they are dormant. CS-MARS keeps time stamps on the rules, marking when they were active or inactive; this allows archived data that is reimported into CS-MARS to be processed by rules that were active at the time CS-MARS originally received the data. Figure 4-4 shows an example of a CS-MARS rule.

Figure 4-4   *CS-MARS Rules*

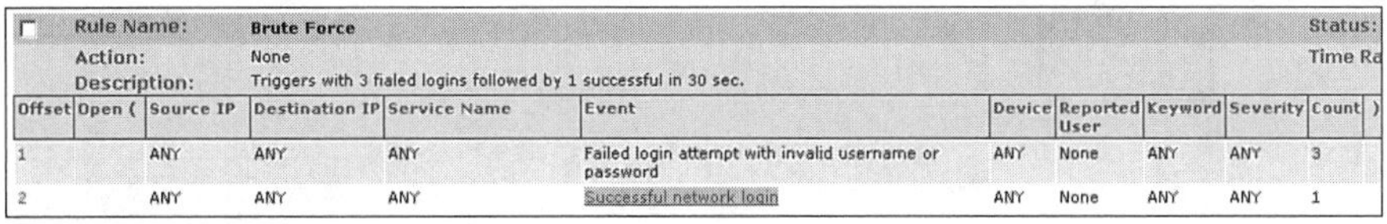

Rule Name:	**Brute Force**									Status:
Action:	None									Time Ra
Description:	Triggers with 3 fialed logins followed by 1 successful in 30 sec.									
Offset	Open (	Source IP	Destination IP	Service Name	Event		Device	Reported User	Keyword	Severity	Count)
1		ANY	ANY	ANY	Failed login attempt with invalid username or password		ANY	None	ANY	ANY	3
2		ANY	ANY	ANY	Successful network login		ANY	None	ANY	ANY	1

CS-MARS Technologies

CS-MARS uses three patented technologies to correlate data, display attack data, and mitigate attacks:

- ContextCorrelation
- SureVector Analysis
- AutoMitigate

ContextCorrelation   This technology groups multiple events and network behavior across NAT boundaries into a session. This CS-MARS process is called sessionization. System- and user-defined correlation rules are then applied to multiple sessions to identify valid incidents.

SureVector Analysis   This technology uses the network topology, host profile information, and vulnerability-assessment information to determine whether a threat is valid and/or whether it can be successful.

AutoMitigate   Mitigation is not done automatically. This technology automatically identifies the devices in the path of the attack that can be used to stop the attack. It then makes recommendations using those devices and gives the user a method to push the appropriate commands to the mitigative device.

The key to understanding how CS-MARS operates is in understanding how it processes the received data. Figure 4-5 simplifies the order of operation for CS-MARS processes.

Figure 4-5 *CS-MARS Event Processing Flow Chart*

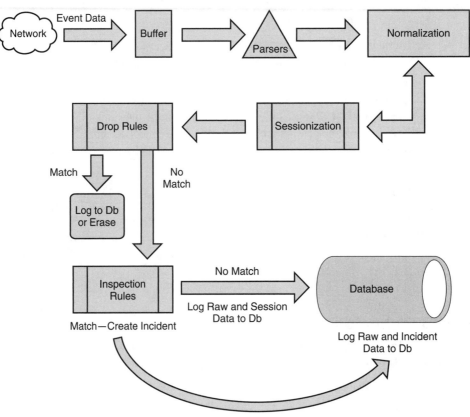

You will also find this flow chart useful in troubleshooting misconfigurations and data-processing issues that might arise.

Database Storage and Utilization

CS-MARS uses an Oracle 9.2i Enterprise database. The database is fully licensed for operation on the appliance and requires no administration whatsoever; therefore, it is completely self-sustaining. Additionally, all remote services and system calls are disabled because they are not used in CS-MARS.

Two subjects about the database are discussed next:

- Database structure
- Database archival

CS-MARS Database Structure

Cisco is pretty tight-lipped about how it structures the database and what modifications (if any) it makes, but the database is optimized for performance. To understand why CS-MARS is so fast, we use a thought process that is not the actual structure, but that enables you to visualize how the database works.

Think of CS-MARS as using hundreds of little databases. Each reporting device, host, and day (March 1, March 2, and so on) of data has its own database. Now, don't think of CS-MARS as using standard database indexing but as using objects that link these databases and create the relationships. When a query or a call for information happens, the object is requested and CS-MARS calls up the data for display.

Each CS-MARS device has its own storage requirements. The actual event-data storage is smaller than the total storage each respective platform offers. For example, the M20 has 120 GB of storage available; however, only 77 GB are for event data. The remaining 43 GB are used for the other databases, configuration files, reports, and much more.

Table 4-4 lists the actual event-database storage sizes for each platform.

Table 4-4   *CS-MARS Events Storage and Total Storage*

Platform	Total Storage	Event Storage
M20	120 GB	77 GB
M50	240 GB, RAID 0	148 GB
M100e	750 GB, RAID 10	565 GB
M100	750 GB, RAID 10	565 GB
M200	1 TB, RAID 10	795 GB

When storing event data in its internal database, CS-MARS stores it in its raw format, uncompressed. It breaks event data into ten different partitions. When writing data to the databases, CS-MARS uses a first-in, first-out (FIFO) approach. When the 77 GB of storage is reached in a M20, it wipes out the oldest day (database) of event data. This data is lost if you are not archiving the data. This process allows CS-MARS to have room for event data in case a network infection or an attack happens. Here is an example to make the point. One day's worth of data could be 70 GB, the next day's could 5 GB, and the following day's could be 2 GB. With this, an M20 has 3 days of on-box storage. The next day, CS-MARS wipes out the 70 GB of data stored for Day 1. In reality, 70 GB for 1 day in an M20 is unheard of; however, you now understand how it stores its event data.

This example brings up some good questions. How do you know what size CS-MARS to get to meet your organizational storage requirements? What if you need 30 days of on-box storage—what platform do you need? Unfortunately, you need to make some assumptions or do some very good measurements with your data.

The following example and formula can be used to determine on-box database storage in your environment.

Assume that, by rough estimation, at 100 events per second and each event having an average of 200 bytes, 1 day of storage capacity is: $(100 \times 200 \times 86,400) = 1,728,000,000$ bytes of data, or 1.72 GB of data per day required. Using an M20 with 61.6 GB of event-data storage available (77 GB, minus 20 percent for the redo tables and indexing), you have 36 days of on-box storage (61.6/1.72).

In this example, we made several assumptions about events per second (EPS) and event-data packet size. These variables differ between products and based on network utilization.

In analyzing storage capacity for your data, it becomes apparent that you need a means of archiving it.

CS-MARS Data Archiving

CS-MARS has the capability of archiving its on-box event data and configuration files. CS-MARS archives its configuration at 2 a.m. every morning and compresses and transfers its event data approximately every hour to a remote networked attached storage (NAS). Archiving serves two purposes:

- To restore the CS-MARS system, in case of hardware failure or physical damage, to its closest running state, either on the same appliance or on the new appliance
- To retrieve the historic event data

CS-MARS uses NFS to archive its data. In future releases, it will use other protocols; however, Cisco has not committed any time frames for releasing this. NFS is a widely supported protocol, allowing data to be transferred to an NFS server that can be placed on just about any common operating system. Using NFS gives organizations the flexibility to use any type of storage mechanism they already have in place.

Various kinds of NAS storage exist, but most types of NAS support both NFS and CIFS protocols. When a NAS box is running the NFS protocol, it acts as an NFS server to any NFS clients that have NFS enabled, including CS-MARS.

CS-MARS compresses the data with the Ziv-Lempel algorithm (also used in GZIP) and stores it in its native format when it archives. The compression ratio CS-MARS can achieve varies depending on the event-data packet size, ranging from 12:1 to 38:1.

The archiving GUI function enables users to specify the capacity of the remote NAS storage used for archiving event data in terms of the number of days. When the specified number of days is reached, the CS-MARS box recycles the storage by deleting the oldest day of data and replacing it with the newest data. Each day of event data is stored in its own folder, with each hour of data in a separate file within the folder. With CS-MARS deleting the oldest archived event data first, it becomes necessary for an organization to use its data-backup mechanisms to copy the previous archived data from the NFS server before it is replenished by the new archived data. CS-MARS archives its configuration data daily.

The archiving GUI can be found at **Admin > System Maintenance > Database Configuration Information > Data Archiving**. Figure 4-6 displays the archiving function.

Figure 4-6   *Archiving Configuration Data*

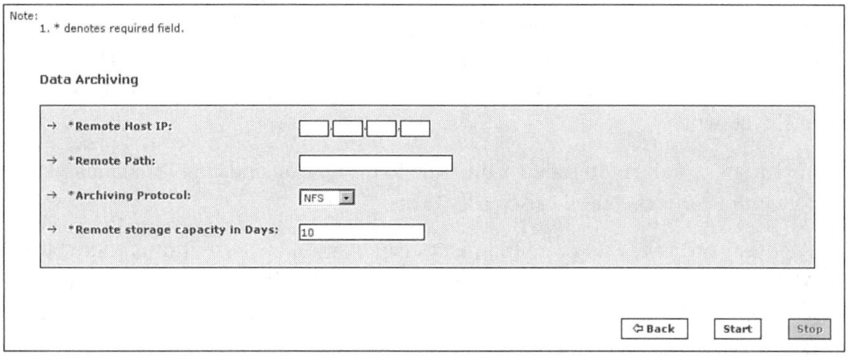

In calculating remote storage capacity, the same formula used for on-box storage is used, but the result is divided by the compression ratio. Being conservative, use 12:1 as the compression ratio for the following example:

Using a rough estimation of 5,000 events per second with a compression ratio of 12:1 and with each event having an average of 200 bytes, 1 day of storage capacity is $(5,000 \times 200 \times 86,400)/12 = 7.2$ GB.

To store 1 year's worth of events at 5,000 EPS, you need a NAS with a storage capacity of $7.2 \times 365 = 2.6$ TB of available disk space.

Restoration of archived data must be done on the exact same model that archived the data or a larger model. You cannot restore data from a larger model to a smaller model. Archive restoration can be accomplished through the command-line interface (CLI) using the **pnrestore** command. This command gives you two options:

- Restore the CS-MARS configuration
- Restore the CS-MARS configuration and retrieve the archived event data

Network Topology Used for Forensic Analysis

Never before has a SIM been capable of offering topology-related information from the event data it reports and correlates. As an enhanced STM, CS-MARS enables operators to weigh important security information against their own network topology.

Using the topology, an operator can drill down into the forensic data in a very easy-to-read and understandable fashion, significantly negating the need for time-consuming and costly analysis.

In this section, you learn what information the topologies provide, how to understand attack diagrams and vectors, and how CS-MARS learns topology information.

CS-MARS Topology Information

CS-MARS enhances forensic analysis by providing visual tools for attack-path analysis and attack propagation. It conducts a step-by-step visual attack replay and provides a graphical means of drilling into the normalized and raw data. Additionally, by enabling users to instantly identify "hot spots" on their network, threat responders, security engineers, and administrators can immediately determine the areas that are most vulnerable to security-related incidents. CS-MARS can accomplish this at both Layer 3 and Layer 2 of the network.

Topology visualization reduces the time to mitigation and enables an analyst or operator to concentrate efforts on other security tasks.

Topology awareness is more than just visualization because it uses route tables, an ARP cache, and CAM tables for deriving the following information, in addition to a topology map:

- **Various events and flows for the same session**—These events might have been generated by network devices across NAT boundaries, with the possibility of having different source and/or destination addresses and ports. CS-MARS uses its internal knowledge of topology and device configurations to correlate multiproduct events into one session. This reduces the amount of event data and creates the entire body of an attack.

- **Events for the same session and an analysis of the path taken by an incident from the true source to the destination**—CS-MARS is capable of determining whether an attack actually reached the intended destination or whether it was dropped by a device such as a firewall, ACL, or IPS between the source and the destination.

- **The best mitigation device, based on an analysis of the path from an attacker to the intended destination**—Using the recommended philosophy of preventing an attack closest to the source, CS-MARS can determine the closest mitigative device and recommended the mitigation point. Having knowledge of device configurations enables CS-MARS to generate accurate device-mitigation commands at Layer 2 or Layer 3.

- **Attack paths and network hot spots**—CS-MARS uses network topology to visualize the attack path and identify the areas containing the most security-related incidents.

- **Detailed forensics**—Because CS-MARS is aware of NAT tables from devices, it can provide enhanced forensics by identifying NAT, PAT, and CAM tables. Therefore, you can derive pre- and post-NAT addresses or MAC addresses in a DHCP environment.

One of the most common questions asked about CS-MARS regarding topology is, "Can it work without the topology information?" The answer is yes; without topology information, CS-MARS becomes an intelligent log aggregator with correlation. You will lose mitigation and vectoring without it. Correlation occurs using common relationships such as IPs, ports, time stamps, and NAT information.

Understanding Attack Diagrams and Attack Vectors

CS-MARS uses attack diagrams to aid in the visualization and display of the sequential propagation of an attack or an incident. Adobe SVG Viewer is required to view the diagrams; if you have not installed this plug-in on your browser, you will be redirected to Adobe's website upon initial login. When using Adobe SVG Viewer, you can manipulate the graphics in two ways. First, you can zoom in by holding down the **Ctrl** key on the keyboard and left-clicking the mouse. Second, you can move the image in all directions by holding down the **Alt** key on your keyboard and simultaneously holding down the left mouse button and dragging the image to where you want to place it. When the diagram exceeds the viewing area, you can use the **Alt** and the mouse to move the diagram around in the viewing pane. You can reference all the commands for graphic manipulation by clicking the **Help** button located on each graphic, where provided.

Four main types of attack diagrams and vectors exist:

- Sequential incident vector information
- Sequential path information
- Standard attack diagram
- Standard path analysis

Sequential incident vector information   To display information, click the **Incident Vector Information** icon under the Path column located at the end of every incident. Incidents can be viewed on the Summary page or the Incidents page of the CS-MARS GUI. When you click this icon, a new page pops up and displays the path vectors for the applicable incident. When an incident has multiple paths, the **Next** button can be clicked to highlight the next sequential propagation path of the attack. Figure 4-7 illustrates the incident vector.

Figure 4-7   *Sequential Incident Vector Diagram*

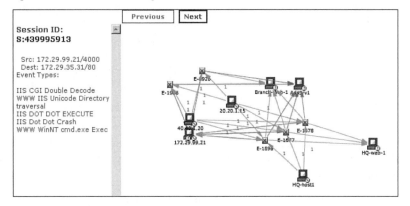

Sequential path information   Information can be displayed by clicking the **Path Information** icon under the Path column located at the end of every incident. Incidents can be viewed on the Summary page or the Incidents page of the CS-MARS GUI. When you click this icon, a new page pops up and displays the complete path, from source to destination, for the applicable incident. Additionally, if more than one session is associated with the incident, it displays the paths for all sessions. When you click the **Next** button at the top of the new popup window, the path for the first session is highlighted and the session information is displayed in the left window pane. If you click the **Next** button again, the next sequential path is highlighted and updated session information appears on the left. In the left pane of the popup window, you can click the session ID; CS-MARS then opens a new window to display the detailed forensic data for that session. Figure 4-8 illustrates the path diagram.

Figure 4-8   *CS-MARS Sequential Path Diagram*

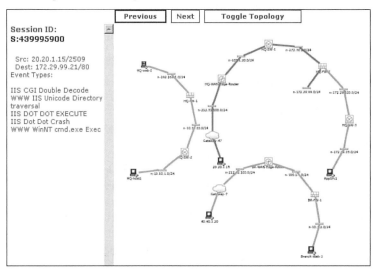

Standard attack vector diagram   Graphical information is located in the Path/Mitigate column after every session or event. This diagram is labeled with a topology and a stop symbol. From this diagram, you can select the Layer 3 path, the Layer 2 path, or the path as set against the entire topology. You will also find the mitigative devices in the left pane of this window. Located on the same page and below the diagram is the enforcement device information. This information contains the configuration data necessary to stop the offending traffic for the selected enforcement device. Figure 4-9 illustrates the attack vector diagram.

Standard path analysis   This diagram, found on the Summary page, maps the vectors for the most current incidents and displays them as a summary of attack vectors. Under high-incident activity, this diagram can look very "busy." Figure 4-10 illustrates the path analysis diagram.

When reviewing vectors, you will see that each path is directional, with the vector ending in an arrow pointing in the direction of the attack propagation. When you move your mouse cursor over the vector, it becomes highlighted in red and allows you to click it. When you click it, another popup window appears detailing the correlated and summarized event data. Also pay attention to the red, yellow, or green icon at the center of every vector. This icon represents the severity level of the event and provides its event ID.

Figure 4-9   *CS-MARS Standard Attack Vector Diagram*

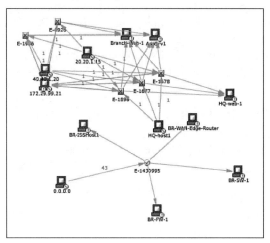

Figure 4-10   *CS-MARS Standard Path Analysis Diagram*

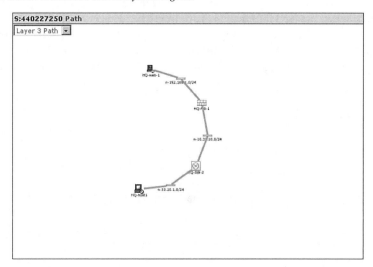

In these diagrams, you will see that every host or network device icon has a color to it. CS-MARS uses four colors to display the status of a host:

- **Clear**—The host or device is in its normal state, with no incident-related information applicable to it.

- **Red**—This is the destination system of the attack.

- **Brown**—This is the source system of the attack.

- **Purple**—This system has been deemed compromised and is now attacking.

CS-MARS also enables you to obtain certain information about each of the hosts or network devices populated in the diagrams. If you click the icon, a popup window appears with basic configuration information about the device. The window also provides a means of obtaining more information about this device by clicking the **More Info for This Device** button. If you click a host or device and nothing appears, CS-MARS is unaware of its information. This is common on hosts that are external to your network.

CS-MARS Network Discovery

For CS-MARS to present and use topology information, it must be told of your topology. CS-MARS becomes topology aware in four primary ways:

- SNMP discovery

- Seed file input

- Manual entry

- Device event reporting

SNMP discovery   This is based on Layer 3 network discovery. Beginning at an SNMP target, CS-MARS discovers its Layer 3 neighbors and then uses each of its neighbors as starting points to learn Layer 3 information to discover other devices. Only SNMP read access (RO) is required. SNMP discovery configuration in CS-MARS is located under **Admin > System Setup > Topology Discovery Information (Optional)**. Configuration information is discussed in Chapter 5. Figure 4-11 displays the SNMP Discovery Configuration screen.

Figure 4-11 *CS-MARS Community String and Networks Configuration GUI*

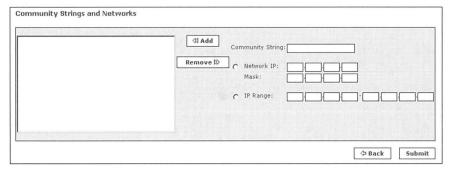

Seed file input   This can be derived from most common network-management systems (NMS), such as HP Open View or CiscoWorks, or can be manually created. An NMS typically exports its topology information through a .csv file. This file contains the attributes CS-MARS needs to populate its device tables to circumvent manual entry. To view a sample of this file, refer to Appendix C, "CS-MARS Supplements," or pages 2 through 16 of the CS-MARS 4.1 Users Guide.

Manual entry   This involves the management protocols of the respective device. Refer to Chapter 5 for detailed steps for manually discovering devices. These primary protocols are used in manual entry:

- SNMP RO (required for L2 devices)
- Telnet
- SSH
- FTP
- CPMI
- RDEP/SDEE

Device event reporting   This involves teaching CS-MARS about hosts on the network and information about them. CS-MARS then places them in the applicable network topology cloud, based on their IP addresses. Examples of the reporting devices are VA scanners, IDS/IDP systems, firewalls, HIDS/HIPS, and the built-in NMAP tool. Additionally, CS-MARS maintains important information about these hosts, such as operating systems, open ports, and applications. This information can also be manually entered in CS-MARS after the host has been discovered.

The average length of time it takes CS-MARS to discover a 300-node network is about 2 hours. Network discovery can be scheduled for periodic updates using the Topology Scheduling tool, found under **Admin > System Setup > Topology Discovery Information (Optional)**. When scheduling a periodic update, it uses the configured method of discovery for the devices. Therefore, it can use a combination of SNMP, Telnet, and SSH. The default update is scheduled as Run on Demand and is set to discover all devices in all networks it is aware of. You can add any discovery scheme you want using this tool and set it up for any period of time. Figure 4-12 displays the Topology Update UI.

Figure 4-12   *CS-MARS Topology/Monitored Device Update Scheduler GUI*

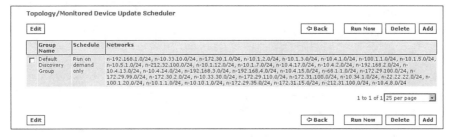

The following are the Management Information Bases (MIBs) that CS-MARS uses in discovering devices and reading their configuration data:

- mib-2(1) .System
- mib-2(1) .Interface.iftable
- mib-2(1) .ip.iproutetable

- mib-2(1) .ip.ipaddrTable
- mib-2(1) .ip.forwarding
- mib-2(1) .At.attable (for ARP info)
- mib-2(1) .dot1dBridge(17)
- vtpVlanState EMIB

NetFlow in CS-MARS

An often-overlooked technology, NetFlow is a powerful tool that can be used to profile and baseline network activity from a security perspective. Typically, NetFlow has been used by networking departments to analyze traffic patterns, billing by bandwidth, application monitoring, and user monitoring.

CS-MARS uses the information provided by NetFlow for similar purposes but takes a different approach in analyzing the data.

This section discusses the following NetFlow topics:

- Understanding NetFlow
- Using NetFlow in CS-MARS
- Conducting behavioral profiling using CS-MARS

Understanding NetFlow

NetFlow is a Cisco technology for monitoring network traffic; most IOS images support it. NetFlow is a UDP-based protocol that reports on flows seen by a router or a switch. A flow is a small packet consisting of session setup, data transfer, and session teardown information. Seven unique keys define NetFlow:

- Source IP address
- Destination IP address
- Source port
- Destination port
- Layer 3 protocol type
- TOS byte (DSCP)
- Input logical interface (ifIndex)

In CS-MARS, all keys are used except the TOS byte, which is used for quality of service (QOS) purposes.

After an IOS or CATOS device is configured for NetFlow, a collection of flows and its associated parameters are packaged in a UDP packet and sent to a defined collector.

Because multiple flows are packed into a single UDP packet, NetFlow becomes an efficient utility for monitoring network traffic in contrast to syslog or SNMP.

You can get more information about NetFlow by visiting www.cisco.com/go/netflow.

Using NetFlow in CS-MARS

CS-MARS uses NetFlow Version 5 or Version 7 to profile the network usage, detect anomalous behavior, monitor bandwidth, and correlate behavior to attacks and other events reported by NIDS and firewall devices. Although there are a few differences in the type of information provided in Versions 5 and 7 of NetFlow, CS-MARS uses the same information from both versions. Therefore, there is no benefit in using one version over the other.

When CS-MARS is in your network, it must first understand the normal flow of data in your network; this is called baselining. CS-MARS measures the network usage between four days to two weeks. When it understands and baselines network activity, it then switches to a detection mode and looks for behavior that is out of its baselined scope. If it finds deviations that exceed its measured baseline by a means of five times or greater, it begins to actively monitor that behavior and continues the measurements until they decrease or exceed the mean by ten times. Then CS-MARS creates an incident and alarms.

CS-MARS profiles the network at a detailed level and keeps a profile of top combinations of flows learned and packets exchanged for every hour, every day of the week.

By default, CS-MARS does not store the NetFlow records in the database because of the high volume of data. However, you can manually configure this capability, if desired. You learn how to configure this parameter in Chapter 5.

Upon detecting an anomalous behavior, CS-MARS starts to dynamically store the full NetFlow records for the anomalous activity. This intelligent collection system provides all the information that a security analyst needs and does not overburden CPU and disk resources.

CS-MARS can be configured to profile hosts that belong to a set of known valid networks. It provides built-in rules for automatically correlating anomalous behavior with alerts reported by network IDS systems.

Conducting Behavioral Profiling Using CS-MARS

Because CS-MARS baselines and monitors host- and network-related activity, it has the capability of reporting deviations from a host's typical behavior in addition to that of monitored networks. As an example of this profiling, imagine that CS-MARS learns that most connections to and from a server are made over ports 137, 138, and 139; then suddenly that server makes multiple outbound port 25 connections through the default gateway. CS-MARS would trigger a "mass-mailing worm" incident to notify the operators of the change in behavior.

Additionally, CS-MARS uses NetFlow information to graphically depict port-level activity on your network using a graph that measures protocol connections over time. Figure 4-13 displays the All Events and NetFlow chart.

Figure 4-13 *CS-MARS Activity: All Events and NetFlow Chart*

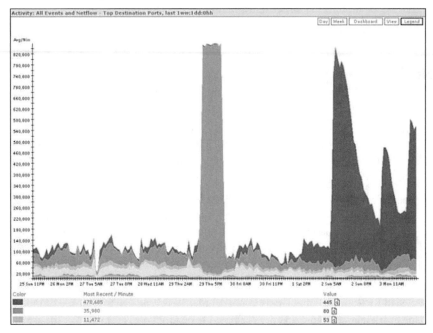

As you can see in Figure 4-13, CS-MARS has reported huge deviations from typical port 80 and 445 activity. This is an example of behaviorally profiling port activity.

This capability is a great method for detecting day-zero worms and viruses. Often when these malicious programs are released, they do not contain names or have detection signatures for them. Your organization's only defense against detecting and mitigating day-zero attacks at a network level is to use CS-MARS. Firewall data and NetFlow information give you this unique capability.

Positive Alert Verification and Dynamic Vulnerability Scanning

Receiving and interpreting log data when you receive thousands of events per second is an overwhelming experience. The process of pulling out legitimate event logs and manually correlating them can be compared to searching a haystack for a needle.

Most SIMs offer correlation capabilities that tie event data together via some relationship, but a security analyst is still required to filter and validate the data. This is a time-consuming process that is often done postmortem. In today's fast-moving world, time is money. Having a system that can automatically and effectively correlate that data and validate it is such a value to security analysts that it can be compared to paying for a compact automobile and receiving a NASCAR.

CS-MARS is such a system. The intelligence that is built into the system effectively reduces incident data through built-in validation tools or with third-party VA tools. This enables analysts to concentrate their efforts on real, legitimate incidents.

This section discusses the following topics to help you better understand how CS-MARS validates incident data:

- False positives
- Vulnerability analysis

Understanding False Positives

Reducing false positives has been a subject that IDS and SIM vendors have struggled with for years. IDS system logs must be reviewed and analyzed to determine their validity and SIM solutions to report event data or incidents when they receive alarm data, even if a firewall or ACLs have denied the traffic. Either way, tuning can be an arduous, painful, and often unproductive process.

As mentioned in Chapter 1, "Understanding SIM and STM," two types of false positives exist. CS-MARS adheres to these same principles:

- When a device classifies data as a possible intrusion or policy violation and it is legitimate authorized data
- When a device classifies data as a possible intrusion or policy violation when the data will not be successful in its intent

Using these two principles, CS-MARS can classify a false positive into two categories:

- System determined
- Unconfirmed

System determined   CS-MARS has determined that the incident was unsuccessful. This could be because a device prevented the incident from occurring or provided data that told CS-MARS that the destination system is not vulnerable to the type of attack.

Unconfirmed   CS-MARS has determined that the incident was not successful but was real data; however, there was a mismatch on the vulnerability assessment data. On the Summary page, this is displayed as "To be confirmed," which simply means that an analyst can confirm or reject the CS-MARS assessment.

In CS-MARS, tuning a false positive actually involves creating a drop rule. Drop rules have two categories:

- **Drop the events completely**—Erases the event from the database and stops logging events
- **Log to database only**—Does not create an incident but maintains the event in the CS-MARS database

You can create a drop rule (or tune a false positive) under **Rules > Drop Rules > Add** or by clicking the False Positive link in the Tune column of any session. Both methods populate the results under the Drop Rule tab. Figure 4-14 displays the False Positive link.

Figure 4-14 *CS-MARS False Positive Link*

Using these tuning wizards makes tuning out false positives as easy as pointing and clicking. Therefore, using CS-MARS, you can tune multiple devices in one drop rule and even be able to tune out events or alarms from systems that do not allow you to do so, such as a firewall or a Windows OS.

Understanding Vulnerability Analysis

Vulnerability assessment information is a key piece of evidence that security analysts use to determine whether an attack was successful. CS-MARS uses VA data to help it understand what vulnerabilities exist for devices on the network and to weigh them against event and session data targeted for specific systems. This process allows CS-MARS to flag an event as a false positive or escalate it as an incident. It is important to mention that VA data cannot be viewed in CS-MARS.

CS-MARS can obtain VA information from two sources:

- Built-in Nessus utility
- Third-party VA tool

Built-in Nessus utility   CS-MARS uses NASL scripts (built in) to do vulnerability correlation. For example, if you receive an event from an IDS system reporting that there is a buffer overflow attack, this triggers an incident (because there is a default rule defined). In the postanalysis of the incident, CS-MARS conducts further investigations by checking its database to see if it has a VA definition of the targeted destination and if it is vulnerable (based on OS, patches, and so on). This is called static data. CS-MARS then checks whether the targeted destination is vulnerable by sending an on-demand, targeted poke through the respective NASL script. CS-MARS does not do a targeted vulnerability scan unless the user gives the system permission to do so. A user can enable vulnerability scanning by browsing to **ADMIN > System Setup > CS-MARS Setup > Networks for Dynamic Vulnerability Scanning**. Not all events have NASL scripts associated with them. Cisco provides updated NASL scripts with the periodic updates available for CS-MARS.

Nessus VA scanning can be very intrusive to a network; CS-MARS customers have expressed concerns about using the tool in a production network and thus have decided not to implement this false-positive reduction technology. It is important to understand that CS-MARS does not use a full version of Nessus and does not conduct a full scan of the host systems; it conducts only a "targeted" scan on the systems under attack for that specific attack.

One CS-MARS customer put it best when speaking about CS-MARS to potential users: "CS-MARS doesn't do a full-blown vulnerability assessment on a target machine, but it selects specific tests to run based on the traffic seen." Network load is a big concern for a lot of people, and the initial impact of thinking about doing something like this is, "If we turn this on, we're going to saturate our network with traffic generated by CS-MARS." First, it's not true. Second, this information is critical in helping to filter the wheat from the chaff and getting the most bang out of the time that you spend with the platform. If you turn CS-MARS onto every device in the network and have every device feed CS-MARS, but you don't do some form of vulnerability analysis on the individual events as they occur, there is little chance for CS-MARS to avoid reporting everything to you as valid. That means more man-hours dedicated to the incident-response capability than are really needed, which directly impacts your ROI, which is likely why you purchased CS-MARS.

Third-party VA tool   CS-MARS integrates with three third-party VA tools: eEye REM, Qualys QualysGuard, and Foundstone Foundscan. The information gleaned from these tools is much more complete and robust than the information gathered from the built-in tool. CS-MARS has the capability to request information from these sources at a scheduled interval or with QualysGuard, so you have the capability to request an on-demand scan.

Third-party VA tools can be configured on CS-MARS as reporting devices under the Admin tab. If you so desire, you can enable the built-in tool along with adding a third-party tool, and then weigh the data against each other. If the data is not congruent, a mismatch occurs and the incident is marked as an "unconfirmed false positive."

Methodology of Communication

CS-MARS obviously needs to communicate with reporting devices to receive and process network, host, server, and security device information. The CS-MARS appliance itself is neither an inline device nor a packet-capture device; it's a device that receives and analyzes information from other devices, queries other devices, probes devices, sends notifications to threat responders, and pushes commands to devices to mitigate attacks. Because of this, communications can be one-way or two-way between CS-MARS and a reporting device.

To enable you to properly configure your network infrastructure and to configure CS-MARS to enforce your security policies, it's important to understand how CS-MARS exchanges data with other devices.

To help you understand how CS-MARS interacts with other devices, this section is divided into three separate parts:

- Communication Methods
- Use of Agents
- Incident Reporting and Notification Methods

Communication Methods

CS-MARS uses a variety of protocols to communicate with reporting devices. Some of the protocols are vendor specific; others are standards based. Because CS-MARS is primarily agentless, a majority of the communications are two-way. The key to understanding whether CS-MARS needs a two-way path for communications is to recognize whether the method of log retrieval is a push or a pull.

With a push, the reporting device sends its log data to CS-MARS at its own predefined interval or in real time. A pull means that CS-MARS needs to request the data from the reporting device. Some reporting devices, such as a Microsoft OS, can be either a push or a pull. Pushing data is typically done in real time; pulling data is usually done at preset intervals that are defined on CS-MARS. Pulling data usually requires an authentication account on the reporting device; thus, CS-MARS provides configuration fields for a username and password when this functionality is required.

CS-MARS uses IP tables to protect the communications with its respective reporting devices. Every time you add a device to CS-MARS, it creates an IP table based upon the access and reporting IP address you program into the device configuration. Logically, it deletes these when you delete the device from CS-MARS.

The following list outlines the communication types and protocols CS-MARS uses to obtain event data:

- Syslog
- SNMP
- RDEP
- OPSEC-LEA (Clear and encrypted)
- POP
- SDEE
- HTTPS
- HTTP
- JDBC
- RPC
- SQLNet

Other forms of communication that CS-MARS uses are for MARS operation and administration, device discovery, and mitigation.

Table 4-5 outlines the protocol for each type of communication.

Table 4-5   *CS-MARS Communication Protocols*

	MARS Admin and Ops	Discovery	Mitigation
HTTPS	x		
SSH	x	x	x
Telnet		x	x
SNMP		x	x
FTP		x	
CPMI		x	
SSL		x	

Use of Agents

CS-MARS is primarily an agentless device; however, because of certain limitations of products that CS-MARS supports, an agent might be necessary. Agents are software applications that convert log data into a different format and transfer the data to a defined source. These agents convert the log data into syslog format for CS-MARS to parse. CS-MARS supports System iNtrusion Analysis & Reporting Environment (SNARE), Cisco pnLog agent, and Cisco Security MARS agent.

SNARE is an open-source application developed under the Intersect Alliance; it is available for free use under the GNU Public License. More information and the SNARE application itself can be found at http://www.intersectalliance.com/projects/Snare/.

The Security MARS agent or pnLog agent can be downloaded from Cisco's Support website with CCO access at the following location: http://www.cisco.com/cgi-bin/tablebuild.pl/cs-mars-misc.

The following devices require an agent:

- Custom application with ASCII logs (SNARE)
- MS IIS web server (SNARE)
- Sun iPlanet web server (Security MARS agent)
- Apache web server (Security MARS agent)
- Cisco Secure Access Control Server (pnLog agent)

Some SIMs offer encrypted transport of log data when the source does not encrypt the data by design; this requires the use of software-encryption agents. CS-MARS does not encrypt data from unencrypted protocols. Cisco believes that if encryption is needed, it should be done at L2 or L3, not at the application layer. Application layer encryption places a toll on CPU and memory resources for the reporting device. CS-MARS is designed to be nonintrusive to its reporting devices. Additionally, transfer of event data is recommended to be done out-of-band, for security and reliability purposes.

Incident Reporting and Notification Methods

Invariably, SIMs and STMs need to notify an external entity when incidents or alarms are generated, when reports are ready for reviewing, or when certain abnormal behaviors are detected. CS-MARS has built-in notification mechanisms that allow it to inform entities remotely. CS-MARS can send notifications of incidents and reports using the following methods:

- E-mail
- Syslog
- SNMP
- SMS
- ASCII text messaging

Built into CS-MARS is a v.92 modem, which can be hooked up to a plain old telephone service (POTS) line and configured to send incident-notification messages to an SMS or text-messaging recipient. Each messaging provider can be uniquely defined on a per-user basis. All notification methods use the information that each user or group account provides. Figure 4-15 displays the configuration UI for users.

Figure 4-15 *CS-MARS User Contact Configuration GUI*

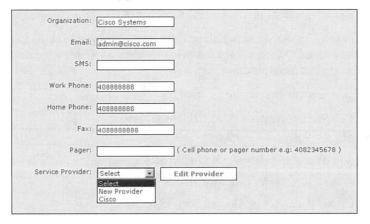

In addition to sending e-mail notifications, CS-MARS has the capability to send incident notifications through SNMP or syslog to another monitoring application, such as HP Openview, CiscoWorks, or IBM Tivoli.

CS-MARS notifications are configured as notification schemes, which can include one or up to all the notification methods per scheme. The scheme is then applied to a rule or a report as an action. When the rule is triggered or a report is complete, the action is taken. Figure 4-16 shows the CS-MARS interface that enables you to create a notification scheme.

Figure 4-16 *CS-MARS Notification Configuration Scheme GUI*

Name:
Description:
Email
Change Recipient
Syslog
Change Recipient
Page
Change Recipient
SNMP
Change Recipient
SMS
Change Recipient
Distributed Threat Mitigation
Change Recipient
ALARM ONLY

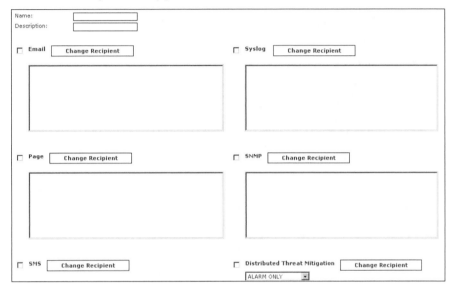

As of CS-MARS v4.1, case management has become more robust. CS-MARS has an internal trouble-ticketing system that enables a case with a unique ID to be opened and the entire history of the case to be recorded.

The built-in case-management tools allow organizations using CS-MARS to increase inner- and interdepartmental communications when assessing or addressing incident handling. Users can assign review or action tasks to other users to keep a record on how they were handled, for use in audit requirements, change control, or accountability. Figure 4-17 displays the Case Summary panel in CS-MARS.

Figure 4-17 *CS-MARS Case Summary GUI*

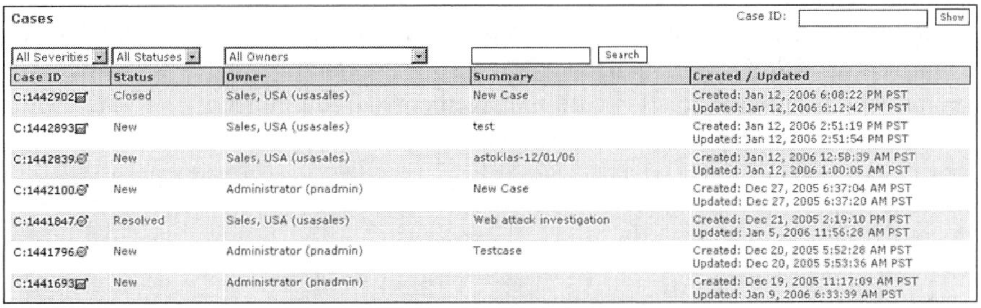

Cases
Case ID:
Show
All Severities
All Statuses
All Owners
Search
Case ID
Status
Owner
Summary
Created / Updated
C:1442902 Closed Sales, USA (usasales) New Case Created: Jan 12, 2006 6:08:22 PM PST Updated: Jan 12, 2006 6:12:42 PM PST
C:1442893 New Sales, USA (usasales) test Created: Jan 12, 2006 2:51:19 PM PST Updated: Jan 12, 2006 2:51:54 PM PST
C:1442839 New Sales, USA (usasales) astoklas-12/01/06 Created: Jan 12, 2006 12:58:39 AM PST Updated: Jan 12, 2006 1:00:05 AM PST
C:1442100 New Administrator (pnadmin) New Case Created: Dec 27, 2005 6:37:04 AM PST Updated: Dec 27, 2005 6:37:20 AM PST
C:1441847 Resolved Sales, USA (usasales) Web attack investigation Created: Dec 21, 2005 2:19:10 PM PST Updated: Jan 5, 2006 11:56:28 AM PST
C:1441796 New Administrator (pnadmin) Testcase Created: Dec 20, 2005 5:52:28 AM PST Updated: Dec 20, 2005 5:53:36 AM PST
C:1441693 New Administrator (pnadmin) Created: Dec 19, 2005 11:17:09 AM PST Updated: Jan 9, 2006 6:33:39 AM PST

The Case Management tool has the following options:

- Case Assignment
- Case Notes and Comments
- Incident ID and Incident Review
- Incident Summary Data (source, destination, and so on)
- Case Reference and Documents Page
- E-mail Case to a User
- Case Severity Set and Change

When a case is closed, it can only be viewed.

Figure 4-18 is an example of the individual Case tool.

Figure 4-18 *CS-MARS Individual Case History and Edit GUI*

In Version 4.1, the only external case-management tool supported is Remedy. CS-MARS supports the required e-mail format for automated case generation by Remedy; thus, an action of CS-MARS can be to send a Remedy system an e-mail with the incident details. In Version 4.2 of CS-MARS, an XML notification method will be available. The XML format will provide detailed case-management and full incident data to an external case-management or reporting tool.

Summary

In this chapter you learned about the hardware specifications, database operations, terminology, and unique technologies used by CS-MARS for data and event correlation, attack data display, and mitigation of attacks. The network topology and forensics section of this chapter describes how CS-MARS learns and displays the devices in your network and then discusses how you can use this information to investigate attacks that have occurred on your network. You also learned that CS-MARS has technology built into it to help reduce reports of attacks that are not valid (false-positive attacks).

This chapter has provided you with critical information that you need to know about how the CS-MARS appliance works. Now that you understand this information, the following chapters go into more detail on the services and value CS-MARS offers you when it is deployed in your network.

In this chapter, you learn the fundamental steps required to configure and deploy your CS-MARS platform. Topics discussed include these:

- Deploying CS-MARS in Your Network
- CS-MARS Initial Setup and Quick Install
- CS-MARS Reporting Device Setup
- Creating Users and Groups
- Configuring NetFlow and Vulnerability Scanning
- Configuring CS-MARS System Maintenance
- Configuring System Parameters

## CHAPTER 5

CS-MARS Appliance Setup and Configuration

In previous chapters, you learned the difference between security threat mitigation (STM) and security information management (SIM). Understanding the advantages of deploying an STM in your environment, you now walk through the steps necessary for the initial configuration and setup of high-level system parameters that enable CS-MARS as an STM system.

This chapter discusses the first step of deploying CS-MARS, which is determining where it can be securely placed in your network. It explains how to configure the information required for network communication and alert notification, and includes instructions on how to use the CS-MARS web interface to add devices that will report to the CS-MARS appliance. You will learn how to add users and groups to administer your CS-MARS appliance and how to use NetFlow and configure vulnerability scanning, which will significantly increase the accuracy of attack recognition. Finally, you will learn about system maintenance tasks and how to configure system parameters.

After applying the information in this chapter, you will have a fully operational CS-MARS STM device.

Deploying CS-MARS in Your Network

Before you start configuring your CS-MARS appliance, you need to make the critical decision of where CS-MARS should be placed in your network. This decision is important for the security of your network and the security of data going to and from your CS-MARS device. Your CS-MARS appliance data and your CS-MARS appliance itself are prime targets for an attacker who wants to compromise your network.

Just some of the information hackers could glean if they had access to the data stream going to and from your CS-MARS appliance would include the following:

- IP addresses
- Device names
- Source and destination pairs
- Attack information

- Vulnerability information
- Operating system information

The CS-MARS box itself would be a prime target because if attackers can access the box, they could change policies and hide attacks that they might launch against your critical assets.

Because of the importance of this device and its data, you don't want to place it where it can be easily compromised or where attackers might be able to run network sniffers and harvest information about your network.

Network Placement

Normally you want to place CS-MARS in a part of your network where normal users don't have access. These networks are called out-of-band networks. Conversely, in-band networks are networks where user, voice, and video data are located. In relation to out-of-band (OOB) networks, in-band networks are considered insecure. In-band networks are susceptible to many types of attacks by which an attacker can gain control of a device and gain leverage to attack other devices in the network or sniff traffic on the network; the attacker might then learn critical information such as device configurations, IP addresses, usernames, or passwords. Because out-of-band networks don't have user workstations, they are considered to be much more secure. Of course, all this information assumes that when the administrator set up the in-band and out-of-band networks, the switches and routers were configured with the proper commands so that attackers can't "hop" between networks.

Because out-of-band networks are considered more secure, we recommend that you place your CS-MARS device and all other security-management devices, such as password servers, syslog servers, Network Time Protocol (NTP) servers, and domain name services (DNS) servers in these networks. Figure 5-1 shows a very simple illustration of components that are commonly found in an OOB network.

OOB networking for management devices is an "ideal" best practice, and sometimes it's not possible to implement them because of distance limitations, interface limitations, and various other factors. At best, if you need to place critical management devices in user networks, you should try to encrypt traffic that is sourced from and destined to those devices. As an alternative, if management traffic needs to traverse your in-band network, you should always keep your management device protected from the user networks with a combination of firewalls and intrusion-prevention appliances.

The bottom line is that, depending on how your network is set up, CS-MARS should be deployed in the most secure area possible. Table 5-1 lists the network types from most secure to least secure and provides an explanation of the presumed security level of each area.

Figure 5-1   *Management Network*

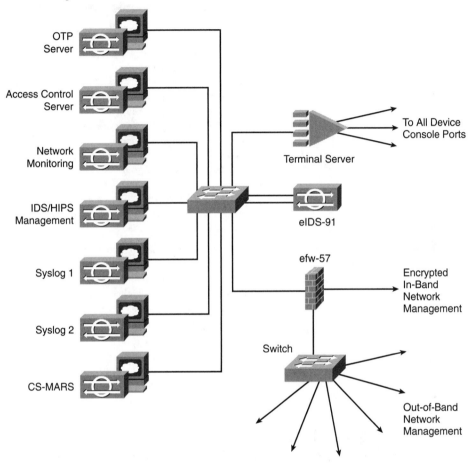

Table 5-1   *Network Placement for CS-MARS*

Network Connection Type	Description
OOB management network segment	This is the preferred network segment for your CS-MARS appliance. There should be no user access except by security administrators. Make sure that all switches are locked down to protect against Layer 2 attacks and that there are no open ports where an attacker can connect a PC.

continues

Table 5-1 *Network Placement for CS-MARS (Continued)*

Network Connection Type	Description
In-band encrypted	You should place CS-MARS in an in-band network only if you can encrypt all data going to and coming from the CS-MARS appliance. This ensures that even if attackers have access to your in-band network, they cannot steal network and attack data going across this network. Also make sure that all switches are locked down to protect against Layer 2 attacks and that there are no open switch ports where an attacker can connect a PC. The greatest risk in this network scenario is that an attacker might be able to guess the IP address of your CS-MARS device and try brute-force password attacks against the appliance. If you have an IPS device on the same network as your management interface, you will be able to recognize and mitigate these types of attacks.
In-band appliance protected	If you can't encrypt data to and from your CS-MARS device, you should have a firewall and a network intrusion-prevention (IPS) device between the CS-MARS box and the user network. The attacker should have his hands full figuring out how to directly compromise the device with these appliances in place.
In-band	This scenario is not recommended and should be avoided at all costs. This gives an attacker free rein to try to sniff data off the network and to try to gain management access to the appliance.

CS-MARS Security Hardening

The earlier "Network Placement" section goes into a lot of detail about how you should treat CS-MARS as a critical secure network component and ensure that it is deployed properly in your network. You should not be intimidated by this; the good news is that this is the only task besides administering usernames and passwords that you need to worry about when installing CS-MARS. Normally, when you deploy a host, server, network, or security device in your business or enterprise network, you want to complete several tasks before using the new device. The following is a list of typical security best practices, depending on the type of device:

- Apply current operating system patches
- Apply current application patches
- Analyze configurations and remove unneeded services that could be exploited by malicious network activity

- Turn off or secure clear-text services to the security appliance
- Correctly apply access control lists limiting connectivity to the inside of your network
- Enable auditing functions
- Apply registry and file-sharing security as recommended by the operating system vendor
- Install antivirus software from a leading vendor
- Install host or server intrusion prevention

On the CS-MARS platform, the developers have done these tasks for you, either by design or based on input that you provided to the CS-MARS appliance when adding devices or setting global parameters.

The CS-MARS appliance is built on a Red Hat Linux operating system that has been heavily modified and security-hardened by CS-MARS developers. Because of this, you will never need to install typical operating system components or application patches. This type of maintenance is common for other vendors that install security software on off-the-shelf operating systems (OS). However, Cisco has assured its customers that if a security vulnerability is found in any of its devices, including CS-MARS, it will immediately provide a patch to protect against malicious software that could exploit this vulnerability. It should be noted, however, that when this book was written, Cisco and Protego had shipped CS-MARS for more than three years, and no vulnerabilities had been identified for this product.

The other major task that you need to do if you purchased an off-the-shelf security product that runs on a commercial operating system is to turn off the unused network services, such as Hypertext Transfer Protocol (HTTP), Simple Mail Transfer Protocol (SMTP), File Transfer Protocol (FTP), and Internet Control Message Protocol (ICMP). Although it's impossible to turn off all network services on a security device installed on an off-the-shelf OS, the developers of CS-MARS either have turned off unnecessary services, have never installed them, or have modified the services that are enabled to eliminate known vulnerabilities. In some cases, such as SMTP, the developers implemented the protocol to allow only the skeleton requirements needed by CS-MARS.

The bottom line is that you need to do a minimal amount of work to secure your CS-MARS appliance; most of these types of tasks have been completed for you by CS-MARS developers or because of the architecture of CS-MARS.

Table 5-2 lists typical network and host-hardening tasks and shows how CS-MARS either does these tasks for you or eliminates the necessity for you to perform the task.

In addition to traditional security-hardening tasks such as those mentioned previously, CS-MARS adds hardening features to protocols that are required for CS-MARS functionality.

Table 5-2 *Security-Hardening Tasks*

Required Security-Hardening Task	Hardening Achieved	User Interaction
Apply current operating system hot fixes	Because CS-MARS is written on a special developer's version of Red Hat Linux operating system, no operating system hot fixes are required.	No action is required on your part unless Cisco releases a security alert in conjunction with a software patch for this appliance.
Apply current application patches	Because CS-MARS is written on a special developer's version of Red Hat Linux operating system, no application patches are required.	No action is required on your part.
Analyze configurations and remove unneeded services that could be exploited by malicious network activity	CS-MARS developers never installed unneeded services, and they modified existing services to reduce or eliminate the possibility of vulnerabilities that attackers could exploit.	No action is required on your part.
Harden or remove clear-text services to the security appliance	The clear-text protocols used by CS-MARS are Telnet and syslog. These clear-text protocols are required to support existing legacy reporting and management applications used by most security and network devices.	As recommended in the previous section, if you are using clear-text protocols, you should either isolate your CS-MARS appliance in an out-of-band network or encrypt the clear-text data if it traverses a user network.
Correctly apply access control lists limiting connectivity to your security device	CS-MARS communicates only with devices that you have added to its device database, so access control lists are not required.	No action is required on your part.
Turn on auditing functions	Full device-auditing features are turned on by default in the CS-MARS appliance.	No action is required on your part.
Apply registry and file-sharing security as recommended by the operating system vendor	CS-MARS developers have written the operating system and the CS-MARS applications so that a registry, as we know it, is not required and file sharing does not exist.	No action is required on your part.
Install antivirus software	Because CS-MARS is a hardened OS with IP tables for inbound and outbound connections, the probability of virus outbreak is very low.	No action is required on your part.
Install host or server intrusion prevention	Because CS-MARS is a hardened operating system that tightly controls its operating environment and controls applications with code that can be executed, the probability of exploit is very low.	No action is required on your part unless Cisco releases a security alert in conjunction with a software patch for this appliance.

Protocol Security Hardening

CS-MARS employs additional protocol security hardening in four ways:

* Enforcing directional control on protocols that it requires on the appliance using IP tables
* Allowing local protocol access only
* Selectively allowing protocol access using device-authentication mechanisms
* Sandboxing your computer command-line execution and the internal database

Enforcing directional control   In some protocols, which would normally be bidirectional, CS-MARS has ensured that inbound traffic is not accepted. SNMP is an example of this. CS-MARS uses SNMP to notify predefined users in the case of a high-severity event, but SNMP on a CS-MARS appliance does not accept inbound traffic; therefore, the SNMP server cannot be exploited from the outside.

Allowing local protocol access only   Because CS-MARS uses the Oracle database to store and organize its device and event data, it requires a piece of software called a Transparent Network Substrate (TNS) listener. CS-MARS architects used the developer's version of Red Hat Linux and built CS-MARS applications from scratch, so access to the TNS listener is restricted to only the CS-MARS appliance itself. The only exception to this is if you elect to deploy a configuration called Local Controllers (LC) and Global Controllers (GC) on CS-MARS. When the LC-to-GC deployment is made, the TNS listener is used only within the HTTPS connection between LC and GC devices.

Selectively allowing protocol access using device authentication   If you decide to use local and global CS-MARS devices as suggested in the previous bullet point, it's required that the Global Controller talk to the Local Controller database. In this case, the TNS listener must accept data from outside devices. Because CS-MARS developers wrote the CS-MARS application with security in mind, they employed a device-authentication mechanism that ensures that the remote CS-MARS appliance that you defined is the only device that can communicate with the local TNS listener.

Sandboxing your command-line execution   The CS-MARS developers wrote a custom command-line parser that restricts operating system command execution to just a few lines. These commands are used solely to troubleshoot, configure CS-MARS, view some global parameters, or view statistics. This ensures that if hackers were able to gain access to your CS-MARS command-line interface (CLI), they would not be able to run traditional Linux commands to manipulate execution or install malicious code such as rootkits. To protect the CS-MARS operating system even more, all compilers and development libraries have been removed from the system. This ensures that in the unlikely event that attackers gained access, they would not be able to create or modify code on the device.

CS-MARS Initial Setup and Quick Install

One of the greatest assets of CS-MARS is that it's extremely simple to set up, regardless of your level of technical expertise. A novice can easily follow the step-by-step process in this chapter and have a fully configured CS-MARS appliance when the steps are completed. In fact, the steps are exactly the same and just as easy, whether you are a novice system administrator or an experienced security or network engineer.

This book describes two different methods for initially setting up and installing CS-MARS. The first method, which is covered in this chapter, involves connecting a keyboard and a video monitor to your CS-MARS appliance and completing the initial setup using direct input through the keyboard. The second method is defined in Appendix F, "CS-MARS Console Access." It involves connecting your PC using the asynchronous serial port of your CS-MARS device and a terminal emulator and entering the initial configuration information on your keyboard. After you have successfully configured your CS-MARS device, you can access the device using the CS-MARS web interface. This requires the Microsoft Internet Explorer v6.x application, the Adobe VGA Viewer IE plug-in, and a network connection to the CS-MARS appliance.

The initial steps you need to perform to enable your CS-MARS device for deployment are the following:

Step 1   Complete the initial CS-MARS configuration.

Step 2   Enter system parameters using the CS-MARS web interface.

Complete the Initial CS-MARS Configuration

Completing the initial configuration for CS-MARS is a simple nine-step process. After you have completed this process, you can access your CS-MARS device with the web interface, complete additional steps required to add devices to the CS-MARS device database, and also configure system parameters. These steps make up the initial configuration process:

Step 1   Connect the video and the keyboard to the CS-MARS backplane.

Step 2   Power on the CS-MARS device.

Step 3   Log into CS-MARS using the factory default username and password.

Step 4   Change the default username and password.

Step 5   Set the time zone or synchronize to an NTP server.

Step 6   Set the desired date.

Step 7   Set the desired time.

Step 8   Set the IP address for your CS-MARS interface.

Step 9   Ensure connectivity between your CS-MARS device and your administrative management workstations.

The following is a description of the steps you need to perform to initialize your CS-MARS appliance:

Step 1   **Connect the video and the keyboard to the CS-MARS backplane**—
While the device is powered off, simply connect a standard computer monitor and video cable to the video out on the CS-MARS backplane. After the video is connected, simply insert a standard keyboard and keyboard cable into the keyboard port on the CS-MARS backplane. See Figure 5-2.

Figure 5-2   *CS-MARS Backplane*

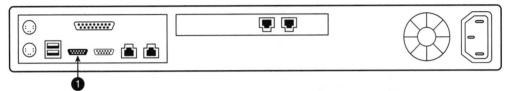

Step 2   **Power on the CS-MARS device**—Plug the CS-MARS power cable into the device backplane then into a standard 110 volt AC outlet. There are two switches used to power on the device; first press the power switch on the CS-MARS backplane, and then remove the face plate and press the power switch on the front of the device.

Step 3   **Log into CS-MARS using the factory default username and password**—When the CS-MARS device has completed its power cycle, you are presented with a username prompt. Enter **pnadmin** for both the username and the password.

Step 4   **Change the default username and password**—Enter the command **passwd**; you are prompted to change the username and password. Because CS-MARS is a critical device in your network and has access to most of your security, network, hosts, and server devices, it's a best practice to use a password that will be very difficult to guess if somebody gains physical or remote access to this device. General guidelines are to use a password with greater than eight characters that contains uppercase, lowercase, numeric, and special characters. Under no circumstances should your password be a word that can be found in a dictionary, English or otherwise.

Step 5   **Set the time zone or synchronize to an NTP server**—The first step you need to do is either manually set the time zone where your CS-MARS device is located or point your CS-MARS device to an NTP server.

Without synchronizing times among your CS-MARS appliance, your management workstations, and your reporting devices, you face several potential problems:

— Management workstations will not be capable of connecting to CS-MARS devices because self-signed certificates will appear to be expired.

— The dates on CS-MARS reports will not be accurate. This is especially a problem if you are using CS-MARS data for forensic analysis or you plan to use this data in a legal deposition or at a trial.

A fundamental feature of CS-MARS is to correlate event logs and alerts from many different network and security devices. These devices can be located anywhere in the world and in any time zone. To enable CS-MARS to accurately correlate information regardless of geographical location to a common time source, you must configure the accurate date, time, and time zone. The date, time, and time zone can be set manually, but it's much easier and much more accurate to simply point your devices to an authoritative Network Time Protocol (NTP) server.

The time zone can be set manually via the CLI using the **timezone set** command. After you enter the command, a text wizard steps you through the process of defining your time zone.

Step 6 **Set the desired date**—For the same reasons you need to synchronize time zones, you also need to ensure that the correct date is set on your CS-MARS device. As with the time zone, the date can manually be set or can be synchronized and set using an NTP server. Use the CS-MARS CLI command **date dd/mm/yyyy** to set the current date.

Step 7 **Set the desired time**—The same logic and reasoning applies to setting the desired time. As with the time zone, the time can manually be set or can be synchronized and set using an NTP server. Use the CS-MARS CLI command **time hh:mm:ss** to set the current time.

Step 8 **Set the IP address for your CS-MARS interfaces**—The **ifconfig** command is used to set the IP address on the CS-MARS interfaces. This command uses the standard UNIX **ifconfig** syntax. In the examples in this book, we use the default IP addresses on the CS-MARS interfaces. The Ethernet 0 default IP address is 192.168.0.100, and the Ethernet 1 default IP address is 192.168.1.100. Either of these IP addresses can be used for management access through an administrative workstation.

To change the IP address on your CS-MARS interfaces, use the CLI command **ifconfig eth0 <ip-address> <subnet-mask>**; if you need to change the IP address on Ethernet 1, use the command **ifconfig eth1**

<ip-address> <subnet-mask>. Note that any changes to IP addresses or time zones require you to boot CS-MARS before the changes take effect.

Every time an IP address is changed, CS-MARS requires a reboot of the system.

Step 9   Ensure connectivity between your CS-MARS device and your administrative management workstations—You need to ensure that you have SSL/HTTPS access and network connectivity between your CS-MARS device and your management workstations. Connectivity can be verified using the **ping** command on either the workstation or the appliance, and management protocol connectivity can be verified using a browser and entering **HTTPS://192.168.0.100** (or the IP address you used for your CS-MARS interface). If either the ping or the browser access fails, you must work with your network administrators to ensure that you have a route between your workstation and the appliance and that no access lists are blocking TCP port 443 or ICMP traffic.

When you have completed these steps, continue to the next section to add devices and set system parameters to activate your CS-MARS appliance.

Enter System Parameters Using the CS-MARS Web Interface

The only supported browser for the CS-MARS web interface is Internet Explorer (IE) v6.0 SP1; it's assumed that higher versions will work. Before you use the browser to access your security appliance, you must make the following changes:

- **Turn off web page caching**—This ensures that current web pages are always returned from the CS-MARS device. If you don't do this step, when you make a change to the CS-MARS configuration and then use your browser to check your configuration, you likely will see old data and not the change that you just made.

- **Configure IE with a medium security level**—This enables ActiveX controls and scripting required by the web interface.

- **Configure IE to a privacy level of medium**—By default, this allows cookies that are required for the correct operation of the CS-MARS web interface.

- **Configure IE to allow popups from the CS-MARS**—CS-MARS uses popup windows to display several different types of information. Without this configuration, you will not be able to use the CS-MARS web interface. Your system might have other popup blockers besides the default IE blockers; you must make sure all of them are set to allow popups from CS-MARS.

If you are having any trouble making these changes on your system, refer to the excellent detailed step-by-step description on the Cisco website. You can access that information by browsing to www.cisco.com/go/mars and clicking on the **Install and Upgrade** link; then follow the links to the CS-MARS 4.1 *Install and Setup Guide*.

Enter System Parameters to Activate Your CS-MARS Appliance

Now that you have the correct browser, the correct browser configurations, connectivity to your appliance, and the appliance IP address, you are ready to make some basic configurations and activate your appliance.

The following is a step-by-step procedure to activate your CS-MARS appliance.

Step 1 Enter your username and password. The screen shown in Figure 5-3 appears. The default username and password are pnadmin/pnadmin.

Figure 5-3 *CS-MARS License Entry Panel*

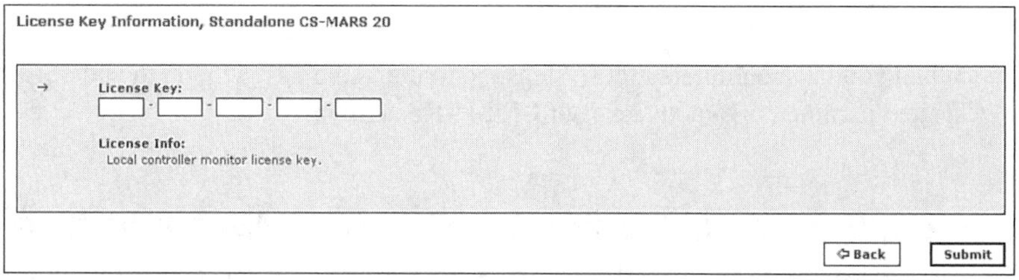

Step 2 Enter the license key for your CS-MARS appliance. This should have been shipped with your device. If it was not included or you have misplaced it, send an e-mail to licensing@cisco.com or browse to Cisco's licensing website to get a license.

You will notice that no matter what selection you chose on the GUI, you are prompted for the license key.

Step 3 After you enter your license key, CS-MARS presents you with a screen to enter the initial configuration for your appliance.

The screen that is displayed contains cells to enter (see Figure 5-4).

— IP address for the second CS-MARS interface

— Default gateway

— Mail gateway

— DNS address information

Step 4 Enter the required values for each of these fields.

Figure 5-4   *CS-MARS Basic Configuration Panel*

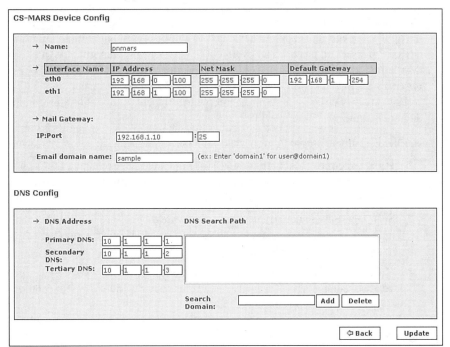

Step 5   Make sure you include DNS addresses. The CS-MARS device generates reports that contain source and destination IP addresses. The CS-MARS appliance will resolve these names as long as you have defined your DNS servers. If you don't define your DNS servers, you must manually resolve addresses, which severely impacts the speed and accuracy of your analysis process.

Step 6   You have flexibility on how you can use the interfaces of your CS-MARS device. The basic functions provided by the CS-MARS interfaces are data collection and device management. The interfaces can be used for either of these purposes. For example, you could use one interface for device management or event collection, or both. You could also choose to use one interface for data collection and the other for device management.

Step 7   CS-MARS uses the mail information to send alerts or reports to certain mail addresses when alerts or reports are generated, so it's important to populate this field appropriately.

Step 8   After the data is entered, click the **Update** button at the bottom of the page. This sends the data to your appliance and saves the configuration.

CS-MARS Reporting Device Setup

Now that you have configured the basic parameters for CS-MARS and have connectivity to the appliance, you must add the devices that will be communicating to your CS-MARS device. This section provides an overview of how to set up reporting devices. For more detailed information on how to configure reporting devices, reference *The User Guide for Cisco Security MARS Local Controller.* This document is located on the Cisco website at www.cisco.com/go/mars. Follow the links to product literature, support, and documentation.

CS-MARS supports three main types of devices:

- **Hardware-based security devices**—These are devices that are traditional network and security appliances, such as routers, switches, security appliances, firewalls, web proxies, and intrusion-prevention devices.

- **Software-based security devices**—Software devices are applications that run on hosts or servers. These include Apache web server, IIS server, or other software-based network or security services.

- **On-demand security services**—These are subscription-based services provided by vendors using a central security operations center or management center.

Adding Devices

Two methods are used to input device information into CS-MARS:

- Manual device entry
- Comma-separated variable (CSV) seed file imports

Manual Device Entry

The first method for device entry is the manual method. Using this function, you enter all your known devices into CS-MARS to enable CS-MARS to use their information for log integration, log correlation, and topology discovery. You are asked to enter the following information for each device. This list isn't absolute, however. For example, in some cases, you won't be able to enter SNMP-RO information; in other cases, you might not be able to enter usernames and passwords. Don't worry about this. Enter what you can, and CS-MARS will use whatever information it can glean from the information that you do give it.

The following is a list of general information you can use to add devices to CS-MARS. Note, however, that most devices require only a subset of this information for CS-MARS to begin communications.

- Device name (required)
- Access IP address (IP used for Telnet, SNMP, or SSH access to the device; required)

- Reporting IP (source IP address of reporting data; required)
- Access type (Telnet, SSH, FTP)
- Username
- Password
- Enable password
- Config path
- Filename
- SNMP-RO community string
- Monitor resource usage
- Interface IP addresses and subnets (needed for path calculation only)

If a device is not entered into CS-MARS or is improperly configured in CS-MARS, the appliance classifies and reports any data it receives as an "Unknown Reporting Device," and the data from these devices is not used in CS-MARS for attack analysis.

One of the more impressive features of CS-MARS is that after you enter the information of your network and security devices, CS-MARS uses that information to access those devices, analyze the device configurations, analyze interface parameters, and analyze route and Content Addressable Memory (CAM) tables to determine your network topology. This is discussed in detail in Chapter 4, "CS-MARS Technologies and Theory."

The following steps are taken when manually adding a device on your CS-MARS appliance.

Step 1   In the CS-MARS GUI, navigate to the panel to add devices: **Admin > Security and Monitoring Information**. Figure 5-5 is the starting panel for adding network devices.

Figure 5-5   *CS-MARS Add Device Panel*

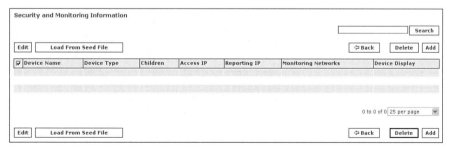

When you've accessed this panel, click the **Add** button to enter a new device. Figure 5-6 appears.

Figure 5-6 *CS-MARS Device-Configuration Panel*

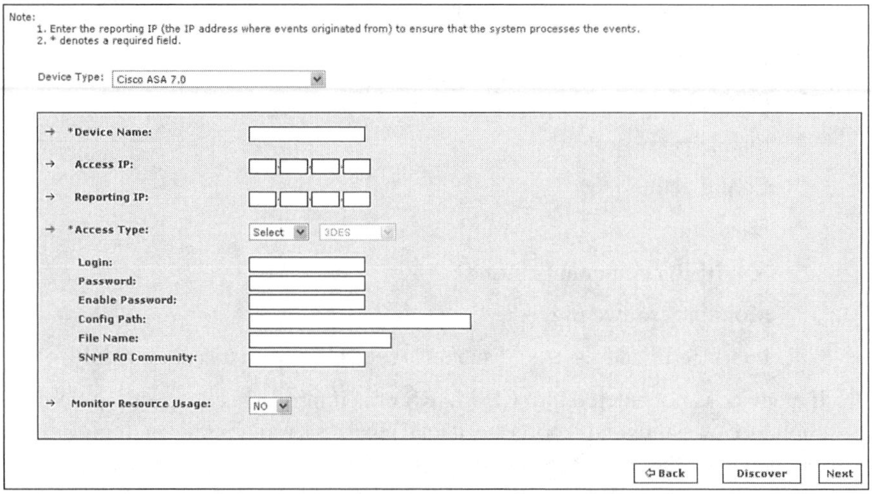

Note:
    1. Enter the reporting IP (the IP address where events originated from) to ensure that the system processes the events.
    2. * denotes a required field.

    Device Type: [Cisco ASA 7.0   ▼]

    →   *Device Name: [   ]

    →   Access IP: [ ][ ][ ][ ]

    →   Reporting IP: [ ][ ][ ][ ]

    →   *Access Type: [Select ▼] [3DES ▼]

         Login: [   ]
         Password: [   ]
         Enable Password: [   ]
         Config Path: [   ]
         File Name: [   ]
         SNMP RO Community: [   ]

    →   Monitor Resource Usage: [NO ▼]

                                          [⇦ Back] [Discover] [Next]

Step 2   You must make a selection from the **Device Type** pull-down list. These
            are the default devices that have reporting features that CS-MARS
            supports. Figure 5-7 shows those devices and categorizes them by
            HW-based security device, SW-based security device, and on-demand
            security device.

Figure 5-7 *CS-MARS Device Pull-Down Menu*

Notice that the devices that are supported in this pull-down list are not
only Cisco devices, but devices from most of the popular security
vendors. Chapter 6, "Reporting and Mitigative Device Configuration,"

has a complete list of supported devices and vendors. The following is a partial list of third-party vendors that CS-MARS supports:

— Cisco Systems

— Extreme Systems

— NetScreen

— Network Appliance

— ISS

— Qualsys

Step 3 In the example for this chapter, you add a Cisco Intrusion Prevention 5.0 device.

Select Cisco IPS 5.x from the **Device Type** pull-down menu. You are presented with the panel to add an IPS 5.x device, illustrated in Figure 5-8. Note that because not all devices have the same configuration characteristics and reporting formats, this screen might differ, depending on the device selected.

Figure 5-8   *IPS Device Entry Panel*

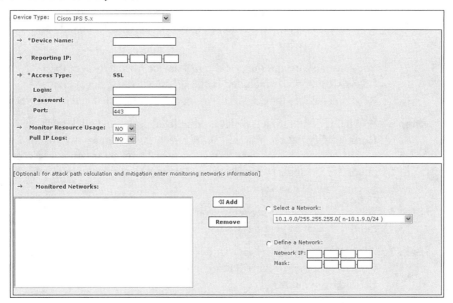

Step 4 You must fill in the following information to enable this device as a CS-MARS reporting device:

— **Device Name**—This is name that has been configured with the IPS CLI or IPS web interface as the device name for this device.

— **Reporting IP**—This is the IP address for the management interface of this device. Make sure this interface is routable to the CS-MARS device. In this example, the IPS device has an address of 192.168.0.222.

— **Login**—This is the administrative username for the IPS device.

— **Password**—This is the administrative password for the IPS device.

— **Port**—Unless otherwise configured on the IPS device, this value should always be 443.

— **Monitor Resource Usage**—Select **Yes** if you want CS-MARS to report when this device uses excessive hardware resources.

— **Monitored Network**—This selection tells CS-MARS that this device will be sending alert information for the IP addresses that are members of the defined subnets in this table. It is important that the proper information is placed in these fields because CS-MARS uses this data for path calculation and alarm data. A best practice is to enter the *exact* subnets from inside your network that this IPS device monitors. Do not summarize these entries! If all your subnets are not present in the Select a Network drop-down list, you can manually put them in using the Define a Network selection. In this example, the monitored networks are 192.168.0.0/24 and 192.168.1.0/24.

You must also ensure that, on the IPS device, the address of the CS-MARS device is included in the IPS's "allowed" access list. Readying devices for CS-MARS access is discussed in depth in Chapter 6.

Step 5 When this configuration panel is completed, you must click the **Test Connectivity** button. You will see a screen that indicates that discovery of this device is in progress. If the discovery fails, an Internet Explorer popup screen appears. If it's successful, an Internet Explorer popup screen reads "Discovery is done."

Step 6 When the device is discovered, you must click the **Submit** button to add the IPS device to your device list.

Step 7 After adding the device to your device list, you need to activate your work. Select the **Activate** button, in the upper-right corner of the CS-MARS window.

Activation is important in the CS-MARS world. When you make changes through the web interface, your changes are written to the CS-MARS database but do not take effect until they are activated. Activation is achieved simply by selecting the **Activate** button.

After activation, your CS-MARS screen looks like Figure 5-9.

Figure 5-9 *CS-MARS Added Device List*

You can also confirm that CS-MARS recognized your device by navigating to the topology page and verifying that an icon for the IPS device has been added to the Summary page, as shown in Figure 5-10. Your topology should show your CS-MARS device, two subnets that are displayed as Layer 2 switches, and the IPS device you just loaded. In this configuration, the address of the IPS device is 192.168.1.222. The two subnets 192.168.0.0 and 192.168.1.0 show up as connected routes to the CS-MARS device because of the interface IP addresses, and the IPS device shows those addresses for two reasons: The management interface of the IPS box is in the subnet 192.168.0.0, and when we added the device, we told CS-MARS that the IPS device is monitoring 192.168.0.0 and 192.168.1.0.

Figure 5-10 *CS-MARS Network Topology Display*

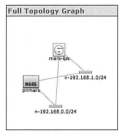

This example using SSL is just one of many different ways to add devices to CS-MARS. SNMP is important and should not be overlooked. CS-MARS extensively uses the information from SNMP device databases to discover network topology and as a method to make configuration changes for attack mitigation. Discovery and mitigation are covered in depth in Chapter 4.

These Cisco devices have SNMP support through the CS-MARS appliance:

- Cisco adaptive security appliances
- Cisco IOS routers, Version 12.2 and higher

- Cisco PIX firewalls
- Cisco Catalyst switches/CATOS
- Cisco Catalyst switches/IOS
- Cisco Virtual Private Network (VPN) concentrators, Version 4.03 and higher

CSV File Import

From the previous section, which explained how to manually add a device, you have probably observed that adding devices is easy but that it would be very time-consuming to add several devices. If you are an enterprise with 20 or more devices you need to add to the CS-MARS database, it might make sense to use CSV file import, which was designed to add multiple devices.

A CSV file must be created in a specific format so that CS-MARS can correctly use the information for its intended purpose. Each entry contains the same information that Figure 5-6 showed.

The detailed format for a CSV file is documented in *The User Guide for Cisco Security MARS Local Controller,* found on the Cisco website at www.cisco.com/go/mars. Follow the links to product literature, support, and documentation until you find the document titled *Install and Setup Guide for Cisco Security Monitoring, Analysis, and Response System, Release 4.1.* Within that document, search for the string "add multiple devices using a seed file."

After you create a CSV file with all your devices and appropriate access information, you must import that file into CS-MARS.

Using a CSV Device Import File (Seed File)

First create the file with an entry for each of the devices you need to add to CS-MARS. This file is called the seed file.

The information for each device and CSV seed file format is listed in Appendix C, "CS-MARS Supplements."

The following is an example of a seed file that could be used to import a PIX firewall, two NetScreen devices, and two IOS devices into CS-MARS.

```
192.168.10.1,,,,PIX,TELNET,,,cisco,,,,,,,,,,,
24.3.24.100,,,,NETSCREEN,SSH,netscreen,ns3146wsdf,,,,,,,,,,,,
192.168.10.2,,,,NETSCREEN,SSH,netscreen,tt160p91,,,,,,,,,,,,,
50.1.1.200,,,,IOS,TELNET,,,Qa$1*5ft,gt$*j15,,,,,,,,,,
10.10.10.1,,,,IOS,TELNET,,,telnetpass123,,,,,,,,,,
```

In this example, for simplicity, we add a single PIX 7.0 firewall and use the following information in the seed file.

```
192.168.0.150,,,,PIX7X,ssh,sshuser,cisco123,,Cisco
```

Step 1   After the seed file has been created, you need to once again navigate to
the **Admin > Security and Monitoring Information** panel. This time,
instead of adding a device, click the **Load from Seed File** button.
A browser popup prompts you for the FTP location of your seed
file. Figure 5-11 shows the prompts and the value used for this
example.

Figure 5-11   *CS-MARS Seed Import Configuration Panel*

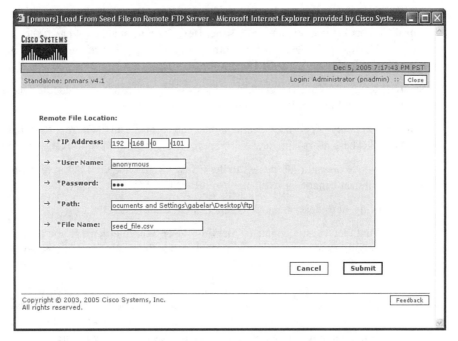

Step 2   After the seed file has been submitted, CS-MARS automatically
discovers the devices that were in your seed file and notifies you with a
browser popup when the devices have been discovered.

Step 3   You must then navigate back to the previous screen and click the
Activate button.

Step 4   Then, as you did when you manually added a device, go to the Summary
page and view the topology map to see your device.

Creating Users and Groups

The next step to get your CS-MARS devices ready for deployment is to create users and
groups that are allowed to interact with your CS-MARS device.

You can create four types of users to manage your CS-MARS environment:

- Admin
- Security analyst
- Notifications only
- Operator

Each of these user types has a specific set of functions it is allowed to perform on a CS-MARS appliance.

Admin—This is the equivalent of a superuser. The admin account has full control on a CS-MARS appliance. The pnadmin account is the only account that can access the CS-MARS through SSH for CLI operation.

Security analyst—This user can access all areas of the CS-MARS web interface and CLI, except for the Admin configuration panel.

Notifications only—These are accounts that can receive e-mails or reports generated by CS-MARS. These users can view only report data related to the notification they received.

Operator—An operator has access to the CS-MARS device GUI but in read-only mode. This type of user cannot make changes to the system.

The following steps describe how to add users to CS-MARS.

Step 1 First, you must navigate to **Admin > User Management**. If you have a default installation, the only user created is the pnadmin user, labeled as Administrator (pnadmin).

Step 2 Before you set up accounts, you need to identify each user that needs access to the CS-MARS device and then what function that user needs to perform. Then you input each user through the **Admin > User Management** configuration panel and associate them with the appropriate group.

CS-MARS enables you to enter a significant amount of informational data for each user. It should be considered a best practice to enter all the data you possibly can. In many industries, regulations require you to do this, but this also can save you significant time if you need to contact CS-MARS users in the middle of a threat response.

Configuring NetFlow and Vulnerability Scanning

At this point, your CS-MARS device is capable of accepting and analyzing logs and security alerts, but with the addition of NetFlow and vulnerability scanning, your CS-MARS appliance will be a much more powerful security solution.

The addition of NetFlow enables CS-MARS to recognize traffic anomalies and baseline network behavior.

The addition of vulnerability scanning enhances the already considerable capability of CS-MARS to tell the difference between a real attack sequence and a false-positive attack sequence.

NetFlow Configuration

Simply speaking, NetFlow is a core technology built into many Cisco routers that reports the number of flows on a per-port, per-IP address basis (source and destination). Cisco defines NetFlow as follows:

> [NetFlow] efficiently provides a key set of services for IP applications, including network traffic accounting, usage-based network billing, network planning, security, Denial of Service monitoring capabilities, and network monitoring. NetFlow provides valuable information about network users and applications, peak usage times, and traffic routing. Cisco invented NetFlow and is the leader in IP traffic flow technology.

NOTE	For an in-depth discussion of NetFlow, go to www.cisco.com/go/netflow on the Cisco website.

Most security experts agree that NetFlow in a CS-MARS environment adds substantial value because its rate of false positives is very low and its capability to recognize previously unknown attacks is very high. Chapter 4 discusses NetFlow and how it is used in conjunction with CS-MARS.

Enabling NetFlow on a CS-MARS appliance is a straightforward task.

Step 1   First you must navigate to the **Admin > System Setup > Device Configuration and Discover Information > NetFlow Config Info** panel.

Step 2   Enter the port that will listen for NetFlow data. The default is UDP 2055, but NetFlow is user configurable on routers, so you might want to verify with a network engineer which port is being used for NetFlow.

Step 3   The next option enables or disables NetFlow on the CS-MARS device. The collection and processing of NetFlow data is enabled by default. If your network is not NetFlow enabled, select No.

Step 4   The next selection provides you with an option to store NetFlow records. If you select Yes, this tells CS-MARS that you want to store every NetFlow record. This can potentially slow down your CS-MARS system because it has to write many more events than if you select No. If you select No, you are telling CS-MARS that you want to store only NetFlow traffic that represents an anomaly or is part of a session that triggered a rule. Generally, unless dictated by industry or government regulations, you select **No** for this option. If you select Yes to store NetFlow data, your CS-MARS counts every flow as an event, thus impacting your CS-MARS appliance EPS rate.

Step 5   The last option is to define which networks you want to evaluate NetFlow data. Because flow anomalies can show up on any device that might inadvertently run malicious software or might be misconfigured, a best practice is to define all the networks over which CS-MARS will be reporting. If this table is left blank, CS-MARS will process flows for all subnets that it learns about.

Step 6   After all the data is entered, select **Submit** to enable NetFlow. This readies your CS-MARS device to listen for NetFlow data. At this point in the setup, you haven't yet configured any devices to send NetFlow, so this won't have an impact on your CS-MARS reporting until you configure your routers as described in Chapter 6. Figure 5-12 shows the completed NetFlow configuration panel.

Step 7   Click **Activate** on the top-right side of the CS-MARS page.

Figure 5-12   *CS-MARS NetFlow Configuration Panel*

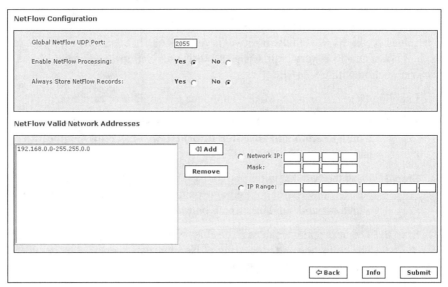

Dynamic Vulnerability Scanning Configuration

Vulnerability scanning is a feature that vastly increases the accuracy of CS-MARS threat reporting.

When vulnerability scanning is enabled on your CS-MARS device, CS-MARS will not conduct a vulnerability scan until a rule is triggered as a result of an event or session.

Configuring CS-MARS to conduct dynamic vulnerability scanning is a very simple process (see Figure 5-13):

Step 1   Browse to **Admin > System Setup > CS-MARS Setup** and click **Networks for Dynamic Vulnerability Scanning (Optional)**.

Step 2   Select the radio button for the method you want to use to enter the network or IP range of the systems in which you want scanning to be enabled.

Step 3   Use the drop-down box to select the network of your choice, manually enter the network and mask, or manually enter a range of IP addresses.

Step 4   Click the **Add** button to add your selection to the pane. Click the Remove button if you want to remove your selection.

Step 5   Repeat steps 2 through 4 until you have entered all networks or IP ranges you want to have scanned.

Step 6   Click the **Submit** button to submit your changes.

Step 7   Click the **Activate** button at the top-right corner of the web page to activate your configuration. When a new popup widow appears indicating that activation is done, click the **Close** button to close the new window.

NOTE   Clicking the Info button on this page opens a new window with a brief explanation of vulnerability scanning on CS-MARS.

For a more detailed description of vulnerability scanning, see Chapter 4.

Figure 5-13   *CS-MARS Dynamic Vulnerability Scanning Configuration GUI*

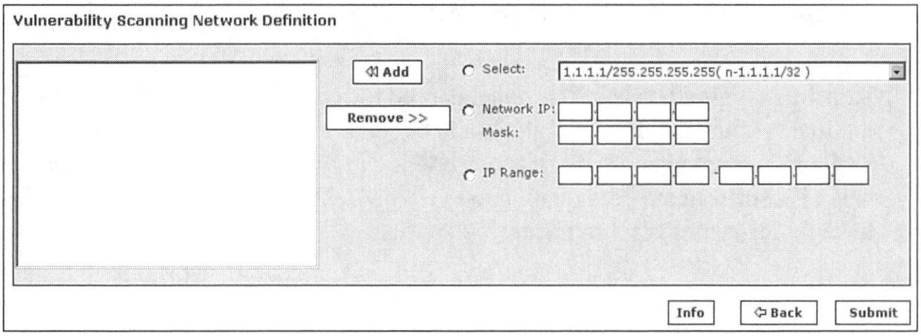

Configuring CS-MARS System Maintenance

At this point in your configuration process, CS-MARS has been configured to be ready to collect syslog messages and events, accurately correlate data, and respond to threats. You still need to configure the network devices and applications, but that is covered in Chapter 6.

This section of this chapter doesn't require you to make any changes on the CS-MARS device; it's just informational. You will learn about the global system variables in CS-MARS. All parameters should be set to the default unless you need to archive or retrieve data.

To configure or view maintenance parameters for CS-MARS, you must navigate to the **Admin > System Maintenance** panel. From this panel, you have the option to configure the following:

- License keys
- Upgrades
- Certificates
- Runtime logging levels
- Viewing of archived or current log files
- Viewing of the audit trail
- Retrieval of raw messages
- Data archiving

License keys   This panel is useful if you need to configure a license key on your CS-MARS device. You simply enter the key and click **Submit**. If you have to do a **pnreset** on your CS-MARS box, you will lose the license key. Before running pnreset, you should go to this panel and write down the key. Then when pnreset is completed, come back to this panel and enter the license key.

Upgrades   This panel is used to upgrade the CS-MARS system software. You must first put the upgrade package on an FTP or HTTPS server. Then enter the server's IP address, username, password, path, package name of the CS-MARS upgrade file, and server type.

Certificates   This panel is used to import Global Controller certificates and export Local Controller certificates for input to a Global Controller. See the MARS 4.1 Local Controller Users Guide for more information.

Runtime logging levels   This panel is used to set the logging levels of your CS-MARS internal system logs. These levels should be set to the default unless requested by the Cisco TAC or Cisco engineering for troubleshooting purposes. Each entry that you see on this panel is a software process running in the CS-MARS operating system; the default logging level for all entries is set to trace.

Viewing of the appliance's log files   Using this panel, you can view the logs of the CS-MARS system processes. These logs show processes and process threads starting and stopping. Under normal circumstances, these logs are used only by Cisco TAC and Cisco engineering teams.

Viewing of the audit trail   This panel enables you to do a query to see what operations were performed by which users on a CS-MARS device. This log shows whether a new user is added or any device database information is changed. This audit log satisfies many requirements as defined by industry or federal regulations.

Retrieval of raw messages   This panel can be used to selectively retrieve raw log data that CS-MARS has received from a device in its database or archived files. You specify a time range and the name of the device whose data you need to view. A text file of the resulting data is zipped, and you are offered an option to download it to your workstation for further analysis. This operation can be done from either your CS-MARS Local Controller database or a device that has been defined as an archive location. This feature also satisfies many requirements as defined by industry or federal regulations.

Data archiving   This panel enables you to define an NFS server and a location on the server to archive CS-MARS data. You also have an option on this panel to define the length of time you would like to store the CS-MARS data on the archive server. One consideration that you need to carefully examine is planning the remote storage capacity and setting the number of days of data to store on the archive location. It might take some ongoing changes before you're satisfied with the balance between the length of time and the amount of data that you are storing on the archive server.

Configuring System Parameters

System parameters define the miscellaneous global variables such as polling intervals and authentication prompts. But this section highlights a new feature in system parameters, called distributed threat management.

These parameters can be configured or viewed in the Admin > System Parameter panel.

- Windows event log pulling time interval
- TACACS/AAA server prompts
- Oracle event log pulling time interval
- Distributed threat mitigation settings
- Proxy settings

Windows event log pulling time interval   This parameter defines how often CS-MARS will pull event logs from devices that are running the Windows operating system. These event logs can be valuable in discovering Microsoft Windows attacks such as brute-force password attacks. CS-MARS indicates this by correlating several Microsoft events that identify failed password attempts. CS-MARS generates incidents to reflect the source IP addresses that generate the failed login attempts and makes a recommendation to put an access list in a router to prevent those failed attempts from reaching their destination. Because the source is identified, threat responders can evaluate and take action on the system or systems that are sourcing the attack. The default polling interval is 300 seconds, or 5 minutes. If you want to lower this parameter, keep in mind that it's possible, depending on the number of hosts you have, that network traffic volume could drastically increase. Most customers find that the default is adequate.

A best practice when polling Microsoft servers and workstations for their security event logs is to take the log data from the domain controller(s) in the network. This drastically reduces the risk of saturating your network with event log data. To accomplish this, you must configure your servers and workstations to send their log data to their respective domain controllers.

TACACS/AAA server prompts   When your network devices use a TACACS/AAA server for user management and access controls, often network administrators choose to modify the login prompts on the remote devices. If the login prompts are modified from the original device defaults, CS-MARS needs to know the new prompts. This setting allows CS-MARS to use the changed prompts to gain access to your network devices for required data and mitigation.

Oracle event log pulling time interval   This setting behaves essentially the same as the one for Windows polling, except it is applied to Oracle database log pulling.

Distributed threat mitigation (DTM) settings   DTM is a new feature in CS-MARS 4.1 that polls Cisco IPS appliances to find out what events are firing most frequently. When CS-MARS determines this information, it calculates the top signatures and pushes the signature-definition files to IOS routers that are capable of running fully functional IPS code.

Proxy settings   This setting configures CS-MARS to communicate with devices through a proxy server. This would be needed, for example, if your organization uses a proxy server for Internet control and security, and you have DNS servers and an IDS device on your DMZ. CS-MARS would need to use the DNS server for DNS resolution and to communicate with the IDS device on the DMZ. Thus, CS-MARS needs proxy settings and an access account.

Summary

This chapter covered the basic functions of installing and configuring the CS-MARS appliance.

You learned that a critical first step is determining the placement of CS-MARS in your network. The basic premise is that, according to *safe* guidelines, CS-MARS should be placed in out-of-band networks when possible. If it's not possible to put CS-MARS out-of-band, you want to ensure that communications between CS-MARS and its management devices and reporting devices are encrypted to protect against network sniffing.

In addition to deployment considerations, this chapter described the steps necessary for the initial configuration and setup of high-level system parameters that enable CS-MARS as an STM system.

In Chapter 6, you will learn how to configure your network devices and hosts to communicate with your CS-MARS device. Enabling communications with these devices will make your CS-MARS device a fully functional threat-response system.

In this chapter, you learn how to configure your network and security devices to send information to the CS-MARS platform. Topics covered in this chapter include the following:

- Identifying CS-MARS–Supported Devices
- Configuring Devices to Communicate with CS-MARS

## CHAPTER 6

Reporting and Mitigative Device Configuration

In this chapter, you learn how to configure your security and network devices, operating systems, and database servers to send events and syslog data to your CS-MARS appliance. This includes the configurations of routers, switches, firewalls, intrusion-prevention systems (IPS), operating systems, web server applications, Virtual Private Network (VPN) concentrators, generic devices, and database servers. Perhaps more important, this chapter includes configurations for not only Cisco products, but almost every popular best-of-breed security vendor.

The need to correlate mixed-vendor event logs and syslogs can't be overstated. Although most of the major system integrators in the United States, Central America, Europe, and Asia now believe that a single-vendor network and security solution provides the strongest possible security posture, the reality is that thousands of networks have a mixed-vendor environment, and this poses an enormous challenge for threat responders to quickly and accurately make decisions on how to respond if a threat is discovered in their networks.

This chapter highlights the steps you must take to configure Cisco and best-of-breed network and security equipment to be used in a CS-MARS–enabled networking environment.

Identifying CS-MARS–Supported Devices

To help you clearly understand the devices and vendors CS-MARS supports, this section is divided into three different topics:

- Types of devices and the information they provide
- The difference between reporting and mitigation devices
- Table of device support for CS-MARS v4.1

The first section describes the different types of devices and how they are used by the CS-MARS appliance. The second section explains the differences between a reporting device and a mitigation device. The final section provides you with a list of devices and vendors that are fully supported by the CS-MARS appliance.

Types of Devices and the Information They Provide

CS-MARS supports three different classes of devices. Each of these classes of devices has a specific function in the network. Not all the functions of these devices are security related; the functions also include routing network data and maintaining host services, application services, and server and host location tables. This section helps you understand how CS-MARS correlates alerts, events, and messages from different devices.

The classifications of devices in CS-MARS are as follows:

- **Hardware-based security devices**—These devices are traditional network and security appliances, such as routers, switches, firewalls, intrusion-detection or -prevention systems (IDSs/IPSs), and others.

- **Software-based security devices**—Software devices are applications that run on hosts or servers and provide network or security services; these can include an Apache web server, a Check Point firewall, or any other software application.

- **On-demand security services**—Security services represent subscription-based services provided by vendors using a central security operations center (SOC) with remote-monitoring nodes. This can include products such as Qualys QualysGuard.

CS-MARS supports the following security and network devices:

- Routers
- Switches
- Firewalls
- VPN devices
- Network IDS/IPS
- Host IDSs
- Antivirus applications
- Vulnerability assessment tools
- Host operating systems
- Web server applications
- Web proxy devices and applications
- Database servers
- Authentication, Authorization, and Accounting (AAA) servers
- Generic syslog devices
- Generic SNMP devices

These different device classifications and types of devices are important to note when configuring CS-MARS because there's a clear difference between a PIX firewall, which is a hardware device, and a Check Point firewall, which is often a software device. Because of this, these two devices are configured differently when configuring them to communicate with CS-MARS and adding them to the CS-MARS appliance device database.

Each of the devices listed has a separate function in the network; because of this, they offer CS-MARS different types of information. Table 6-1 describes each device type and the data that is available from the device type. It also describes how CS-MARS can use the data to determine things such as mitigation recommendations or likelihood of attack success, or to determine your network topology.

Table 6-1   *CS-MARS Device Data Type Definitions and Usages*

Device Type	Definition and Use
Router	**Mitigation and discovery protocols**—The most popular options for device discovery are SSH and SNMP.
	NetFlow data—NetFlow information is used for threat-detection topology maps that show attack traffic paths, baselining protocols, and anomalous behavior detection.
	NAT translations—This information is used for topology maps that show attack traffic paths.
	SNMP-RO—This information is used for topology maps that show attack traffic paths and device discovery. If SNMP was used as the discovery protocol, it also is used for device configurations to determine network topology.
	Syslog data and SNMP queries—These queries are used for device status and resource utilization, such as memory, CPU, and interface/port statistics.
	ARP cache table—This table maps IP addresses to MAC addresses and is used for topology maps that show attack traffic paths and device discovery.
	ARP cache table during investigation and mitigation—When an incident is analyzed, the ARP cache tables are reviewed to map IP addresses to hosts. This data is cached for 6 hours. This information is used for topology discovery and attack mitigation recommendations.
	SSH or Telnet—These are used for DTM signature delivery.
Switch	**Forwarding tables**—These map IP addresses to MAC addresses and are used for topology maps that show attack traffic paths and device discovery.
	SNMP queries—These queries are used to determine device status and resource utilization, such as memory, CPU, and interface/port statistics.
	NetFlow data—NetFlow information is used for threat-detection topology maps that show attack traffic paths.

continues

Table 6-1 *CS-MARS Device Data Type Definitions and Usages (Continued)*

Device Type	Definition and Use
	Syslog data—This information is used for device status and resource utilization, such as memory, CPU, and interface/port statistics. The data is also used for 802.1x logs generated during NAC sessions and configuration change control. **SNMP-RO and SSH**—With these, you can obtain interface configurations that are then used to generate topology maps, determine expected data routes, and issue mitigation commands.
Firewall	**NAT mappings**—These are used to locate the source and destination of attacks and track those attacks as they traverse your network. This information is used for topology discovery and mitigation recommendations. **Firewall logs**—The session setup and teardown information is used to help determine false positive attacks. For example, if CS-MARS sees an event indicating an attack, but the firewall syslog indicates that the session setup was never built, when CS-MARS correlates the two messages, it knows that it's a false positive. **Audit logs**—CS-MARS can use these logs to match users with authenticated sessions, which helps to identify if accounts and administrative sessions have been exploited. **ARP cache table**—This table maps IP addresses to MAC addresses and is used for topology maps that show attack traffic paths and device discovery. **SNMP and syslog**—These are used to identify anomalous network activities based on memory, CPU, interface, and port. **VPN remote user information**—This information is used to map usernames to IP addresses on VPN clients. This helps CS-MARS determine whether the person who logged in had permission to perform the operations reported by the device. This information is also used to determine the true user of the host that could be part of an attack.
VPN	**User logging records**—These records can identify the source address of a user. When correlated to an outbreak such as a worm, this can help identify the source of the outbreak. **SNMP and syslog**—These are used to identify anomalous network activities based on memory, CPU, interface, and port. **Signature alerts**—Some VPN devices also include IPS functionality. Because of this, CS-MARS processes signature events to identify attack threats. CS-MARS learns and correlates this information and determines either a mitigation response or a false positive.

Table 6-1   *CS-MARS Device Data Type Definitions and Usages (Continued)*

Device Type	Definition and Use
Network IDS/IPS	**IPS alert**—This information provided by an IPS device includes the source and destination of the attack and the signature that was fired, to identify the attack itself. This starts a chain of correlation events in CS-MARS that includes correlation with other device logs to verify the accuracy of the alert, verify the vulnerability of the destination, generate a network topology map of the source and destination of the attack, determine whether mitigation is possible, and recommend a mitigation command and location. **Trigger packet information**—This data includes the payload of the packet that caused the IPS signature to fire. **IPS blocked events**—When a signature is fired, depending on the IPS device, an event might be blocked. CS-MARS uses this information to determine whether an event is successful. For example, if an event is blocked, CS-MARS knows that the likelihood of success is low; if the event was a report-only event, CS-MARS must correlate with other logs to determine the likelihood of attack success. These blocked events could be between any network devices: hosts, servers, routers, firewalls, and so on. **Device status information**—Depending on the IPS device, this can be an IPS alert or a syslog message. This information is used to identify anomalous network activities based on memory, CPU, and interface and port.
Host IDS	**HIPS events**—CS-MARS can use this information to know whether a host has been compromised. For example, if a CSA agent reported that a buffer-overflow was followed by an attempt to execute code off the stack, but the action was denied, and CS-MARS at the same time correlated a buffer-overflow event to the same host, it would be determined that the attack was not successful. **AV and HIPS server logs**—CS-MARS can use this information to determine what hosts in the network have been infected with viruses. For example, CS-MARS might get an event from a network AV server that saw a possible virus sent to an address. It then could correlate that information with an AV server to see if that host has an AV data file that can protect against the virus. If not, CS-MARS reports a possibly infected host.

continues

Table 6-1 *CS-MARS Device Data Type Definitions and Usages (Continued)*

Device Type	Definition and Use
Antivirus	**Antivirus server logs and queries**—CS-MARS can use this information to determine the host OS and patch levels. When correlating an IPS alert, CS-MARS can use this information to determine whether the destination system is vulnerable to the attack.
Vulnerability assessment	**Vulnerability assessment data**—CS-MARS uses this information to determine the likelihood of a successful attack. Several different types of vulnerability assessment tools can be used with CS-MARS. Depending on the tool you choose, you'll get different information: Operating system and version Open network ports Applications associated with an open port Version of applications associated with an open port Known vulnerabilities of a network device CS-MARS correlates this information with other device alerts to determine the likelihood of a successful attack.
Host OS security event	**Security events**—CS-MARS pulls security events and then correlates them to other events to determine information such as the likelihood that an attack was successful, host privilege escalation, modification of the system logs, excessive failed logins, spoofed IP addresses, network interface cards configured for promiscuous mode, abnormal termination of system processes, resource-utilization events, application events generated by web servers, and application events generated by database servers.
Web server	**Web server logs**—Web server logs correlated with OS security events can show the compromise of a web server from a web attack.
Web proxy	**Web proxy logs**—These logs are used to map users to sites and to translate addresses that may pass through the proxy to determine network topology and attack topology maps. In addition, CS-MARS can use web proxy logs for regulatory compliances such as URL filtering and reporting.
Database	**Database logs**—CS-MARS can use database logs to determine possible brute-force attacks against the database server. These logs also can help determine attacks such as privilege escalation. In addition, CS-MARS can use them for regulatory compliances associated with database tracking and object modification.

Table 6-1   *CS-MARS Device Data Type Definitions and Usages (Continued)*

Device Type	Definition and Use
AAA	**AAA logs**—AAA server syslogs can be used to track the following: NAC logins and NAC functionality such as denied admission attempts Passed authentications Failed attempts Specific NAC radius accounting logs Information similar to Windows events on some vendors' products
Generic syslog	**Syslog data**—This information is used to identify anomalous network activities based on memory, CPU, interface, and port. CS-MARS maps syslog messages to CS-MARS rules for supported devices and vendors. Generic syslogs can easily be imported into CS-MARS using the custom parser.
Generic SNMP	**SNMP data**—This information is used to identify anomalous network activities based on memory, CPU, and interface and port. CS-MARS maps syslog messages to CS-MARS rules for supported devices and vendors. Generic SNMP can easily be imported into CS-MARS using the custom parser.

The Difference Between Reporting and Mitigation Devices

Most devices in your network are either both reporting and mitigation devices or only-reporting devices. As you could see from the information in the previous section, CS-MARS uses both types of devices in its operation. Mitigation devices are devices for which CS-MARS can push or recommend commands to stop attacks. CS-MARS cannot modify reporting devices, but they provide critical logs and events that CS-MARS uses to make important decisions related to threat identification and mitigation. It's important that you understand the distinction between these two types of devices before adding them to your CS-MARS device database.

Reporting Devices

Reporting devices are generally devices deployed on your network that CS-MARS does not use to mitigate attacks, but whose information is correlated to determine valuable threat and response information. These software and hardware devices fall into this category:

- Network hosts and servers
- VPN concentrators not equipped with NAC functionality

- Software applications and software security systems that can't be configured remotely
- Database servers
- Web servers
- Web proxies
- Syslog servers
- Vulnerability scanners
- Network IPS and IDS devices incapable of running distributed threat management

In the world of CS-MARS, don't discount the importance of these network devices; the events and logs from these devices are absolutely critical for CS-MARS to accurately and quickly correlate threats and threat-response actions.

Mitigation Devices

Mitigation devices are simply devices deployed on your network that CS-MARS uses to mitigate attacks or make mitigative recommendations. These devices are typically hardware devices and sometimes, but not always, include the following:

- Routers
- Switches
- Firewalls
- IPS or IDS
- Cisco Integrated Security Routers (ISR)

The protocol for routers, switches, and firewalls is generally Secure Shell (SSH) or the Simple Network Management Protocol (SNMP). For IPS devices, the protocol is normally secure Hypertext Transfer Protocol (HTTPS).

CS-MARS first correlates all its data to determine the best device and command that can be used to mitigate the attack. When this determination is made, CS-MARS presents you with the mitigation command it has determined will best stop the attack. CS-MARS also offers you a single-click option to deploy the command to the mitigation device.

Chapter 9, "CS-MARS Uncovered," and Chapter 4, "CS-MARS Technologies and Theory," provide more in-depth discussions on how CS-MARS performs attack mitigation.

Table of CS-MARS–Supported Devices

Table 6-2 lists all Cisco and third-party security vendors whose devices are supported by CS-MARS. This list can also be found on the Cisco website at http://www.cisco.com/go/mars (follow the links to the CS-MARS 4.1 user guide).

The definitions for the headers in Table 6-2 are as follows:

- **Device Type/Vendor**—The vendor and the device type.
- **Supported Versions**—The versions that CS-MARS supports.
- **Protocol: Configuration Retrieval**—The protocols that CS-MARS can use to retrieve device configuration and topology information.
- **Protocol: Event Retrieval**—The protocols that CS-MARS can use to retrieve events from this device.
- **Protocol: Mitigation**—The protocols that CS-MARS can use to send its mitigation commands to this device.
- **Device Classification**—The device classification.
- **CSV Keyword**—The keyword that you would use in a CSV seed file to define this device type. Note that a CSV keyword is not available for every type of device.

Table 6-2   *CS-MARS–Supported Devices*

Device Type/ Vendor	Supported Versions	Protocol: Configuration Retrieval	Protocol: Event Retrieval	Protocol: Mitigation	Device Classifi- cation	CSV Keyword
Router/Switch Devices						
Cisco Router	Cisco IOS 11.*x*, 12.2	FTP, SNMP, SSH, Telnet	Syslog (from device), NetFlow v5, v7	SNMP	HW	IOS
Cisco Router Module	Cisco IOS 12.2	FTP, SNMP, SSH, Telnet	Syslog (from device), NetFlow v5, v7	SNMP	HW-switch	SWITCH-IOS
Cisco Switch	CATOS 6.*x*, IOS 12.2	FTP, SNMP, SSH, Telnet	Syslog (from device), NetFlow v5, v7	SNMP	HW	SWITCH-CATOS
Extreme Extreme-Ware	6.*x*	SNMP	Syslog (from device)	SNMP	HW	EXTREME
Generic Router	Unknown	SNMP	Syslog (from device)	—	HW	—

continues

Table 6-2 *CS-MARS–Supported Devices (Continued)*

Device Type/ Vendor	Supported Versions	Protocol: Configuration Retrieval	Protocol: Event Retrieval	Protocol: Mitigation	Device Classifi- cation	CSV Keyword
Firewall Devices						
Cisco PIX	6.0, 6.1, 6.2, 6.3	FTP, SSH, Telnet	Syslog (from device)	—	HW	PIX
Cisco PIX	7.0	FTP, SSH, Telnet	Syslog (from device)	—	HW	PIX7X
Cisco Adaptive Security Appliance (ASA)	7.0.1	FTP, SSH, Telnet	Syslog (from device)	—	HW	—
Cisco Firewall Services Module (FWSM)	1.1, 2.2, 2.3	FTP, SSH, Telnet	Syslog (from device)	—	HW-switch (IOS 12.2 or CATOS)	FWSM
Cisco IOS Firewall Feature Set	12.2(T) and later	FTP, SNMP, SSH, Telnet	Syslog (from device)	—	—	—
Juniper NetScreen	ScreenOS 4.0, 5.0	SNMP, SSH, Telnet	Syslog (from device)	—	HW	NETSCREEN
Check Point OPSEC NG and Firewall-1	NG FP3, NG AI (R55), NGX (R60)	SSLCA, CLEAR, ASYMSSLCA (OPSEC-CPMI)	OPSEC-LEA (from log server or manage-ment server)	—	SW-host	—
Nokia Firewall (running Check Point)	NG FP3, NG AI (R55), NGX (R60)	SSLCA, CLEAR, ASYMSSLCA (OPSEC-CPMI)	OPSEC-LEA (from log server or manage-ment server)	—	SW-host as Check Point	—

Table 6-2   *CS-MARS–Supported Devices (Continued)*

Device Type/ Vendor	Supported Versions	Protocol: Configuration Retrieval	Protocol: Event Retrieval	Protocol: Mitigation	Device Classification	CSV Keyword
VPN Devices						
Cisco VPN 3000 Concentrator	4.0.3, 4.7	SNMP	Syslog (from device)	—	HW	—
Network IDS						
Cisco Network IDS	3.1	SSH, Telnet	POP (from device)	—	HW	—
Cisco IDSM	3.1	SSH, Telnet	POP (from device)	—	HW-switch	—
Cisco Network IDS	4.0	SSL	RDEP (from device)	—	HW	—
Cisco IDSM	4.0	SSL	RDEP (from device)	—	HW-switch	—
Cisco Intrusion Prevention System (IPS) ASA module	5.0, 5.1	SSL	SDEE (from device)	—	HW	—
Cisco IPS ASA module	5.0, 5.1	—	SDEE (from device)	—	HW-ASA	—
Cisco IOS IPS (software only)	12.3(8)T or later	FTP, SNMP, SSH, Telnet	SDEE (from device)	—	HW-switch, HW-router	—
IntruVert IntruShield	1.5	—	SNMP (from management server)	—	SW-host	—

continues

Table 6-2 *CS-MARS–Supported Devices (Continued)*

Device Type/ Vendor	Supported Versions	Protocol: Configuration Retrieval	Protocol: Event Retrieval	Protocol: Mitigation	Device Classifi- cation	CSV Keyword
Juniper Net-Screen IDP	2.1	—	SNMP (from manage-ment server)	—	SW-host	—
Symantec ManHunt	3.*x*	—	SNMP (from device)	—	SW-host	—
ISS Real-Secure Sensor	6.5, 7.0	—	SNMP (from device)	—	SW-host	—
Snort	2.0	—	Syslog (from device)	—	SW-host	—
Enterasys Dragon	6.*x*	—	Syslog (from manager)	—	SW-host	—
Host IDS						
Cisco Security Agent	4.0, 4.5, 5.0	—	SNMP (from CSA MC)	—	SW-host	—
McAfee Entercept	2.5, 4.0	—	SNMP (from manage-ment server)	—	SW-host	—
ISS RealSecure Host Sensor	6.5, 7.0	—	SNMP (from device)	—	SW-host	—
Antivirus						
Symantec AntiVirus	9.*x*	—	SNMP (from manage-ment server)	—	SW-host	—

Table 6-2   *CS-MARS–Supported Devices (Continued)*

Device Type/ Vendor	Supported Versions	Protocol: Configuration Retrieval	Protocol: Event Retrieval	Protocol: Mitigation	Device Classifi- cation	CSV Keyword
Cisco Incident Control System (Cisco ICS), Trend Micro Outbreak Prevention Service (OPS)	1.0	—	Syslog (from CICC server)	—	SW-host	—
McAfee ePolicy Orchestrator	3.5	—	—	—	SW-host	—
Network Associates VirusScan	8.*x*	—	SNMP (from manage- ment server)	—	—	—
Vulnerability Assessment						
eEye REM	1.0	MS SQL	JDBC (from REM server)	—	SW-host	—
Qualys Qualys-Guard	3.4	—	HTTPS	—	ODS	—
Foundstone Foundscan	3.0	MS SQL	JDBC (from manage- ment server)	—	SW-host	—
Host OS						
Windows	NT, 2000, 2003	—	Syslog (from SNARE agent) or MS-RPC event pull	—	Host	WINDOWS

continues

Table 6-2 *CS-MARS–Supported Devices (Continued)*

Device Type/ Vendor	Supported Versions	Protocol: Configuration Retrieval	Protocol: Event Retrieval	Protocol: Mitigation	Device Classifi- cation	CSV Keyword
Solaris	8.*x*, 9.*x*, 10.*x*	—	Syslog (from device)	—	Host	SOLARIS
Red Hat Linux	7.*x*, 8.*x*	—	Syslog (from device)	—	Host	LINUX
Web Servers						
Microsoft Internet Information Server	Any	—	Syslog (from SNARE agent)	—	SW-host	—
Sun iPlanet	Any	—	HTTP (from Cisco Security MARS agent)	—	SW-host	—
Apache	Any	—	HTTP (from Cisco Security MARS agent)	—	SW-host	—
Web Proxy Devices						
Network Appliance NetCache	Generic	—	HTTP	—	HW	—
Database Servers						
Oracle Database	9i, 10g, Generic	TCP	SQLNet (from host)	—	SW-host	—
AAA Servers						
Cisco Secure Access Control Sever (ACS)	3.3	—	Syslog (from Cisco Security MARS agent)	—	SW-host	—

Table 6-2   *CS-MARS–Supported Devices (Continued)*

Device Type/ Vendor	Supported Versions	Protocol: Configuration Retrieval	Protocol: Event Retrieval	Protocol: Mitigation	Device Classifi- cation	CSV Keyword
Syslog Servers and SNMP Devices						
Generic devices	Any	—	SNMP (from device), syslog (from device)	—	—	—

Configuring Devices to Communicate with CS-MARS

You are now ready to begin configuring devices to communicate with CS-MARS. In previous chapters, we showed you how to configure CS-MARS to add devices to its database. Now it's time to learn how to configure the network devices to send reporting information to CS-MARS and also to accept mitigation commands from CS-MARS.

You will now see how to configure both Cisco and other third-party vendor devices. The types of devices include the following:

- Routers
- Switches
- Firewalls
- IDS and IPS
- Operating systems and web servers
- VPN concentrators
- Antivirus hosts and servers
- Database servers

Configuring Routers

Cisco routers and switches report events to CS-MARS using various protocols. The protocols most often used are syslog and SNMP, but to enable Network Admission Control (NAC) reporting, specific commands need to be applied to your routers.

In this section, we cover the commands necessary to enable the following protocols:

- SNMP
- NetFlow
- Syslog
- NAC-specific messages

This section also describes configuring a generic router.

Before you configure your Cisco IOS router to communicate with CS-MARS, you must ensure that you're running IOS version 11.0 or greater.

Configuring SNMP on Cisco IOS Routers

When you added your routers to the CS-MARS database, if you elected to use SNMP, you must also enable SNMP on the routers themselves. CS-MARS uses SNMP for four primary purposes:

- To read configuration data for mitigative recommendations
- To achieve topology discovery
- For reporting
- For device resource reporting

To fully define SNMP, you need to provide read and write community strings, enable traps, and define the SNMP server, which, in your case, is the CS-MARS appliance.

Now you must log into the router using either Telnet or SSH and enter the following commands. In this example, the community string is marstring and the IP address of the CS-MARS device is 192.168.0.100.

```
IOS Router (config)# snmp-server community marstring RO <ACL name if required>
IOS Router (config)# snmp-server community marstring RW
IOS Router (config)# snmp-server enable traps
IOS Router (config)# snmp-server host 192.168.0.100 marstring
```

You can limit the IP addresses used by SNMP by using a combination of a named access control list and the **snmp-server community** command.

Configuring NetFlow on Cisco IOS Routers

NetFlow is a protocol that Cisco routers use to summarize and track paired source and destination IP addresses that traverse a router. CS-MARS uses this information to recognize anomalous traffic, which is helpful in identifying day-zero attacks.

NetFlow needs to be first globally enabled in CS-MARS through the Admin panel, as discussed in Chapter 5, "CS-MARS Appliance Setup and Configuration." After CS-MARS is enabled to accept NetFlow data, IOS routers need to be configured to send NetFlow data to the CS-MARS device. The IOS commands define the following NetFlow information:

- NetFlow version to be used (v5 or v7)
- The destination device where NetFlow will send the data
- The UDP or TCP port to be used for sending NetFlow data
- The router interface where the NetFlow data will be sourced
- The interface on the router that will be enabled to sense the data flow that is fed into the IOS NetFlow engine

The following is an example of the IOS commands to enable NetFlow. Note that CS-MARS recognizes only NetFlow major and minor releases of Version 5 and Version 7.

In the example, the IP address of the CS-MARS device is 192.168.0.100 and the interface that has a route to the CS-MARS device is FastEthernet 0/1.

The **ip-flow-export source** command, shown next, is used to ensure that the source IP address of the NetFlow data is the same as the reporting address that you configured when you added your CS-MARS device.

```
IOS Router (config)# ip flow-export version 5
IOS Router (config)# ip flow-export destination 192.168.0.100 2055
IOS Router (config)# ip flow-export source interface FastEthernet 0/1
IOS Router (config)# interface FastEthernet 0/1
IOS Router (config-int)# ip route-cache flow
```

CS-MARS can accept only one reporting IP address per device, so it is important to have the NetFlow reporting IP the same as the router's syslog reporting IP. Both syslog and NetFlow use different default reporting IPs in the same device.

If you have two IOS devices in an HSRP configuration, the reporting IP of NetFlow and the syslog will always be the HSRP address as seen by CS-MARS, regardless of what source addresses you configure in the MFSC.

Configuring Syslog on Cisco IOS Routers

Now you must log into the router using either Telnet or SSH and enter the following commands. In the example, the IP address of the CS-MARS device is 192.168.0.100 and the interface that has a route to the CS-MARS device is FastEthernet 0/1.

```
IOS Router(config)#logging source-interface FastEthernet 0/1
IOS Router(config)#logging trap
IOS Router(config)#logging 192.168.0.100
```

CS-MARS can accept only one reporting IP address per device, so it is important to have the syslog reporting IP the same as the router's NetFlow reporting IP. Both syslog and NetFlow use different default reporting IPs in the same device.

Configuring NAC-Specific Reporting

NAC reporting from IOS devices is sourced from syslog. NAC messages are reported in a syslog reporting class called EoU, which stands for EAP over UDP. The following are the message types reported as EAPoUDP messages:

- EAPoUDP Session Creation/Removal
- EAPoUDP Posture Validation Status
- EAPoUDP Cisco Trust Agent Detection
- EAPoUDP Authentication Type
- Host Policy
- Match with Identity Policy
- Status Query Result STATUSQUERY=VALIDATED
- EAPoUDP Version Mismatch
- Process Creation Error
- Interface-Specific EAPoUDP Configurations
- Start of Posture Validation
- Posture Session State Changes
- AuthProxy Posture Cache Limit Exceeded

CS-MARS uses these message types in different ways. Some message types have only information that is interesting to host administrators or network administrators. CS-MARS collects and displays this information using the CS-MARS reporting and query engine.

CS-MARS can use some NAC reporting message types to help determine the likelihood of the successful attack for attack-mitigation decisions. The messages used in this manner include the following:

- EAPoUDP Posture Validation Status
- Posture Session State Changes

When CS-MARS receives an alert from a device such as an IPS that a possible attack is in progress, CS-MARS correlates all events that it has for the targeted host by time and flow information. If NAC has reported that this host has passed posture validation, it knows that the likelihood of an attack is less than if there were no posture validation for this device. No mitigation commands are presently available to communicate with the NAC infrastructure.

The following example shows the commands to enable NAC reporting on an IOS router. Because NAC reporting is a class of events that are part of syslog, that syslog also is enabled on this device. All NAC IOS commands are configured in global mode; no commands are required at the interface level. These commands are valid only for NAC phase 1; for NAC phase 2 commands, see the section on configuring Cisco switches.

```
ios-router#conf t
ios-router (config)#eou logging
ios-router (config)#ip auth-proxy auth-proxy-audit
ios-router #sh eou -> to verify that NAC and NAC reporting are enabled on this router
```

NOTE   All Critical/Warning/Alert messages come unsolicited as a result of the IP **auth-proxy** command.

CS-MARS offers several options for NAC reporting for administrators who might require this level of data. Data can be queried by requesting either all NAC records or a combination of source address, destination address, and event time. CS-MARS collects NAC information, not only from Cisco IOS routers, but also from Cisco switches and Cisco Access Control servers. See Figure 6-1 for the CS-MARS NAC query and reporting panel.

Figure 6-1   *NAC Reporting*

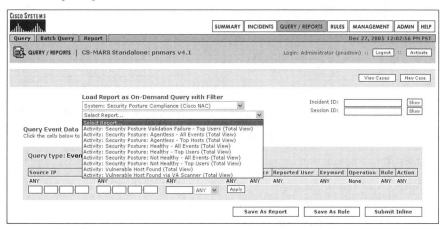

Generic Router Support

Configuring a generic router to communicate with CS-MARS is almost exactly the same as configuring an IOS router, except that the generic router must use SNMP and an operating system is not specified.

On the router itself, you must specify the SNMP community string so that CS-MARS can receive information from the router. Because the generic router can be any operating system, CS-MARS does not have the capability to recommend mitigation commands to these devices. Just as with an IOS router, you must also specify the following:

- Device name
- Access IP
- Reporting IP
- Access type (SNMP only)

Figure 6-2 shows a CS-MARS configuration panel for a generic router. Notice that the main difference between this panel and an IOS router panel is the device type, which, of course, is labeled as a generic router, and there is no access type such as Telnet or SSH.

Figure 6-2 *Generic Router Configuration*

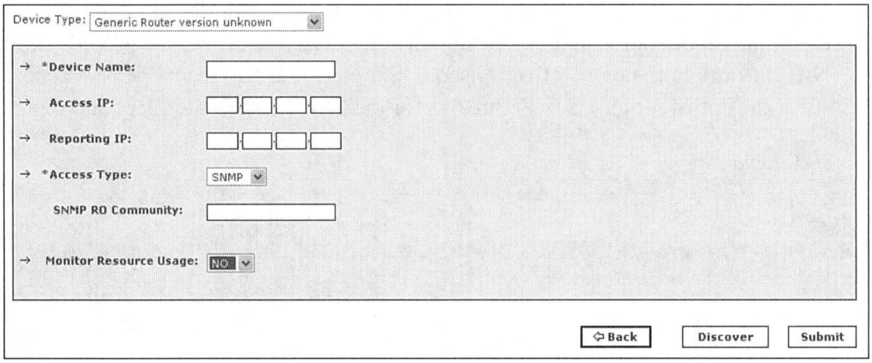

The steps to enter this device in CS-MARS are the same as for any other device:

Step 1 Enter the DNS device name.

Step 2 Enter the management IP address, also called an access IP.

Step 3 Enter the IP address that will source the SNMP or syslog protocol, also called the reporting IP.

Step 4 When the information in the panel is completely filled in, you must click **Discover** to make sure you can communicate with the device.

Step 5 Then click **Submit** to add the device to your CS-MARS database.

Step 6 Click **Activate** to enable communications with CS-MARS. You should see this device on the CS-MARS Security and Monitoring Information page.

Your generic routing device now will be sending syslog messages and SNMP messages to CS-MARS for correlation with other security and network events.

Configuring Switches

Cisco switches report events to CS-MARS using various protocols, but mainly syslog or SNMP. To report NAC events, specific commands need to be applied to your switches.

Cisco switches can provide valuable information to CS-MARS using various methods at several different levels. The Cisco switches can provide this information:

- Logging information required for message correlation with other network and security devices
- Topology information that shows the location of a host, a server, or any device in your network
- MAC to host IP address translation
- Layer 2 information that resolves confusion caused by the commonly used attack methodology of IP address spoofing

For the switches to provide this type of information, you must configure the switches to use specific protocols. This section describes how to configure the switches to use the following protocols:

- L2 discovery
- SNMP
- Syslog
- NAC-specific messages

Configuring Switches to Enable L2 Discovery

Layer 2 device discovery is one of the most critical features of CS-MARS. This feature allows CS-MARS to accurately determine the source and destination path of an attack. This feature becomes especially important when attacks that use IP spoofing are launched in your network. Switches use a combination of forwarding tables and Address Resolution Protocol (ARP) tables to map the source switching port of the attack. CS-MARS can use this information, in conjunction with routing and network topology information discovered from Layer 3 devices such as firewalls and routers, to determine the exact source or destination of an attack. CS-MARS queries switches using SNMP to scan their forwarding tables and send the resulting information back to CS-MARS for topology reporting. The result of this process is that CS-MARS can determine the source of an attack in your network even though an IP spoofing methodology was used.

The resulting Layer 2 information, after correlation with other device topology information, can be very detailed, as shown in Figure 6-3.

Figure 6-3 *CS-MARS Attack Vector*

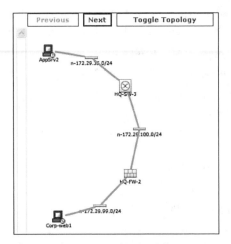

Configuring switches to communicate with CS-MARS is only slightly more complex than configuring IOS routers. Cisco Catalyst switches commonly have two different operating systems:

- **CATOS Hybrid**—A legacy operating system used initially in Catalyst 6000 series routers, still commonly used today

- **Cisco IOS**—The mainstream router operating system, which now supports many Catalyst switches and is emerging as the standard operating system for Cisco switches

These two operating systems use completely different configuration commands, but from the CS-MARS perspective, they yield the same results.

Cisco IOS 12.2 Switches—Enabling L2 Discovery SNMP

To enable Layer 2 discovery in a Cisco switch running Cisco IOS 11.0 or higher, you must enable SNMP.

On a switch, SNMP is enabled using the same steps as an IOS router. You must log into the router using either Telnet or SSH and enter the following commands. In this example, the community string is marstring and the IP address of the CS-MARS device is 192.168.0.100. If you plan to use SNMP as a mitigation technology, you must define the RW (read-write) community string the same as the RO string.

```
IOS Switch (config)# snmp-server community marstring RO <ACL name if required>
IOS Switch (config)# snmp-server community marstring RW
IOS Switch (config)# snmp-server enable traps
IOS Switch and (config)# snmp-server host 192.168.0.100 marstring
```

NOTE   You can limit the IP addresses used by SNMP by using a combination of a named access control list and the **snmp-server community** command.

To fully enable Layer 2 discovery on a Catalyst switch, you must turn on spanning tree. Spanning tree ensures that there is a single path to a host on a specific port and eliminates any possible loops in your switching topology. When this is established, you can be sure that the port and host information generated by SNMP is accurate. Spanning tree is enabled by default on Cisco switches. For more information on spanning tree, acquire a username and password from the Cisco website and access the following URLs:

> http://www.cisco.com/en/US/partner/products/hw/switches/ps708/
> prod_configuration_examples_list.html

> http://www.cisco.com/univercd/cc/td/doc/product/lan/cat6000/sw_8_4/confg_gd/
> spantree.htm

During active investigation, which is triggered by an incident that needs to be investigated, CS-MARS sends SNMP requests to the switch asking for information regarding its Layer 2 information. As indicated previously, that information is used for topology discovery and attack tracking.

For an example of attack-tracking maps and topology maps, see Figures 6-3 and 6-4.

CATOS Switches—Enabling L2 Discovery SNMP

To enable Layer 2 discovery in a Cisco switch running Catalyst OS (CATOS, also known as the Catalyst Hybrid and operating system), you must enable SNMP.

Very few similarities exist between native CATOS and Cisco IOS running on the Catalyst switch. We still use the same example information to communicate to CS-MARS, but the commands to deploy that information are quite different.

To fully enable Layer 2 discovery on a Catalyst switch, you must turn on spanning tree. Spanning tree ensures that there is a single path to a host on a specific port and eliminates any possible loops in your switching topology. When this is established, you can be sure that the port and host information generated by SNMP is accurate. Spanning tree is enabled by default on Cisco CATOS switches. For more information on spanning tree, see the following URLs:

> http://www.cisco.com/en/US/partner/products/hw/switches/ps708/
> prod_configuration_examples_list.html
> http://www.cisco.com/univercd/cc/td/doc/product/lan/cat6000/sw_8_4/confg_gd/
> spantree.htm

In the example, the community string is marstring and the IP address of the CS-MARS device is 192.168.0.100. If you plan to use SNMP as a mitigation technology, you must define the RW community string the same as the RO. Following are the native CATOS commands to enable SNMP to communicate with the CS-MARS device. These configurations are covered in the CS-MARS user guide, so a detailed explanation of each command is not provided here. For more information, go to http://www.cisco.com/go/mars.

```
Catos-switch > enable
Catos-switch > (enable)
Catos-switch > (enable) set snmp community read-only marstring
Catos-switch > (enable) set snmp community read-write marstring
Catos-switch > (enable) set snmp community read-write-all marstring
Catos-switch > (enable) set snmp rmon enable
Catos-switch > (enable) exit
```

NOTE Note that the read/write strings are required only if you plan to use your Catalyst switch as a mitigation device. Using the Catalyst for mitigation is considered a best practice when deployed with CS-MARS because it enables you to stop the host attack right at the port switch. This completely isolates the attacking device, effectively stopping the attack from spreading to even a single additional device in your network. This is one of the most potent and effective mitigation location points that CS-MARS can deploy.

During active investigation, which is triggered by an incident that needs to be investigated, CS-MARS sends requests to the switch asking for information regarding its Layer 2 information. As indicated earlier, that information is used for topology discovery and attack tracking. Figures 6-3 and 6-4 illustrate how CS-MARS displays this information.

Figure 6-3 shows an attack vector that uses information from a combination SNMP switch, router, and firewall. One of the significant and useful features of CS-MARS is that it gives you the option to click on any device in this attack vector to discover network information and, in some cases, attack information associated with the device. Just this single click saves attack responders hours of traditional research compared to using SIM-based software.

Figure 6-4 illustrates the topology map associated with Figure 6-3. It used topology information from all network devices to come up with this topology map gleaned from a combination of switch, router, and firewall SNMP information. Again, on this topology panel, CS-MARS gives you the option to click any device to find out device and, in some cases, attack information, which saves attack responders hours of threat research.

Figure 6-4   *CS-MARS Topology Map*

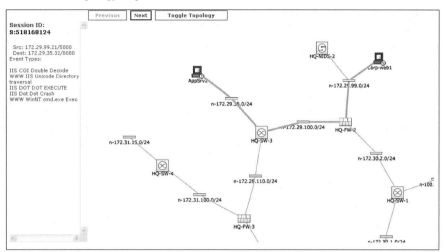

Configuring Switches to Enable Syslog

Syslog messages from all network devices should be sent to CS-MARS so that CS-MARS can have as much correlation data as possible to analyze threats accurately.

As with routers, configuring syslog on switches is a very straightforward process. The procedure for enabling syslog is different for each operating system.

IOS Switches—Enabling Syslog

The process of configuring syslog using Cisco IOS on a router is exactly the same as configuring syslog on a switch.

To be consistent, we once again use the CS-MARS IP address of 192.168.0.100 as the destination of the syslog data. Essentially, this makes CS-MARS the syslog server. The interface on the switch that routes data to CS-MARS is FastEthernet 0/1. All IOS commands are entered in global config mode, as shown here:

```
CATIOS (config)#logging source-interface FastEthernet 0/1
CATIOS (config)#logging trap
CATIOS (config)#logging 192.168.0.100
```

CATOS Switches—Enabling Syslog

The process of configuring syslog using Catalyst OS on a router is exactly the same as configuring syslog on a switch, although you will see in the next example that IOS and CATOS commands are not similar.

To be consistent, we once again use the CS-MARS IP address of 192.168.0.100 as the destination of the syslog data. Essentially, this makes CS-MARS the syslog server. The interface on the switch that routes data to CS-MARS is FastEthernet 0/1. All IOS commands are entered in enable or privileged mode.

```
catos(enable) set logging server enable
catos(enable) set logging server 192.168.0.100
```

In CATOS, you have the option to set each syslog message that you want to send by protocol and level. You can elect to send some or all of these messages to the CS-MARS appliance; the messages that don't have meaning to CS-MARS will simply not be used. Although you can enable any of these SNMP traps on a per-protocol basis, you should consider two best practices:

- If you aren't using the protocol, don't turn on the trap.
- Keep an eye on your switch performance.

In general, these traps should not cause performance issues, but if they do, prioritize the traps that you want to see and turn off the others.

This is a list of example CATOS syslog traps:

```
set logging level cdp 7 default
set logging level mcast 7 default
set logging level dtp 7 default
set logging level dvlan 7 default
set logging level earl 7 default
set logging level fddi 7 default
set logging level ip 7 default
set logging level pruning 7 default
set logging level snmp 7 default
set logging level spantree 7 default
set logging level sys 7 default
set logging level tac 7 default
set logging level tcp 7 default
set logging level telnet 7 default
set logging level tftp 7 default
set logging level vtp 7 default
set logging level vmps 7 default
set logging level kernel 7 default
set logging level filesys 7 default
set logging level drip 7 default
set logging level pagp 7 default
set logging level mgmt 7 default
set logging level mls 7 default
set logging level protfilt 7 default
set logging level security 7 default
set logging server facility SYSLOG
set logging server severity 7
set logging buffer 250
set logging timestamp enable
```

Configuring Switches to Enable NAC-Specific Messages

The functionality and feature set of NAC has expanded considerably in NAC phase 2. NAC phase 2 gives the capability to deploy security posture assessment and access control at

Layer 2, whereas NAC phase 1 limited you to deploying NAC at Layer 3 or the network routing layer. In this section, you will learn how to enable NAC specific messages for Catalyst switches. Again, the procedures are different for CATOS and Cisco IOS.

The major feature enhancement of NAC phase 2 was to enable Cisco switches to act as a network-access device based on a security policy that you defined. A summary of how NAC works is provided here, but for a more detailed description, visit http://www.cisco.com/go/nac.

NAC phase 2 is deployed with the combination of the following components:

- 802.1x on a Cisco switch
- 802.1x supplicant on a host
- Cisco ACS server
- A Cisco switch, acting as a proxy authenticator to a Cisco Access Control Server (ACS)

The following steps describe how a NAC-enabled switch authenticates a host before letting it access your network:

Step 1   When a host attempts to bring up a Layer 2 connection with a Cisco switch, the switch interrogates the host, asking for its authentication credentials and its security posture. The unique identity of the host is its Media Access Control (MAC) address.

Step 2   The Cisco switch forwards this information to a Cisco ACS server and verifies that the identity information and the security posture of the host matches the policy that you have defined on the ACS server.

Step 3   If the host passes this authentication process, it is allowed access to the network.

Step 4   If the host fails this authentication process, either it is given limited access to the network or access is denied.

The resulting logs from this process provide CS-MARS with some valuable information about the location of hosts in your network, the IP and MAC addresses of those hosts, user-level ACLs associated with those hosts, and the security posture of those hosts. CS-MARS can use this information to correlate with other logs and determine the host topology of your network, mitigation points for NAC-enabled hosts, and the probability that certain attacks were successful.

IOS Switches—Enabling NAC-Specific Messages

NAC-specific information can be configured on IOS-enabled switches through syslog. The instructions for enabling syslog are given in the earlier section "IOS Switches—Enabling Syslog." CS-MARS reads NAC-specific syslog messages and parses them to be used in accordance with each message.

CATOS Switches—Enabling NAC-Specific Messages

NAC-specific information can be configured on CATOS-enabled switches through syslog. The instructions for enabling syslog are given in the earlier section "CATOS Switches— Enabling Syslog." CS-MARS reads NAC-specific syslog messages and parses them to be used in accordance with each message.

Configuring Switches to Enable NetFlow

NetFlow can also be configured on the internal switches in your network. Traditionally, NetFlow data has been collected on perimeter devices and sent to NetFlow collectors, such as CS-MARS or older traditional SIM applications. However, there is value to collecting NetFlow data on switches inside your network. For example, if you have a denial-of-service (DoS), distributed denial-of-service (DDoS), or day-zero attack that was triggered by a mail virus on your campus network and started to flood the rest your campus network, the data would traverse only your campus switches, not your perimeter. In this case, NetFlow on your campus switches could be the only device that would be capable of identifying anomalous network flows. If you enable NetFlow on your internal switches as recommended in this section, CS-MARS would see this anomaly, report it to threat responders, and also make a recommendation to mitigate the threat.

IOS Switches—Enabling NetFlow

NetFlow on IOS switches is configured exactly the same as NetFlow on IOS routers. Using the example of a CS-MARS device with an IP address of 192.168.0.100, a switch interface of FastEthernet 0/1 that has access to the CS-MARS network, and a main trunk of Gig 0/1 that carries the bulk of your campus network, the following is an example of commands to enable NetFlow:

```
IOS Switch (config)# ip flow-export version 5
IOS Switch (config)# ip flow-export destination 192.168.0.100 2055
IOS Switch (config)# ip flow-export source interface FastEthernet 0/1
IOS Switch (config)# interface Gig 1/0
IOS Switch (config-int)# ip route-cache flow
```

CATOS Switches—Enabling NetFlow

Cisco Catalyst switches that don't have a Multilayer Switch Feature Card (MSFC) support a different implementation of NetFlow. With the cache-based forwarding model implemented in the Catalyst 55xx with the Route Switch Module (RSM) and NetFlow Feature Card (NFFC), the following steps must be taken to configure NetFlow:

```
set mls flow full
set mls nde version 5
set mls nde < CS-MARS IP > 2055
set mls nde enable
```

The operating system that runs on an MSFC is also IOS code. Because of this, the commands are the same as earlier, except for one CATOS command to get access into Layer 3 or IOS mode.

Using the example of a CS-MARS device with an IP address of 192.168.0.100, a switch interface of FastEthernet 0/1 that has access to the CS-MARS network, and a main trunk of Gig 0/1 that carries the bulk of your campus network, the following is an example of commands to enable NetFlow:

```
Layer2 (enable) sess 15 -> this command enables connectivity to the MSFC
Enter- the username and password for your MSFC
Enter the enable password for your MSFC.
Enter the following commands to enable NetFlow on your MSFC
IOS Switch (config)# ip flow-export version 5
IOS Switch (config)# ip flow-export destination 192.168.0.100 2055
IOS Switch (config)# ip flow-export source interface FastEthernet 0/1
IOS Switch (config)# interface Gig 1/0
IOS Switch (config-int)# ip route-cache flow
```

Configuring Extreme Network Switches

One of the most powerful features of CS-MARS is its capability to collect and correlate messages and events from platforms other than Cisco devices.

In this section, you learn how to configure an Extreme Network switch to communicate with the CS-MARS device, and also add an Extreme Network switch to the CS-MARS device database. When properly configured, the ExtremeWare switch will be capable of sending syslog events to CS-MARS, performing L2 discovery, and accepting L2 threat mitigation commands from the CS-MARS appliance.

Configuring ExtremeWare SNMP and Syslog

The ExtremeWare switch must first be configured for SNMP reading and writing and also syslog reporting.

Using the example of a CS-MARS device with an IP address of 192.168.0.100, a switch interface of FastEthernet 0/1 that has access to the CS-MARS network, and a main trunk of Gig 0/1 that carries the bulk of your campus network, the following is an example of commands to enable syslog on the ExtremeWare switch:

```
configure syslog add 192.168.0.100 local7 debug
enable syslog
```

Enter the following commands to enable SNMP on the ExtremeWare switch:

```
enable snmp ecrypthisword
configure snmp delete community readonly all
configure snmp delete community readwrite all
configure snmp add community readonly encrypted ecrypthisword configure snmp add
community readwrite encrypted ecrypthisword
```

Your ExtremeWare switch is now ready to communicate with CS-MARS, but first you must add the ExtremeWare switch to the CS-MARS database.

Add ExtremeWare to the CS-MARS Device Database

You add the ExtremeWare switch to the CS-MARS database just like any other device.

Step 1   Navigate to **Admin > Security and Monitoring Device > Add** panel.

Step 2   Select Extreme ExtremeWare 6.X as the device type.

Step 3   Enter the device name for your ExtremeWare switch.

Step 4   Enter the management access IP address.

Step 5   Enter the IP address that will be the source of the SNMP and syslog reporting records.

Step 6   Select SNMP as the access type.

Step 7   Enter the encrypted SNMP community string.

Step 8   Click **Discover** to ensure that CS-MARS can contact your ExtremeWare switch.

Step 9   Click **Submit** to add your ExtremeWare device to the CS-MARS device database.

Step 10   Click **Activate** to enable communications between your ExtremeWare switch and your CS-MARS appliance.

Configuring Firewalls

In the traditional self-defending network, as described in the "Defense-in-Depth and the Self-Defending Network" section of Chapter 2, "Role of CS-MARS in Your Network," firewalls provide a critical function of protecting the perimeter of enterprise networks and also isolating smaller networks inside enterprises and protecting smaller remote-access networks. Because of the deployment locations of firewalls, they often can see traffic inbound from unprotected networks. Thus firewalls can see traffic and trigger events that many other network devices don't have the opportunity to process. However benign these events might seem, they can prove to be very useful to CS-MARS. CS-MARS can correlate these events with other network and security events and syslog to make important determinations regarding threats to your network. Consider the following example: At exactly 10:00 a.m., an IPS device reports an attempted attack on the web server 10.1.1.1. But between the IPS device and the targeted web server was a firewall that generated the syslog message indicating that all port 80 traffic to 10.1.1.1 is being blocked and no flow was ever established to the web server. CS-MARS can correlate this data to clearly see that even though IPS reported an event that could be very serious, the firewall blocked the event and no threat to the web server exists. Thus, CS-MARS marks it as a system-determined false positive.

CS-MARS allows communications between many different types and brands of firewalls. In addition to Cisco-branded firewalls, CS-MARS works with the Juniper NetScreen firewall, Check Point firewall, and Check Point Nokia Appliance firewall equally well. CS-MARS also interoperates with web caches from Network Appliance and NetCache.

Each of the following sections describes how to configure the devices just mentioned to communicate with CS-MARS and how to add these devices to the CS-MARS database.

Cisco PIX, ASA, and Firewall Service Module

The Cisco PIX firewall is the most popular hardware firewall on the market today. Its longevity is a testament to its performance and its capability to provide security and customer satisfaction at the highest possible levels. In this section, all references to the PIX firewall also apply to the Cisco Adaptive Security Appliance (ASA) and the Firewall Service Module (FWSM).

The following tasks must be done on the Cisco firewall devices to enable access from the CS-MARS appliance:

- Configure Administrative Access SSH. (Telnet access is not recommended.)
- Configure syslog to be sent to CS-MARS.

Configuring Telnet on Your Cisco Firewall Device

The first thing that you need to do to allow CS-MARS to access your PIX firewall device is to enable a protocol that can access the firewall command-line interface (CLI).

Telnet is an access protocol for Cisco firewalls, but it's not recommended because the username, password, and firewall configuration are displayed in clear text as this information traverses your network. The impact of this is that if a hacker has access to your network and is running a network sniffer, he or she can see all your critical security information, including the login credentials of your firewall. Because of this, in this book, you will not learn to configure Telnet access on your PIX firewall. If Telnet is a requirement in your network, refer to the firewall documentation on the Cisco website, located at http://www.cisco.com/go/pix or http://www.cisco.com/go/asa.

Configuring SSH on Your Cisco Firewall Device

SSH access can be configured using either the PIX, CLI, Adaptive Security Device Manager (ASDM), or the VMS firewall device manager. For CLI commands enabling SSH, see the following example. You simply need to tell SSH which IP address are allowed access and what interface the access is allowed through. In this case, we specified the management interface, but it could be any demilitarized zone (DMZ) or inside interface, depending on the layout of your network. It's not recommended to use the outside interface because even though SSH is encrypted, it opens your firewall to the possibility of brute-force password attacks.

```
ssh 192.168.0.100 255.255.255.255 management
```

NOTE   A self-signed certificate is normally required for SSH, but when you enable web access on devices, that key is normally generated. Because of this, you should not have to enter a separate command to generate a self-signed certificate.

After this command is applied and this device is added, CS-MARS should be capable of adding the device to its database and using the device for event correlation, threat mitigation, and network topology.

Next you need to configure your firewall to export syslog messages so that CS-MARS can interpret these messages and correlate them with other network and security events.

To properly configure your Cisco firewall to send syslog messages, you need to enable logging and select the logging facility that you want to use. The following example shows the commands required to configure your Cisco firewall to export syslog messages to your CS-MARS appliance:

```
logging enable
logging host management 192.168.0.100
logging trap debugging
```

Cisco engineering recommends that you use the syslog debugging facility with CS-MARS. This gives you more detailed logging information, which, in turn, gives you more flexibility to write keyword-based rules on your CS-MARS appliance.

If **logging trap debugging** results in high CPU usage, CS-MARS will still work well with informational syslog enabled instead of debugging. Informational syslog is enabled with the following command:

```
logging trap informational
```

The commands in this section encompass all Cisco firewalls, with one exception. To enable logging on the Firewall Service Module (FWSM) instead of the command **logging enable**, you need to use the command **logging on**. Also, the Firewall Service Module enables you to rate-limit the number of syslog messages that are generated. The theory behind this is to protect CPU cycles if the FWSM is sustaining a high-volume attack such as a DOS or DDOS attack. The following is an example of the rate-limiting command:

```
logging rate-limit <event per second rate desired> 1
```

NOTE   If you are running your firewalls with multiple contexts, you must enable SSH, syslog, and
SNMP in each context.

Configuring SNMP on Your Cisco Firewall Device

CS-MARS uses SNMP on firewalls to retrieve utilization and usage information from
the firewall, which helps CS-MARS recognize that a device could be under attack.
Mitigation commands cannot be pushed to Cisco firewalls because no write SNMP
options are available on Cisco Firewall devices. These are examples of Cisco firewall
SNMP commands:

```
snmp-server host inside 192.168.0.100 community cisco123
snmp-server location Building 42, Sector 54
snmp-server contact Greg Abelar
snmp-server community cisco123
```

Adding a Cisco Firewall Device to CS-MARS

As is true with adding any device with CS-MARS, it's a very straightforward process:

Step 1   First navigate to **Admin > Security and Monitoring Device > Add**
panel.

Step 2   Select the device type you would like to add to the CS-MARS database.
Your options for Cisco firewalls are Cisco ASA 7.0, Cisco PIX 6.0, Cisco
PIX 6.1, Cisco PIX 6.3, and Cisco PIX 7.0. See Figure 6-5.

Figure 6-5   *Device Type Menu*

Step 3   Enter the device name for your Cisco firewall.

Step 4   Enter the firewall-management access IP address.

Step 5 Enter the IP address that will be the source of the SNMP and syslog reporting records.

Step 6 Select **SSH** as the access type.

Step 7 Enter the SNMP community string. In this case, we used cisco123.

Step 8 Select **Yes** to activate the health checking on this device.

Step 9 Click **Discover** to ensure that CS-MARS can contact your Cisco firewall.

Step 10 Click **Submit** to add your firewall device to the CS-MARS device database.

Step 11 Click **Activate** to enable communications between your firewall and your CS-MARS appliance.

NOTE   If your firewall is already in the CS-MARS device database, you can just edit that entry and add the SNMP information.

Configuring a Juniper NetScreen Firewall

This section describes the tasks that you must complete to configure a NetScreen firewall for communication with CS-MARS.

Enable Juniper NetScreen Firewall for CS-MARS Access

First you must configure the Juniper NetScreen firewall to allow the CS-MARS device to access it through SSH.

Step 1 On the **NetScreen Network Interfaces** panel, select the interface that CS-MARS will use to access the NetScreen device.

Step 2 Select **SSH** as the management access method. This enables CS-MARS to use SSH to add and discover this device.

Step 3 Go to **Configure > Report Settings > SNMP** panel and add the CS-MARS IP address as an SNMP device.

Step 4 Enter the community string enabling communication between the NetScreen device and the CS-MARS appliance.

Enable Juniper NetScreen Firewall for Syslog Reporting

Now you must configure the Juniper NetScreen firewall to send syslog messages to the CS-MARS device.

Step 1 Navigate to **NetScreen Configure > Report Settings > Syslog** panel, enable syslog, and ensure that the **Include Traffic Log** boxes are checked. For NetScreen 5.0, also select the event log.

Step 2   Enter the IP address of the CS-MARS appliance to configure it as a syslog listening device and ensure that it is using the default syslog port UDP 514.

Step 3   Select **AUTH/SEC** for Security Facility and **LOCAL0** for Facility.

Step 4   Click **Apply** to enable your configurations.

The next step is to add the Juniper NetScreen firewall to the CS-MARS device database. Then it should be ready to communicate with the CS-MARS appliance.

Adding the Juniper NetScreen Firewall to CS-MARS

Now that you have completed the steps necessary to configure your Juniper NetScreen firewall to communicate with CS-MARS, you must add that device to CS-MARS so that CS-MARS can start processing and analyzing events and topology.

Step 1   First navigate to **Admin > Security and Monitoring Device > Add** panel.

Step 2   Select the device type you would like add to the CS-MARS database. In this case, select either NetScreen ScreenOS 4.0 or NetScreen ScreenOS 5.0. See Figure 6-6.

Figure 6-6   *CS-MARS NetScreen Addition Panel*

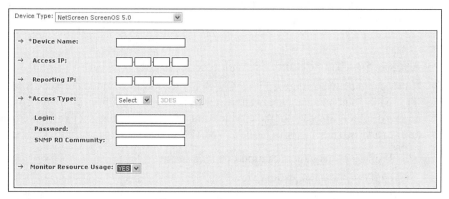

Step 3   Enter the device name of your Juniper NetScreen firewall.

Step 4   Enter the Juniper NetScreen firewall-management access IP address.

Step 5   Enter the IP address that will be the source of the SNMP and syslog reporting records.

Step 6   Select **SSH** as the access type.

Step 7   Enter the SNMP community string.

Step 8   Select **Yes** to activate the resource health checking on this device.

Step 9   Click **Discover** to ensure that CS-MARS can contact your Juniper NetScreen firewall.

Step 10   Click **Submit** to add your Juniper NetScreen firewall device to the CS-MARS device database.

Step 11   Click **Activate** to enable communications between your Juniper NetScreen firewall and your CS-MARS appliance.

NOTE   If your firewall is already in the CS-MARS device database, you can just edit that entry and add the SNMP information.

Check Point Firewall and Check Point Nokia Firewall Appliances

Check Point firewall appliances and Check Point software firewalls can also be configured to work with the CS-MARS appliance. Check Point has several different models, devices, versions, and deployments. Because of this and the fact that the CS-MARS user guide has done an excellent job of documenting the configuration of Check Point devices to communicate with CS-MARS appliances, we cover only how to add a Check Point device to the CS-MARS database. See the CS-MARS 4.1 user guide for configuring your specific Check Point security device.

Adding the Check Point Firewall to CS-MARS

Now that you have configured your Check Point firewall with the correct CS-MARS information and policies, you need to add your Check Point firewall to the CS-MARS device database. Because of the Check Point architecture, this is a two-step process. You need to add two device types to the CS-MARS database:

- Primary Management Station
- Child Enforcement Module(s)

The Primary Management Station is called a SmartCenter server. This server performs centralized policy management for your Check Point firewalls. When you add SmartCenter to the CS-MARS device database, this is defined as a software application running on a host. The Child Enforcement Module is a Check Point device such as a firewall or log server that is managed by the SmartCenter server. When you add the Child Enforcement Module to the CS-MARS device database, it is defined as a child of the Primary Management Station.

Adding these devices requires a thorough knowledge of the Check Point features, functions, and architecture. Instead of reinventing the wheel, to install your Check Point device reference the CS-MARS 4.1 user guide, located on the Cisco website at http://www.cisco.com/en/US/products/ps6241/products_user_guide_book09186a00804efe32.html.

Configuring Web Caches to Work with CS-MARS

Web proxies and web caches have been used for several years now as security devices. Generally, they are multipurpose devices that proxy outbound and even inbound web connections. These proxy devices have the capability to scrub data returning from the Internet and clean any potentially malicious code such as viruses that could be embedded in the returning traffic. In addition, when used as a proxy, these devices hide the source IP address of the requesting host, making it more difficult for hackers to gain access to internal devices.

CS-MARS is designed to work with the Network Appliances NetCache device.

Configuring Network Appliances NetCache

To configure your NetCache device to communicate with CS-MARS, you must follow these steps:

Step 1   Using Internet Explorer, enter the URL and press **Enter** to access your NetCache device.

Step 2   Click the **Setup** tab.

Step 3   Select **HTTP**, then select **Logging**.

Step 4   Under Web Access Log Enable, click the **Enable the Web Access Log** check box.

Step 5   Under Log Format, select one of the top four formats: Web Access Log Default Format, Common Log Format, Netscape Extended Format, or Squid Type Format.

Step 6   Ensure that the Web Details Log Enable box is not selected.

Step 7   Click **Commit Changes** to update the NetCache device with your changes.

Step 8   Select **Streaming** and then select **Logging**.

Step 9   Under Streaming Access Log Enable, select the box labeled **Enable Access Logging for Streaming Protocol Clients**. This selection is license dependent; if you don't have a license for streaming protocol clients, you will not be able to select this box.

Step 10 Under Streaming Access Log Format, select either of the options. If you select Custom, replace x-client-port with x-username.

Step 11 Verify that Streaming Details Log Enable is not selected.

Step 12 Click **Commit Changes** to update the NetCache device with your changes.

Step 13 Select **Streaming**, then **MMS**.

Step 14 Verify that the **Enables MMS Protocol Support** check box is selected under MMS Enable.

Step 15 Click **Commit Changes** to update the NetCache device with your changes.

Step 16 Select **System**, then **Logging**.

Step 17 Enter a number less than or equal to 100 (megabytes) to set the Maximum Log File Size.

Step 18 In the section labeled How to Switch Log Files, select **Push the Log File to the Following URL**.

Step 19 Enter **http://<CS-MARS IP Address>/upload/UploadWebLogServlet** as the URL to push the log file.

Step 20 Ensure that the Username and Password fields are empty.

Step 21 Ensure that the box labeled Push the Log Files in Compressed gzip Format is *not* selected. This would send the logs to CS-MARS in a format it would not be capable of reading.

Step 22 Select the option that prevents the log files from becoming greater than 100 MB in the section When to Switch.

Step 23 Click **Commit Changes** to save the changes to your NetCache device.

For a more in-depth description of how to configure your NetCache appliance, reference the CS-MARS 4.1 user guide on the Cisco website at http://www.cisco.com/en/US/products/ps6241/products_user_guide_book09186a00804efe32.html.

Your NetCache device is now ready to be added to the CS-MARS device database so that CS-MARS can start processing and analyzing threats using logging information from this device.

Adding Network Appliances NetCache to the CS-MARS Device

Now that you have completed the steps necessary to configure your NetCache device, you must add that device to CS-MARS so CS-MARS can start processing and analyzing events and topology.

Step 1   First navigate to **Admin > Security and Monitoring Device > Add** panel.

Step 2   Select the device type you would like add to the CS-MARS database. In this case, you select **Network Appliance NetCache Generic**. See Figure 6-7 for an illustration of the CS-MARS Device Type drop-down box, located on the Add Device panel.

Figure 6-7   *CS-MARS Add Device Panel: Device Type Selection*

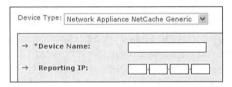

Step 3   Enter the device name for your NetCache appliance.

Step 4   Enter the IP address that will be the source of the NetCache reporting records.

Step 5   Select **Yes** for monitor usage so you will see messages about excessive resource usage for this device.

Step 6   Select the same web log file format that you configured when you set up your NetCache device for CS-MARS reporting.

Step 7   Select the streaming media log format that you configured when you set up your NetCache device for CS-MARS reporting. See Figure 6-8 for the CS-MARS GUI.

Figure 6-8   *Streaming Media Add Panel*

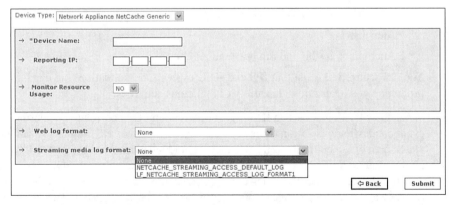

Step 8   Click **Submit** to add your NetCache appliance to the CS-MARS device database.

Step 9   Click **Activate** to enable communications between your NetCache appliance and your CS-MARS appliance.

You've now successfully configured your NetCache security appliance and added it to your CS-MARS database. CS-MARS can now process and correlate logs from this appliance with other network and security events and logs.

Enabling IDS and IPS in a CS-MARS Environment

Intrusion-detection and -prevention security devices could be viewed as the most critical devices in the CS-MARS environment. These devices inspect packets all the way up to the Layer 7 (application layer) payload to see if there is possible malicious data within the packet. Some vendors refer to this as deep packet inspection. In many cases, IDS and IPS compare the inspected traffic with signatures, but many modern-day IDS and IPS devices also use protocol-enforcement rules and anomaly-detection algorithms to recognize various types of attacks and trigger events.

In most cases, these devices can recognize the following threats:

- Worms
- Viruses
- Spyware
- Adware
- Protocol misuse, such as HTTP and FTP tunneling
- IDS and IPS evasion attacks
- Point-to-point tunnel abuse
- Instant-messaging abuse
- Denial-of-service attacks
- Attempts to install Trojans and back doors
- Antispam
- Attempts to install and run bots and zombies

You can see from this list that IPS and IDS devices and applications are capable of protecting you against a wide variety of malicious activities.

When CS-MARS receives an IDS/IPS alarm, it attempts to correlate the alarm with other event data. After correlation (or lack of correlation), CS-MARS attempts to validate the attack path of the alarm to verify whether it could have traversed the network from the alarm's source IP. The next step CS-MARS takes is to use vulnerability assessment (VA) data to validate whether the attack could be successful. If all steps are positive or all do not return data, CS-MARS creates an incident from the alarm or session data. If one of these steps provides information negating the alarm, CS-MARS reports the alarm or session data as a "to be confirmed" false positive.

Configuring IPS devices and adding them to CS-MARS is critical in helping you successfully defend your network.

As was true with routers, switches, firewalls, and web proxies, CS-MARS has full built-in support for not only Cisco devices, but also third-party IDS/IPS devices. The following is a list of the IDS and IPS devices CS-MARS supports:

- Cisco IPS appliance
- Cisco IDS router line cards
- Cisco IPS Catalyst switch modules
- Cisco IPS enable routers (Integrated Security Routers, ISR)
- Cisco IPS modules for ASA
- IntruVert IntruShield
- Juniper NetScreen IDP
- Symantec ManHunt
- ISS RealSecure Sensor
- Snort
- Enterasys Dragon

This section provides you with step-by-step instructions on how to configure and add all these devices and to enable communication with CS-MARS.

This section consists of two parts. The first part describes how to configure your IDS and IPS devices to communicate with CS-MARS. The second part describes how to add and activate these devices in your CS-MARS appliance.

Cisco IPS Appliance Configuration

Enabling communications between the Cisco IPS appliance and CS-MARS is a fairly simple process. It must be noted, however, that Cisco made a major change to the way it reports IPS events between Versions 4.0 and 5.0 of its IPS software. Cisco IDS 4.0 software used a protocol called Remote Data Exchange Protocol (RDEP) to report events to logging servers; IPS 5.0 uses a new standard called Secure Device Event Exchange (SDEE). SDEE allows a device to log into it as a server, as long as the device has authenticated itself with a valid self-signed certificate. CS-MARS subscribes to IPS devices using SDEE, which runs over the SSL protocol. When subscribed, the IPS device sends CS-MARS security events in real time.

Even though there is a slight difference in the way CS-MARS retrieves data from these devices, the process of adding the device to the CS-MARS appliance is almost exactly the same.

One of the unique characteristics to keep in mind when configuring your Cisco IPS appliance is that the action that you request the appliance to take when an event is fired affects the data reported to you in the CS-MARS appliance. Specifically, if you want CS-MARS to report the payload of the data that triggered the event, you must tell the IPS appliance to Produce Verbose Reporting when a critical action is fired. Otherwise, CS-MARS reports only the name and number of the signature that is fired.

NOTE   It is important to note that CS-MARS stores only 500 bytes of data per alarm. If payload data is sent to the CS-MARS, it is displayed in its ASCII format but could be truncated because of its length. Cisco is aware of this limitation and will address it in a future release.

Configuring a Cisco IPS 3.x Appliance

CS-MARS supports the Cisco IDS 3.x appliance, which uses the Post Office Protocol (POP). To configure a Cisco IDS 3.x appliance, refer to the CS-MARS 4.1 user guide, page 6-1.

NOTE   CS-MARS does not receive payload or trigger packet data from IDS 3.x devices.

Configuring a Cisco IPS 4.x Appliance

To enable a Cisco IPS appliance running the 4.x IPS operating system, you must perform the following tasks:

Step 1   Use the IPS 4.X CLI setup utility to ensure that the CS-MARS appliance IP address is in the permit list and that the web management interface is enabled.

Step 2   A self-signed x.509 certificate (TLS) should be generated when the management interface is enabled. You can verify this in the CLI by entering **show TLS fingerprint**. If there is no value, you must enter the command **TLS generate-key**.

Step 3   If you want CS-MARS to display the payload of a packet that triggered an event, you must use IDM or IPSMC to ensure that events have an action of Produce Verbose Alert.

Configuring a Cisco IPS 5.x Appliance

Keep one thing in mind when using Cisco IPS 5.X or any IPS device that is capable of blocking an attack: If CS-MARS sees a message informing it that an attack has been dropped or blocked, CS-MARS will not generate a mitigation suggestion. From the point of view of CS-MARS, if your IPS device blocked the attack, mitigation has already been performed and the alarm is reported as a system-determined false positive.

Some customers are concerned about in-line IPS devices blocking valid traffic. Because of this, it's common in a CS-MARS–enabled network for customers to remove all the blocking actions and let CS-MARS decide how to mitigate an attack after the fact. The downside of this is that some attacks will succeed, but the upside is that it's virtually impossible for your IPS devices to block valid traffic. You need to assess the risk of allowing some successful attacks against the threat of blocking valid traffic, and build this decision into the security policy of your enterprise.

To enable a Cisco IPS appliance running the IPS 5.x operating system, you must perform the following tasks:

- Use the IPS 5.X CLI setup utility to ensure that the CS-MARS appliance IP address is in the permit list and that the web-management interface is enabled.

- Ensure that a self-signed x.509 Transport Layer Security (TLS) certificate exists on your IPS appliance. This certificate should have been generated when the management interface was enabled. You can verify this in the CLI by entering **show TLS fingerprint**. If there is no value, you must enter the command **TLS generate-key**.

- If you want CS-MARS to display the payload of a packet that triggered an event, you must use Intrusion Detection Manager (IDM) or the Intrusion Prevention System Management Console (IPSMC) to ensure that IPS events have an action of Produce Verbose Alert. The default alert is usually only Produce Alert.

This is an example of using IPS 5.x CLI commands to initialize a sensor and configure it to communicate with a CS-MARS device:

```
sensor# setup <CR>
    --- System Configuration Dialog ---
At any point you may enter a question mark '?' for help.
User ctrl-c to abort configuration dialog at any prompt.
Default settings are in square brackets '[]'.

Current Configuration:

service host
network-settings
host-ip 1.1.1.1/24,1.1.1.254
host-name sensor
telnet-option disabled
service web-server
port 443
exit
Current time: Thu Dec 29 20:41:55 2005
Setup Configuration last modified: Thu Dec 29 20:41:50 2005
```

```
Continue with configuration dialog?[yes]: <CR>
Enter host name[sensor]: mars-ips<CR>
Enter IP interface[1.1.1.1/24,1.1.1.254]:
192.168.0.222/24,192.168.0.1<CR>
Enter telnet-server status[disabled]: <CR>
Enter web-server port[443]: <CR>
Modify current access list?[no]: yes<CR>
Current access list entries:
  No entries
Permit: 0.0.0.0/0<CR>
Permit:
Modify system clock settings?[no]: <CR>
Modify virtual sensor "vs0" configuration?[no]: <CR>

The following configuration was entered.
.
.
.
host-ip 192.168.0.222/24,192.168.0.1
host-name mars-ips
access-list 0.0.0.0/0
service web-server
port 443
[0] Go to the command prompt without saving this config.
[1] Return back to the setup without saving this config.
[2] Save this configuration and exit setup.
Enter your selection[2]: <CR>
```

Adding Cisco IPS Appliances to CS-MARS

The following steps guide you through adding a Cisco IPS appliance as a reporting device to CS-MARS. It is important to note that these steps should be completed after you configure your Cisco IPS device to report to CS-MARS, not before.

Step 1 First navigate to **Admin > Security and Monitoring Device > Add** panel.

Step 2 Select the device type you want to add to the CS-MARS database. In this case, select either Cisco IDS 4.0 or Cisco IPS 5.0 (see Figure 6-9).

Step 3 Enter the device name for your Cisco IPS appliance.

Step 4 Enter the Cisco IPS appliance management access IP address.

Step 5 Enter the IP address that will be the source of the SDEE IPS events. This will be the same address as the management interface of your Cisco IPS appliance.

Step 6 The access type default is SSL and cannot be changed.

Step 7 Enter the Cisco IPS appliance username and password.

Figure 6-9   *CS-MARS IPS Add Panel*

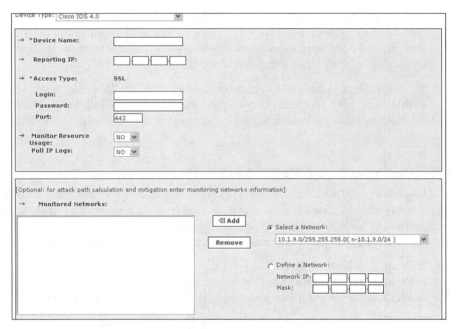

Step 8   Select **Yes** to activate monitor resource usage.

Step 9   Select **Yes** to pull IP logs from the appliance.

Step 10   To provide CS-MARS with critical attack path calculation information to be used for mitigation recommendations, specify the networks being monitored by the sensor. This can be done using the network pull-down menu labeled Select a Network or by manually entering the network information in the Define a Network field.

Step 11   Click **Test Connectivity** to ensure the CS-MARS can contact your Cisco IPS appliance.

Step 12   Click **Submit** to add your Cisco IPS appliance to the CS-MARS device database.

Step 13   Click **Activate** to enable communications between your Cisco IPS appliance and your CS-MARS appliance.

Your Cisco IPS appliance now should be communicating with your CS-MARS appliance. You can easily test and verify this by enabling ping signatures, which are 2000 and 2004 on your Cisco IPS appliance. Then ping a device on the other side of your Cisco IPS appliance. The appliance should fire ping events, and CS-MARS should report the events.

Cisco IPS Catalyst Switch Modules

A Catalyst Intrusion Detection Service Module (IDSM) operates in the exact same way and runs the same software as Cisco IPS appliances. The switch module can run 4.*x* or 5.*x* versions of the IPS operating system. Physically, it's different from the IPS appliance in that it plugs directly into the data bus of a Catalyst switch.

The steps to enable the IDSM to communicate with CS-MARS are the same as the steps to enable a Cisco IPS appliance. Likewise, the steps to add IDSM to the CS-MARS device database are exactly the same. See the earlier section "Cisco IPS Appliance Configuration."

Cisco IPS Enable Routers (Integrated Security Routers)

Cisco Integrated Security Routers (ISR) are specialized routers that are optimized with security features. One of the most popular features of ISR is intrusion prevention. ISR routers run the IPS 5.*x* operating system. Because of this, CS-MARS can process ISR intrusion-prevention events exactly the same as events from other Cisco IPS appliances.

ISRs are significant devices when you are considering a CS-MARS deployment. Starting at Version 4.1, CS-MARS has a new feature called distributed threat mitigation, also known as DTM. These are the important considerations, features, and functions of DTM:

- ISR routers are generally deployed on the edge of a network or in a remote office or network.

- ISR routers are multipurpose devices. They are fully functioning routers that need to make packet-forwarding decisions and route packets to the appropriate interface.

- Because they are fully functional routers, CPU and memory are critical resources.

- When IPS is running on an ISR router, although the IPS module is hardware optimized, it still takes some CPU and memory from the route processor to forward packets to the IPS processor.

- For ISR routers to perform optimally, their signature sets need to be carefully tuned or reduced for the environment they're protecting. Unused signatures should be turned off to save memory.

- DTM running on CS-MARS helps save CPU and memory by keeping track of frequently fired IPS events. It then sends those events to the ISR routers as threats are detected.

- In essence, DTM allows your routers to run with a minimum number of signatures and dynamically sends new signatures to these routers when needed.

Because ISR routers run a full version of IOS, you configure these routers to communicate with CS-MARS exactly as any other IOS router. Also, because ISR is running a fully functional version of the IPS 5.*x* operating system, it can be configured exactly the same as a Cisco IPS appliance.

Instead of repeating how to configure these devices to communicate with CS-MARS and repeating how to add these devices to the CS-MARS device database, we refer you to the two earlier sections in this chapter titled "Configuring Routers" and "Cisco IPS Appliance Configuration."

Cisco Security Service Modules (IPS Modules) for ASA (ASA/SSM)

The Cisco Security Service Module (SSM) is a module that plugs into the backplane of a Cisco Adaptive Security Appliance (ASA). This module, SSM, runs a fully functional Cisco IPS 5.x operating system.

To get the SSM module to communicate with CS-MARS and to add the device to the CS-MARS device database, follow the same instructions given in the earlier section titled "Cisco IPS Appliance Configuration."

IntruVert IntruShield V1.8

The IntruShield product is an intrusion-prevention system and security-management system by McAfee.

This book covers how to configure IntruShield Version 1.8 to communicate with CS-MARS and how to add it to the CS-MARS device database. To perform the same process for IntruShield Version 1.5, reference the CS-MARS 4.1 users guide.

Configuring IntruShield to Communicate with CS-MARS

The primary protocol IntruShield uses to send events to the CS-MARS appliance is SNMP. The following steps describe how to enable IntruShield to communicate with your CS-MARS device:

Step 1 Log into your IntruShield Management device.

Step 2 Click **Configure**.

Step 3 Click **My Company** in the Resource Tree.

Step 4 Click the tab labeled **Alert Notification** to define how to handle alerts.

Step 5 Click the subtab labeled **SNMP Forwarder** to define the CS-MARS device, or you will forward SNMP events.

Step 6 Click the **Add** button.

Step 7   Click **Enter** on the SNMP Forwarder page. On the panel where you
define the new SNMP forwarder, do the following:

  (a)   Select the **Yes** radio button to enable the SNMP forwarder.

  (b)   Enter the CS-MARS IP address in the field Target Server.

  (c)   In the field Target Server Port Number, enter port number
  162, which will be used to communicate between CS-MARS
  and the SNMP forwarder.

  (d)   Select **SNMP Version 1**.

  (e)   Select **Forward Alerts**.

  (f)   Select **Informational and Above** for the alert severity.

  (g)   Enter a community string of your choice in the field
  Customize Community. Note that this must match the
  SNMP community string when you add this device to the
  CS-MARS device database.

Step 8   Click **Apply** to save your changes and exit the program.

Adding an IntruShield Device to CS-MARS

When you add your IntruVert device to the CS-MARS database, you must perform two
distinct steps:

- Add configuration information for the management station
- Add configuration information for the IntruVert IPS sensors

You must do the following to add the IntruShield device manager to the CS-MARS
database:

Step 1   First navigate to the **Admin > Security and Monitoring Device > Add** panel.

Step 2   Select **Add SW Security Apps on a New Host** or **Add SW Security
Apps** from the Device Type list.

Step 3   Enter the device name and IP addresses if you are adding a new host (see
Figure 6-10).

Step 4   Click **Apply**.

Step 5   Click the **Reporting Applications** tab.

Step 6   From the Select Application list, select **IntruVert IntruShield 1.5**, as in
Figure 6-11.

Step 7   Click **Add**.

Figure 6-10 *New Host Configuration Panel*

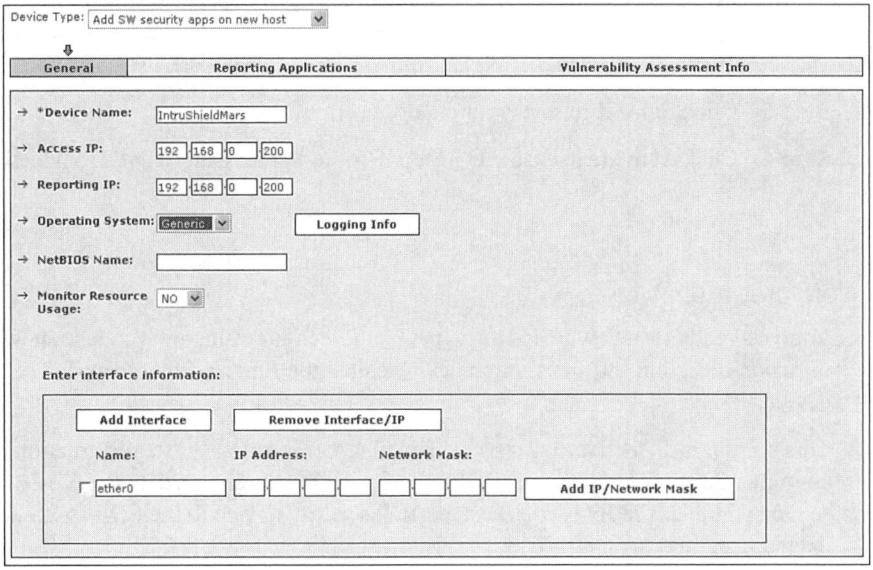

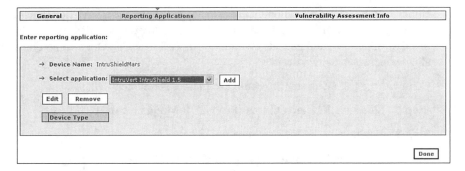

Figure 6-11 *Reporting Applications Configuration Panel*

The manager station now has been added to CS-MARS. Now you need to add the IPS sensor; this step should be repeated for each sensor.

Step 1   Click the **Add Sensor** button.

Step 2   Enter the following information for the IPS sensor: device name, sensor name, and reporting IP address. Note that the reporting IP address is the IP address that the agent uses to send logs to the management console.

Step 3   Add the interface information.

Step 4   Specify the networks that are monitored by the IntruShield sensor so that CS-MARS can accurately calculate the attack path and mitigation possibilities. As with other IPS sensors, you can either define networks manually or select networks from the Select a Network list.

Step 5   Click **Submit** to save your changes.

Step 6   Click **Activate** to enable CS-MARS to start processing events from these devices.

Juniper NetScreen IDP

You've already seen how to add a Juniper NetScreen firewall; now you learn how to add an intrusion-detection and -prevention device called the Juniper NetScreen IDP security device.

This section is divided into two parts. The first part is a step-by-step instruction on how to configure the Juniper NetScreen IDP security device to send its data to CS-MARS; the second part adds the Juniper NetScreen IDP security device to the CS-MARS device database.

Configuring Juniper NetScreen IDP to Communicate with CS-MARS

Notice that in this configuration there are no steps to enter the CS-MARS IP address. This is because, similar to Cisco IPS, Juniper uses SDEE to exchange IPS events. This means that CS-MARS first authenticates with its x.509 certificate, and then communication is allowed between the two devices.

Complete the following steps to configure Juniper NetScreen IDP:

Step 1   Select **NetScreen > Global Pro > IDP Manager > IDP**.

Step 2   Log into the Juniper NetScreen IDP Manager.

Step 3   Select **Tools > Preferences** from the main menu.

Step 4   Click **Management Server** from the tree on the left and click **OK**.

Step 5   Click **Security Policies** and the name of your policy.

Step 6   In the Notification column, right-click anywhere in the cell in the field and select **Configure**.

Step 7   Check **Enable Logging and Syslog** for each policy, and click **OK**. Repeat for all your policies.

Step 8   From the main menu, select **Policy > Install**.

Now you are ready to add your IDP device to CS-MARS.

Adding a Juniper NetScreen IDP Device to CS-MARS

The Juniper NetScreen IDP is classified as an SW security application in CS-MARS, so adding this device is similar to adding the IntruShield device. It's done in two steps:

- Add configuration information for the management station
- Add configuration information for the IntruVert IPS sensors

To add the security management device, you must do the following:

Step 1   First navigate to **Admin > Security and Monitoring Device > Add** panel.

Step 2   Select **Add SW Security Apps on a New Host** or **Add SW Security Apps** from the Device Type list.

Step 3   Enter the device name and IP addresses if you are adding a new host.

Step 4   Click **Apply**.

Step 5   Click the **Reporting Applications** tab.

Step 6   From the Select Application list, select **NetScreen IDP 2.1**.

Step 7   Click **Add**.

The management station now has been added to CS-MARS. Now you need to add the IPS sensor; this step should be repeated for each sensor.

Step 1   Click the **Add Sensor** button.

Step 2   Enter the following information for the IPS sensor: device name, sensor name, and reporting IP address. Note that the reporting IP address is the IP address that the agent uses to send logs to the management console.

Step 3   Add the interface information.

Step 4   Specify the networks that are monitored by the NetScreen IDP sensor so that CS-MARS can accurately calculate the attack path and mitigation possibilities. As with other IPS sensors, you can either define networks manually or select networks from the Select a Network list.

Step 5   Click **Submit** to save your changes.

Step 6   Click **Activate** to enable CS-MARS to start processing events from these devices.

Symantec ManHunt

ManHunt is an IPS solution developed and sold by Symantec Corp. ManHunt is a standalone IPS solution and is fairly easy to configure. You just need to specify it as a software IPS device that uses SNMP to report its events.

Configuring Symantec ManHunt to Communicate with CS-MARS

The following steps are required to enable communication from ManHunt to CS-MARS.

Step 1   Log into the ManHunt IPS device using the correct username and password.

Step 2   Navigate to **Setup > Policy > Response Rules**.

Step 3   When the Response Rules panel is displayed, select **Action > Add Response Rules**.

Step 4   Click the **Response Action** field.

Step 5   Click **SNMP Notification** in the menu on the left.

Step 6   Enter the IP address of CS-MARS in the SNMP Manager IP Address field.

Step 7   Enter **100000** as the maximum number of SNMP notifications.

Step 8   Enter **1 minute** as the delay between SNMP notifications.

Step 9   Click **OK** to save your changes and return to the main screen.

Adding a Symantec ManHunt Device to CS-MARS

You must now follow these steps to add your ManHunt security device to the CS-MARS device database as an SW security application:

Step 1   Navigate to **Admin > System Setup > Security and Monitor Devices > Add** panel.

Step 2   Select **Add SW Security Apps on a New Host** or **Add SW Security Apps** from the Device Type pull-down menu.

Step 3   If you are adding a new host, enter the device name and IP addresses.

Step 4   Click **Apply**.

Step 5   Click the **Reporting Applications** button.

Step 6   Select **Symantec ManHunt 3.x** from the Select Application list.

Step 7   Click **Add**.

Step 8   Specify the networks that are monitored by the ManHunt device so CS-MARS can accurately calculate the attack path and mitigation possibilities. As with other IPS sensors, you can either define networks manually or select networks from the Select a Network list.

Step 9   Click **Submit** to save your changes in CS-MARS.

Step 10 Click **Activate** to enable CS-MARS to start evaluating events from your ManHunt device.

Events from your ManHunt security devices are now being analyzed and correlated by your CS-MARS appliance.

ISS RealSecure Sensor

The ISS RealSecure Sensor is rated in marketing reports as one of the top intrusion-prevention security solutions on the market. It functions as a suite of products that CS-MARS can recognize as a network intrusion-prevention device and a host intrusion-prevention device. ISS RealSecure sends its security events to CS-MARS using the SNMP protocol. RealSecure runs on Microsoft Windows and the Linux operating system. To get RealSecure operational on CS-MARS, you must make configuration changes on the host operating system devices and add it to CS-MARS.

Configuring a RealSecure Sensor to Communicate with CS-MARS

When you configure ISS RealSecure to communicate with CS-MARS through SNMP, you must make modifications to several different configuration files in either Windows or Linux, depending on the platform where you have installed the software. The following steps enable your ISS RealSecure security device to communicate with CS-MARS and include the ISS Network Sensor in addition to the Server Sensor.

NOTE   The objective of getting an ISS Network Sensor or host reporting to CS-MARS is to configure every signature to report through SNMP. The method outlined in this book is to make modifications to the common.policy and current.policy files. Another method exists as well: In the recent release of SiteProtector, ISS's management console, you have the capability of making these same configuration changes to each sensor using the SiteProtector management GUI. Refer to the SiteProtector configuration manual to understand how to accomplish this.

In this example, you use the default IP address for your CS-MARS device, which is 192.168.0.100.

First, you need to enable CS-MARS as the SNMP server that will receive events from RealSecure. Complete the following steps:

Step 1 Log into the operating system that is running the sensor software.

Step 2 Find the common.policy files in these directories, depending on the operating system:

Microsoft Windows:

Program Files\ISS\issSensors\server_sensor_1
Program Files\ISS\issSensors\network_sensor_1

Linux:

/opt/ISS/issSensors/server_sensor_1

Step 3 Edit the common.policy files.

Modify the line

```
Manager =S
```

to this:

```
Manager =S 192.168.0.100 (CS-MARS interface IP address)
```

If in your network you have Network Address Translated the IP address of your CS-MARS device, you must enter the translated IP address in the previous line, not the actual configured IP address of the CS-MARS device interface you are sending the data to.

Step 4 Save these files in their default location.

Now you must modify the security policy files to trigger an SNMP message when a security event fires.

Step 1 Find the current.policy files in these directories, depending on the operating system:

Microsoft Windows:

Program Files\ISS\issSensors\server_sensor_1
Program Files\ISS\issSensors\network_sensor_1

Linux:

/opt/ISS/issSensors/server_sensor_1
/opt/ISS/issSensors/network_sensor_1

Step 2 Edit the current.policy files.

Step 3 Edit each signature to use SNMP as an event response, and set the choice for SNMP trap as the default.

For example, in this original signature:

```
[\template\features\AOLIM_File_Xfer\Response\];
[\template\features\AOLIM_File_Xfer\Response\DISPLAY\];
```

```
Choice =S Default;
[\template\features\AOLIM_File_Xfer\Response\LOGDB\];
Choice =S LogWithoutRaw;
```

Insert the following lines to make it look similar to the following (notice that SNMP has been added):

```
[\template\features\AOLIM_File_Xfer\Response\];
[\template\features\AOLIM_File_Xfer\Response\DISPLAY\];
Choice =S Default;
[\template\features\AOLIM_File_Xfer\Response\SNMP\];
Choice =S Default;
[\template\features\AOLIM_File_Xfer\Response\LOGDB\];
Choice =S LogWithoutRaw;
```

Step 4   Restart the ISS daemon.

For sensors installed on Microsoft Windows, restart it in the Services menu.

For sensors installed on Linux, run

```
/etc/init.d/RealSecure stop
/etc/init.d/RealSecure start
```

Your ISS RealSecure devices are now configured to communicate with CS-MARS and have been modified to send SNMP messages when events trigger.

In Appendix C, "CS-MARS Supplements," there are two Perl scripts that automate this process. Note, however, that they might need some modifications, and Perl must be installed on the sensor for the scripts to work.

Adding a RealSecure Network Sensor to CS-MARS

You must do the following steps to add a RealSecure network sensor to your CS-MARS database:

Step 1   Navigate to **Admin > System Setup > Security and Monitor Devices > Add** panel.

Step 2   From the Device Type pull-down menu, select **Add SW Security Apps on a New Host** or **Add SW Security Apps on the Existing Host**.

Step 3   Enter the device name.

Step 4   Enter the IP addresses for the following: access IP, reporting IP, and interface address.

Step 5   Click **Apply**.

Step 6   Click the **Reporting Applications** tab and select **RealSecure (6.5 or 7.0)** from the Select Application pull-down menu.

Step 7   Click **Add**.

Step 8   Click the **NIDS** radio button. (NIDS stands for Network Intrusion Detection System.)

Step 9   Specify the networks that are monitored by the RealSecure device so that CS-MARS can accurately calculate the attack path and mitigation possibilities. As with other IPS sensors, you can either define networks manually or select networks from the Select a Network list.

Step 10 Click **Submit** to save your changes in CS-MARS.

Step 11 Click **Activate** to enable CS-MARS to start evaluating events from your ManHunt device.

Adding a RealSecure Host Sensor to CS-MARS

You must do the following steps to add a RealSecure host sensor to your CS-MARS database:

Step 1   Navigate to **Admin > System Setup > Security and Monitor Devices > Add** panel.

Step 2   From the Device Type pull-down menu, select **Add SW Security Apps on a New Host** or **Add SW Security Apps on the Existing Host**.

Step 3   Enter the device name.

Step 4   Enter the IP addresses for the following: access IP, reporting IP, and interface address.

Step 5   Click **Apply**.

Step 6   Click the **Reporting Applications** tab and select **RealSecure (6.5 or 7.0)** from the Select Application pull-down menu.

Step 7   Click **Add**.

Step 8   Click the **HIDS** radio button.

Step 9   Click **Submit**.

Step 10 To add multiple interfaces, click the **General** tab and add the new interfaces' names, IP addresses, and network masks.

Step 11 Click **Apply**.

Your RealSecure IPS software devices have now been configured to send their data to CS-MARS, and CS-MARS has been configured to begin processing RealSecure events.

Snort IPS Sensor

The Snort IPS Sensor is one of the oldest (if not *the* oldest) IPS solution on the market. It has had a great history of being a no-cost application supported by open-source programmers for both code and signature updates for years. It is revered and debated by many as being the solution that has signatures available before other competitors. Because of its history and its good name, there are many deployments of Snort in the marketplace today. Because Snort is a point product, it's "always" in a mixed-vendor environment, which makes it an excellent candidate to be used in a network with the CS-MARS appliance. CS-MARS can analyze and correlate Snort data with other network and security applications to quickly and accurately detect the severity of a threat and to make threat-mitigation suggestions to security responders.

Snort also comes commercially sold and packaged. In this form, it is called SourceFire. Because SourceFire is Snort signatures repackaged with hardware and improved management software, it works with CS-MARS. Just add SourceFire as a Snort device and configure the SourceFire appliance to send SNMP traps to CS-MARS. It is important to note that this is not a supported configuration.

Configuring a Snort IPS Sensor to Communicate with CS-MARS

Snort uses syslog to report security events, and its flexibility has made it very easy to configure it to communicate with CS-MARS. You need to perform the following steps to enable Snort to work with CS-MARS. In this example, we once again use the CS-MARS IP address 192.168.0.100.

Step 1   Configure Snort's events to go to syslog with log facility local4 by modifying snort.conf, usually located in the /etc/snort directory. (You can pick any local facility that's unused.)

Step 2   Add a redirector in your /etc/syslog.conf on your Snort platform to send syslog to CS-MARS.

```
local4.alert @192.168.0.100
```

Step 3   Restart the Snort daemon.

Step 4   Restart the syslogd daemon.

Your Snort device is now ready to be added to CS-MARS.

Adding a Snort IPS Sensor to CS-MARS

CS-MARS views Snort simply as an IPS sensor sending events in syslog. CS-MARS analyzes these logs with its syslog parser to recognize which attacks these events represent and which rules within CS-MARS should fire. Of course, CS-MARS then correlates these Snort events with other network and security events.

Step 1 Navigate to **Admin > System Setup > Security and Monitor Devices > Add** panel.

Step 2 From the Device Type pull-down menu, select **Add SW Security Apps on a New Host** or **Add SW Security Apps on the Existing Host**.

Step 3 If you are adding a new host, enter the device name and IP addresses of your Snort device.

Step 4 Click **Apply**.

Step 5 Click the **Reporting Applications** tab.

Step 6 Select **Snort 2.0** from the Select Applications list.

Step 7 Click **Add**.

Step 8 Specify the networks that are monitored by the Snort device so that CS-MARS can accurately calculate the attack path and mitigation possibilities. As with other IPS sensors, you can either define networks manually or select networks from the Select a Network list.

Step 9 Click **Submit** to save your changes.

Step 10 Click **Activate** to enable CS-MARS to start processing your Snort events.

Enterasys Dragon

The Enterasys Dragon IPS software is similar to some other third-party security software vendors in that there are various different architectures and applications that need to be configured. Refer to the CS-MARS user guide, located on the Cisco website at http://www.cisco.com/en/US/products/ps6241/products_user_guide_book09186a00804efe32.html, to configure your Enterasys Dragon.

Operating Systems and Web Servers

Another of the very powerful features of CS-MARS is that it has the capability to pull or receive logs from operating systems and web servers. This information can be used to determine, for example, brute-force login attacks against hosts and servers as well as web servers. The information can also be correlated with other network and security events and logs to determine whether a perceived threat is valid or a false positive. In this section, we cover the following host and server operating systems and web servers:

- Microsoft Windows operating systems
- Solaris and generic Linux operating systems (includes Red Hat)

- MS IIS web server
- iPlanet web server
- Apache web server

Microsoft Windows Operating Systems

The Microsoft Windows operating system is, of course, the most popular operating system in the world. Depending on the market research that you read, a Microsoft OS is installed on more than 95 percent of PCs worldwide. Because of this, correlating security event log data from this operating system is a key component of CS-MARS to ensure that threats are accurately reported and mitigated.

Configure Microsoft Windows to Allow CS-MARS to Pull Security Event Logs

Two modes are used to get the event log data from Microsoft Windows to CS-MARS:

- Configure Windows to allow its event logs to be pulled by CS-MARS
- Configure Windows to push its event logs to CS-MARS

You must take the following steps to configure your Microsoft hosts and servers to allow their event logs to be pulled by your CS-MARS appliance.

On your Windows host, you must first ensure that you have a user that belongs to the administration group and has permission to manage audit and security logs. This can be done at the local and domain account levels.

For a domain user, do the following on the domain controller before you enable Windows event pulling on your client. This enables the account that CS-MARS will be using to pool the event log data from your Microsoft devices.

Step 1   Select the domain user with privileges to pull, such as CORP\syslog.

Step 2   Then on your domain controller, click **Administrative Tools > Default Domain Security Policy > Security Settings > Local Policies > User Rights Management**.

Step 3   Grant the permission Manage Auditing and Security Log to the domain user CORP\syslog.

To enable Windows event log pulling from Windows NT, you must do the following:

Step 1   From **Start > Programs > Administrative Tools > User Manager**, in the menu bar, choose **Policies**.

Step 2   In the submenu, choose **User Rights**. Make sure the right of Manage Auditing and Security Log is granted to the user account used for pulling event log records.

Step 3 In the submenu, choose **Audit**. Configure the audit policy according to your site's security auditing policy.

To enable Windows event log pulling from Windows 2000, you must do the following:

Step 1 Go to **Start > Settings > Control Panel > Administrative Tools > Local Security Policy > Local Policies**.

Step 2 In User Rights Assignment, make sure the right of Manage Auditing and Security Log is granted to the user account used for pulling event log records.

Step 3 In Audit Policy, configure the audit policy according to your site's security auditing policy.

To enable Windows event log pulling from Windows 2003, you must do the following:

Step 1 Go to **Administrative Tools > Local Security Policy > Local Policies**.

Step 2 In User Rights Assignment, make sure the right of Manage Auditing and Security Log is granted to the user account used for pulling event log records.

Step 3 In Audit Policy, configure the audit policy according to your site's security auditing policy.

NOTE   The pulling of an event log itself generates security event logs if certain events, such as Log On/Off, are audited. We recommend that you either set a default domain policy or set the retention method for security event logs on your Windows system to be Overwrite as needed. Otherwise, when the log is full, no new event log can be generated on the Windows system.

Configure CS-MARS to Pull Microsoft Windows Event Logs

To enable CS-MARS to pull event logs from Windows NT, 2000, and 2003, you must do the following:

Step 1 Navigate to **Admin > Security and Monitor Devices > Add** panel.

Step 2 From the Device Type pull-down menu, select **Add SW Security Apps on a New Host** or **Add SW Security Apps on the Existing Host**.

Step 3 Enter the device name and IP addresses if you are adding a new host.

Step 4 Select **Operating System > Windows** from the list.

Step 5 (Optional) Enter the NetBIOS name.

Step 6 Click **Logging Info** to configure OS logging. A new window appears.

(a) Select your Windows operating system: 2000/2003/ Generic/NT.

(b) Check the **Pull** box and leave the Receive box unchecked.

(c) Enter your domain name, host login, and host password. This entry should match the domain username and password that you configured when you set up the domain user and password for CS-MARS.

(d) Click the **Submit** button to save your changes; the new window closes, taking you back to the original screen.

Step 7 Add the interface IP address after the host or server and network mask.

Step 8 Click **Apply**.

Step 9 Click the **Vulnerability Assessment Info** link to define the operating system host information that CS-MARS uses to determine false positive attacks against this host. This step is optional and is not required to complete the configuration.

Step 10 Click **Done** to save the changes.

Step 11 Click **Activate** to enable CS-MARS to start pulling these event logs and correlating them with other network and security events.

CS-MARS is now enabled to pull event logs from your various Windows devices, and critical operating system information has been entered to help CS-MARS to determine false positives while investigating new threats.

Configure Microsoft Windows to Push Event Logs to CS-MARS

To enable Microsoft Windows to push event logs to your CS-MARS appliance, you must install the InterSect Alliance application called SNARE on your Windows computer.

Step 1 First click **Setup > Audit Configuration**.

Step 2 In the Enter the Local Host Name field, enter the IP address or DNS name of the local host.

Step 3 Enter the remote IP or DNS address field. This will be the IP address or DNS name for your CS-MARS device.

Step 4 Select the following options: **Enable Syslog Header**, **Automatically Set Audit Configuration**, and **Automatically Set File System Audit Configuration**.

Step 5 Click **OK** to enable and save your chances.

SNARE has now been configured to receive Windows event logs, convert them to syslog events, and send those events to the CS-MARS appliance.

NOTE   MS Windows has the capability to send its event log data to an SNMP trap destination. You can enable this feature in any Microsoft OS by installing the SNMP services and then configuring them. This pushes MS event data to the CS-MARS as well.

Enable CS-MARS to Receive Pushed Windows Security Event Logs

The process to enable CS-MARS to receive logs is the same as it is to push logs, except that you check the Receive box instead of the Pull box. You must take the following steps to enable CS-MARS to receive pushed Windows event logs:

Step 1   Navigate to **Admin > Security and Monitor Devices > Add** panel.

Step 2   From the Device Type pull-down menu, select **Add SW Security Apps on a New Host** or **Add SW Security Apps on the Existing Host**.

Step 3   Enter the device name and IP addresses if you are adding a new host.

Step 4   Select **Operating System > Windows** from the list.

Step 5   (Optional) Enter the NetBIOS name.

Step 6   Click **Logging Info** to configure OS logging. A new window appears.

        (a) Select your Windows operating system: 2000/2003/ Generic/NT.

        (b) Check the **Receive** box and leave the Pull box unchecked.

        (c) Enter your domain name, host login, and host password. This entry should match the domain username and password that you configured when you set up the domain user and password.

        (d) Click the **Submit** button to save your changes; the new window closes, taking you back to the original screen.

Step 7   Add the interface IP address(es) for the host or server and network mask.

Step 8   Click **Apply**.

Step 9   Click the **Vulnerability Assessment Info** link to define the operating system host information that CS-MARS uses to determine false positive attacks against this host. This step is optional and is not required to complete the configuration.

Step 10   Click **Done** to save the changes.

Step 11   Click **Activate** to enable CS-MARS to start pulling these event logs so it can correlate them with other network and security events.

Sun Solaris and Generic Linux Operating Systems

UNIX operating systems are the second-most-popular host and server operating systems in terms of market penetration. Typically, UNIX operating systems have been used in server type environments, but because of in-roads made in the last few years by Sun, Red Hat, and other vendors, UNIX has also been gaining popularity in the host workstation environment. Because of this, CS-MARS developers have now added support for processing syslog data sourced from UNIX- and Linux-based operating systems.

The configuration steps in this section will likely work for almost any UNIX or Linux operating system deployment with very few, if any, changes. However, different versions might have different syslog messages that CS-MARS might not recognize.

The following two sections step you through how to get UNIX or Linux and CS-MARS communicating with each other so that CS-MARS can process and correlate operating system logs from the systems.

Configure Solaris or Linux to Communicate with CS-MARS

You must perform the following steps to enable Solaris UNIX or Red Hat Linux to communicate with the CS-MARS appliance. We again use the CS-MARS IP address 192.168.0.100.

You need to change parameters for three applications to enable communications with CS-MARS. Changes are required to xferlog, inetd, and syslogd applications.

Step 1 Log into your UNIX or Linux operating system with root privileges.

Step 2 Modify xferlog. Change the FTP parameters, which include FTP login access.

Add the following to /etc/ftpd/ftpaccess:

```
log transfers real,guest,anonymous inbound,outbound log syslog+xferlog
```

Step 3 Enable inetd trace messages, which provide the authentication information for services provided using inetd. Find the line in /etc/rc2.d/ S72inetsvc that reads:

```
/usr/sbin/inetd –s
```

Change it to:

```
/usr/sbin/inetd -t -s
```

Other log messages will automatically appear in the syslog and do not need additional configuration.

Step 4 Modify syslogd to send messages to CS-MARS. Edit the /etc/syslog.conf file and add the following line:

```
*.debug @192.168.0.100
```

When these configurations are complete, FTP authentication information and inetd information will be sent to syslogd. Syslog messages also will be sent directly to your CS-MARS device for processing and correlation.

Add Solaris or Linux to the CS-MARS Device Database

Now that your UNIX or Linux operating system has been modified to send syslog messages to CS-MARS, you must perform the following steps to enable CS-MARS to add UNIX or Linux hosts to its device database:

Step 1   Navigate to **Admin > Security and Monitor Devices > Add** panel.

Step 2   Select **Add SW Security Apps on a New Host** from the Device Type pull-down menu.

Step 3   Enter the device name and its reporting IP address of your UNIX or Linux device.

Step 4   Select **Generic** as the operating system.

Step 5   Select **Logging Info** and select **Receive**; then click **Submit**.

Step 6   Click **Apply** to add the device and to enable CS-MARS to start processing the syslog data.

Microsoft Internet Information Web Server

The Microsoft Internet Information (IIS) web server is a standard part of the Windows 2000 Server, Windows 2003 Server, and Windows NT server operating systems. It can also be installed as an option on other popular Windows platforms. Because of the penetration of the Windows operating system—and, by default, the Microsoft IIS web server—this is an important component that can be used in conjunction with CS-MARS when correlating network and security events messages.

Configure Microsoft IIS Web Server to Communicate with CS-MARS

You must follow these steps to enable the Microsoft IIS web server to communicate with the CS-MARS appliance.

You must first install InterSect Alliance SNARE for IIS on the machine that you want to communicate with CS-MARS. SNARE is a freeware product and can be found at http://www.intersectalliance.com/projects/SnareIIS/index.html#Download.

The next step is to configure SNARE to trap IIS events. You must do the following:

Step 1   Click **Start > Programs > InterSect Alliance > Audit Configuration**.

Step 2   Enter the IP address of the CS-MARS 192.168.0.100 as the IP target.

Step 3 In Log Directory, enter the directory where the logs are to be placed.

Step 4 Click the **Syslog** radio button in Destination.

Step 5 Click **OK** to save and activate your changes.

SNARE has now been configured to send log data to CS-MARS. However, you must take the following steps to configure IIS to send its logs to SNARE:

Step 1 Click **Start > Programs > Administrative Tools > Internet Services Manager**.

Step 2 Right-click **Default Web Site** in the Tree tab on the left.

Step 3 Select **Properties** in the shortcut menu.

On the Web Site tab, check **Enable Logging** and select **W3C Extended Log Format** from the Active Log Format list.

Step 4 Select **Properties**.

Step 5 In the General Properties tab, set New Log Time Period to **Daily**.

Note that the log file directory *must* match the one previously set using the Audit Configuration program.

Step 6 On the Extended Properties tab, make sure all available properties are selected.

Step 7 Click **OK**.

Step 8 Click **OK** to enable and activate your changes.

IIS now can send its logs to SNARE, and SNARE can send the logs to CS-MARS.

Add Microsoft IIS Web Server to the CS-MARS Device Database

You now need to configure CS-MARS to add the IIS web server to its device database. Note that these steps are very similar to the steps to enable receipt of Microsoft Windows host and server event logs.

Step 1 Navigate to **Admin > Security and Monitor Devices > Add** panel.

Step 2 From the Device Type list, select **Add SW Security Apps on a New Host** or **Add SW Security Apps on the Existing Host**.

Step 3 Enter the device name and IP addresses if you're adding a new host.

Step 4 Select **Windows** from Operation System list.

Step 5 Click **Logging Info**.

Step 6 Click the **Receive Host Log** box.

Step 7   Click **Submit**.

Step 8   Add interfaces as required.

Step 9   Add as many IP addresses and masks to the interface as you need by clicking **Add IP/Network Mask**.

Step 10 Click **Apply**.

Step 11 Click the **Reporting Applications** tab.

Step 12 From the Select Application list, select **Generic Web Server Generic**.

Step 13 Click **Add**.

Step 14 Select **W3C_EXTENDED_LOG** format.

Step 15 Click **Submit** to add this device and enable CS-MARS to process and correlate its events.

CS-MARS has now been configured to add this device to its device database and can process and correlate IIS events to more accurately evaluate threats and mitigation recommendations.

iPlanet Web Server

Because there are varying ways to deploy the iPlanet web server, and the variations are covered well in the CS-MARS 4.1 user guide, refer to http://www.cisco.com/en/US/ products/ps6241/products_user_guide_book09186a00804efe32.html for instructions on how to configure the iPlanet web server.

Apache Web Server

The Apache web server is the most popular multiplatform web server installed on the Internet today. It commonly runs on both Microsoft Windows operating systems and UNIX/ Linux operating systems. Because of its popularity, CS-MARS fully supports the processing and correlation of the Apache web server event logs.

Configure the UNIX Apache Web Server and iPlanet Web Server to Communicate with CS-MARS

To enable web server communication, Cisco provides an open-source logging agent and an associated configuration file for you to use. This agent can be downloaded from the software download center at http://www.cisco.com/cgi-bin/tablebuild.pl/cs-mars-misc.

Complete the following steps to install and configure the logging agent:

Step 1   Log into the host as the root user.

Step 2   Create a directory called /opt/webagent.

Step 3   Copy the files agent.pl and webagent.conf to the /opt/webagent directory.

Step 4   Set the protection of the agent script (agent.pl) so it can be read and executed by all:

```
cd /opt/agent
chmod 755 agent.pl
```

Step 5   Edit the configuration file (webagent.conf):

```
logfile_location = access_log_path
MARS_ip_port = MARS_ip_address:port
username = a
password = b
```

Replace *access_log_path* with the full path to the CS-MARS URL, 192.168.0.100 with the IP host number of the CS-MARS appliance, and *port* with the port number. You do not need to edit the username or password in the file.

Step 6   You need a separate webagent.conf file for each access log you want to pull. We recommend naming them webagent1.conf, webagent2.conf, and so forth.

Put these in the /opt/webagent directory.

Step 7   To run the agent using a configuration file other than webagent.conf, use this command:

```
agent.pl other_config_file
```

Replace *other_config_file* with the name of the web agent configuration file.

Step 8   Edit the crontab file to push the logs to CS-MARS at regular intervals. The following example pulls new entries from the access log every five minutes:

```
crontab -e
in 5,10,15,20,25,30,35,40,45,50,55,0 * * * *
(cd /opt/webagent;./agent.pl webagent1.conf)
5,10,15,20,25,30,35,40,45,50,55,0 * * * *
(cd /opt/webagent;./agent.pl webagent2.conf)
```

You must now configure your Apache web server and your iPlanet web server to send logs to the CS-MARS UNIX-based web agent. You must enter the following commands to configure your Apache web server to send its logs to the CS-MARS web agent:

Step 1   In the file httpd.conf, make sure the LogFormat is either Common or Combined *and* matches the format set on CS-MARS.

Step 2   Stop and restart the Apache server for your changes to take effect.

You must enter the following commands to configure your iPlanet web server to send its logs to the CS-MARS web agent:

Step 1 In the iPlanet server administration tool, click the **Preferences** tab.

Step 2 In the left menu, click the **Logging Options** link.

Step 3 Make sure Log File matches the log filename set on CS-MARS.

Step 4 Make sure the Format radio button **Use Common Logfile Format** is checked.

Step 5 Click OK to activate changes.

Step 6 Shut down and restart the iPlanet web server.

Your UNIX-based Apache web server and iPlanet web server have now been configured to send logs to the CS-MARS appliance.

Add Apache Web Server and iPlanet Web Server to the CS-MARS Device Database

Complete the following steps to add the Apache and iPlanet web servers to the CS-MARS device database:

Step 1 Navigate to **Admin > Security and Monitor Devices > Add** panel.

Step 2 From the Device Type list, select **Add SW Security Apps on a New Host** or **Add SW Security Apps on the Existing Host**.

Step 3 Enter the device name and IP addresses if you are adding a new host.

Step 4 Select **Solaris** or **Linux** from the Operation System list.

Step 5 Click **Logging Info**.

Step 6 Click the **Receive Host Log** box.

Step 7 Click **Submit**.

Step 8 Add interfaces as required.

Step 9 Add as many IP addresses and masks to the interface as you need by clicking **Add IP/Network Mask**.

Step 10 Click **Apply**.

Step 11 Click the **Reporting Applications** tab.

Step 12 From the Select Application list, select **Generic Web Server Generic**.

Step 13 Click **Add**.

Step 14 Select the log format you chose when setting up the web server.

Step 15 Click **Submit** to add this device and enable CS-MARS to process and correlate its events.

CS-MARS is now ready to process data from your iPlanet and Apache UNIX-based web servers.

VPN Concentrators

VPN concentrators are remote-access devices used to create and terminate virtual network connections, facilitating the access of remote hosts. Some of the data captured in the VPN concentrator logs is critical for CS-MARS when determining the location of IP addresses within the network, associating usernames with IP addresses, and associating MAC addresses with IP addresses. In addition, CS-MARS uses event logs or syslogs for VPN concentrators to help improve the accuracy of its threat recognition and mitigation.

The only VPN concentrator currently supported by CS-MARS is the Cisco VPN 3000 series concentrators. CS-MARS supports VPN 3000 operating system Versions 4.0.1 to 4.7.

Configure VPN 3000 Series Concentrators to Communicate with CS-MARS

Configuring your VPN concentrator to communicate with CS-MARS is a fairly straight-forward task. The concentrator uses syslog as its communication protocol, so essentially you need to define syslog and set CS-MARS as the device to send your syslog events.

You must perform the following steps to configure your VPN 3000 series concentrator to communicate with your CS-MARS appliance:

Step 1 Use your browser to connect to your VPN concentrator.

Step 2 Select **Configuration > System > Events > General**.

Step 3 Select **Save Log Format as Multiline**.

Step 4 Configure the Syslog Format as **Original**.

Step 5 Select **Severities 1–5** in the Events to Log field.

Step 6 Select **Severities 1–5** in the Events to Syslog field.

Step 7 Select **Severities 1–3** in the Events to Trap field.

Step 8 Select **Configuration > System > Events > Syslog Servers**.

Step 9 Define a target syslog server by clicking **Add**.

Step 10 Enter the IP address or host name of the CS-MARS appliance in the Syslog Server field.

Step 11 Save your settings by clicking **Add**.

Step 12 Click **Save** in the top-right corner to save all changes.

Add VPN 3000 Series Concentrators to the CS-MARS Device Database

You must perform the following steps to configure your CS-MARS device to add your VPN 3000 series concentrator to its device database:

Step 1   First navigate to **Admin > Security and Monitoring Device > Add** panel.

Step 2   Select the device type you want to add to the CS-MARS database—in this case, the VPN concentrator and your operating system version.

Step 3   Enter the device name for your VPN concentrator.

Step 4   Enter the VPN concentrator management access IP address.

Step 5   Enter the IP address that will be the source of the SNMP and syslog reporting records.

Step 6   Enter the SNMP community string; in this case, we used cisco123.

Step 7   Select **Yes** to activate the health checking on this device.

Step 8   Click **Discover** to ensure that CS-MARS can contact your Cisco VPN concentrator.

Step 9   Click **Submit** to add your VPN concentrator device to the CS-MARS device database.

Step 10   Click **Activate** to enable communications between your VPN concentrator and your CS-MARS appliance.

CS-MARS and your VPN concentrator have now been configured to communicate with each other. CS-MARS can now process and correlate the events it receives from the concentrator.

Antivirus Hosts and Servers

CS-MARS recognizes events from three major antivirus vendors:

* Symantec
* McAfee
* Trend Micro

CS-MARS uses events from antivirus hosts and servers to help determine whether an attack has been successful.

The process for configuring antivirus security software and adding it to the CS-MARS database is well documented in the CS-MARS 4.1 user guide. Refer to this user guide on the Cisco website at http://www.cisco.com/en/US/products/ps6241/products_user_guide_book09186a00804efe32.html for instructions on how to configure antivirus software.

Database Servers

In almost every web application in use on the Internet today, there is a database server that is storing data and handling the back-end transactions. These database servers are critical software devices that need to be protected by various network and security applications and appliances. Because of this, CS-MARS can collect and correlate their security logs. Oracle is the most popular database engine and is the only one fully supported and tested in the CS-MARS environment.

Oracle

Oracle database servers have the largest installed base in the current computer networking market. These servers are used not only in Internet applications, but also in standalone enterprise financial, marketing, manufacturing, asset-tracking, and human resource applications, and the list goes on. Obviously, this is a resource that needs considerable security focus, and CS-MARS meets that need.

Configure an Oracle Database Server to Communicate with CS-MARS

You need to perform the following steps to enable your Oracle database server to be made available to your CS-MARS appliance. Note that additional information regarding Oracle applications is located in the CS-MARS 4.1 users guide.

Step 1   As sysdba, execute cataudit.sql to create audit trail views:

```
[oracle@server]$ sqlplus /nolog
SQL> conn / as sysdba;
SQL> @$ORACLE_HOME/rdbms/admin/cataudit.sql
```

Step 2   Enable auditing to the database by adding the following entry to the Oracle instance initialization file, usually named init<SID>.ora:

```
AUDIT_TRAIL=DB
```

This file is usually located in $ORACLE_BASE/admin/<SID>/pfile, where <SID> is the name of the Oracle instance.

If a binary initialization file is used for this instance, make sure you update it first. This file is usually located in $ORACLE_HOME/dbs and is named spfile<SID>.ora. Ask your DBA about the location of these files and the policies applied for this server.

Step 3   Restart the database to activate the change made to the initialization file.

```
[oracle@server]$ sqlplus /nolog
SQL> conn / as sysdba;
SQL> shutdown immediate;
SQL> startup;
```

Step 4 Turn on all the logs that you want to audit. The following example turns on the audit session:

```
SQL> audit session;
Audit succeeded.
```

Step 5 Repeat the previous step for all the logs that you want to audit.

Step 6 Create a user account on this server and grant select privilege for the view dba_audit_trail. Our example assumes that the user has the login name pnuser.

```
SQL> grant select on dba_audit_trail to pnuser
```

You use **pnuser** as the value for User Name in the CS-MARS setup.

Step 7 To test that everything was properly configured, audit logs were written to the database, and pnuser has read access to them, execute the following commands:

```
[oracle@server]$ sqlplus pnuser/<password>@<oracle_server>
SQL> select count(*) from dba_audit_trail;
COUNT(*)
----------
3
```

If this count is anything but zero, congratulations—you have successfully configured the Oracle server. You must repeat the previous procedure for every Oracle server that you want to report audit logs to CS-MARS. You are now ready to configure CS-MARS to recognize events from your Oracle database server. If the count is zero, double-check your step-by-step procedure. If the count is still zero, contact the Cisco Technical Assistance Center for help.

Add an Oracle Database Server to the CS-MARS Device Database

You must perform the following steps to add your Oracle server into your CS-MARS device database:

Step 1 Click **Admin > Security and Monitor Devices > Add**.

Step 2 From the Device Type list, select **Add SW Security Apps on a New Host** or **Add SW Security Apps on the Existing Host**.

Step 3 Enter the device name and IP addresses if you are adding a new host.

Step 4 Click **Apply**.

Step 5 From the Select Application list, select **Oracle Database Server Generic**.

Step 6 Click **Add**.

Step 7 Enter the username, password, and Oracle service name:

— **User Name**—The Oracle database username

— **Password**—The Oracle database user password

— **Oracle Service Name**—The Oracle service name

The Oracle Service Name is the GLOBAL_DBNAME=username.server, which can be found inside a file called listener.ora.

Step 8 Click **Test Connectivity** to verify the configuration.

Step 9 Click **Submit**.

Summary

In this chapter, you first learned about the types of devices, how they can be used in the CS-MARS–enabled network, and how these devices are classified by CS-MARS. Classification is important because CS-MARS can perform separate operations on reporting devices versus mitigation devices. The classes of devices are as follows:

- **Hardware-based security devices**—These devices are traditional network and security appliances, such as routers, switches, and security appliances such as firewalls and intrusion-prevention devices.

- **Software-based security devices**—Software devices are applications that run on hosts or servers. This can include an Apache web server, an IIS server, or any other software application.

- **On-demand security services**—Security services represent subscription-based services provided by vendors using a central security operations center (SOC) with remote monitoring nodes, such as Qualys QualysGuard.

Devices that CS-MARS supports fall into these categories, which together represent almost any device you could imagine installing in your network. But most important, the devices that CS-MARS supports are from many vendors besides Cisco Systems.

CS-MARS is as effective in a mixed-vendor environment as it is in an all-Cisco environment. Although it is beyond the scope of this book, one thing that's important to understand is that, even though CS-MARS effectively reports, analyzes, and mitigates security, network, and host events in a mixed-vendor environment, it is still to your advantage to have end-to-end Cisco network and security equipment because Cisco network and security devices communicate with each other to dynamically change their configurations based on what they have learned from each other. This interaction provides you with a much stronger and more dynamic security posture than you can achieve by inserting third-party security devices in different parts of your network.

PART III

CS-MARS Operation

In this chapter, you learn the basic operation of the CS-MARS platform and become proficient in general operation and incident investigation. Topics in this chapter include the following:

- Using the Summary Dashboard, Network Status Tab, and My Reports Tab
- Using the Incidents Page
- Simple Queries

## CHAPTER 7

CS-MARS Basic Operation

This chapter introduces you to the basic operation of the CS-MARS appliance. It begins with a detailed look at the Summary Dashboard, which familiarizes you with interpreting a "snapshot" of your network from a security perspective and enables you to customize views of data based upon your requirements. A look at the Incidents page takes you one step further into CS-MARS operation by guiding you through incident investigation and basic data forensics. Finally, this chapter helps you tune your data-mining skills by explaining several methods of querying data.

These three functions can be accessed via the tabs located in the upper-left corner of the web page.

Using the Summary Dashboard, Network Status Graphs, and My Reports Tab

The Summary Dashboard is unique in that it enables you to instantly look into your network from a security perspective. This capability presents itself as a sort of "state of the security union" for your data by providing you with the latest information about where incident or policy violations are occurring and what they are. This section explains how you can make well-informed security decisions by doing the following:

- Reading incidents and viewing path information
- Using the HotSpot graph and Attack diagram
- Interpreting event and NetFlow and false positive charts
- Understanding data on the Information Summary column
- Interpreting the graphs
- Using the Network Status tab
- Using My Reports

Reading Incidents and Viewing Path Information

Within the Summary page, recent incidents are presented in CS-MARS as represented by Figure 7-1. These incidents can be filtered for display based upon their severity, the matched rule, or case status.

Figure 7-1 *CS-MARS Summary Dashboard Incident Summary Data*

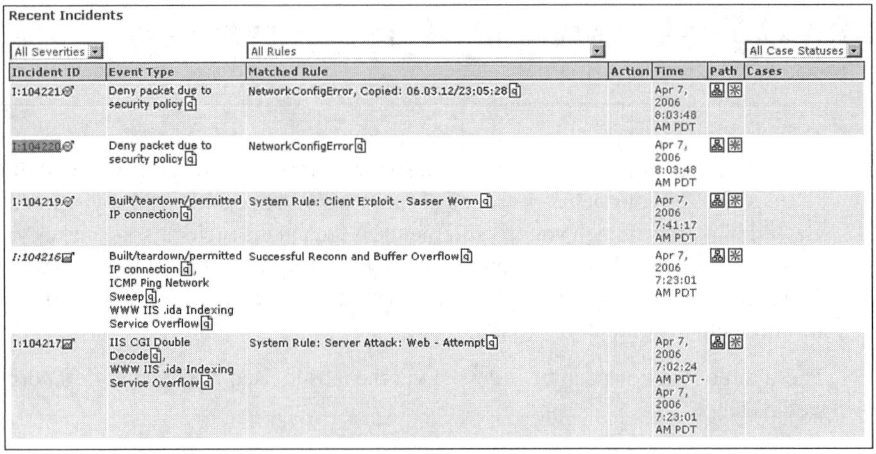
Recent Incidents
All Severities
All Rules
All Case Statuses
Incident ID
Event Type
Matched Rule
Action
Time
Path
Cases
I:104221
Deny packet due to security policy
NetworkConfigError, Copied: 06.03.12/23:05:28
Apr 7, 2006 8:03:48 AM PDT
I:104220
Deny packet due to security policy
NetworkConfigError
Apr 7, 2006 8:03:48 AM PDT
I:104219
Built/teardown/permitted IP connection
System Rule: Client Exploit - Sasser Worm
Apr 7, 2006 7:41:17 AM PDT
I:104216
Built/teardown/permitted IP connection, ICMP Ping Network Sweep, WWW IIS .ida Indexing Service Overflow
Successful Reconn and Buffer Overflow
Apr 7, 2006 7:23:01 AM PDT
I:104217
IIS CGI Double Decode, WWW IIS .ida Indexing Service Overflow
System Rule: Server Attack: Web - Attempt
Apr 7, 2006 7:02:24 AM PDT - Apr 7, 2006 7:23:01 AM PDT

In presenting the summary of incident data, seven fields are displayed to provide you quick information:

- **Incident ID**—CS-MARS uniquely assigns this ID, which pertains specifically to the data being presented. You can click the ID to go to the detailed data presented to begin analysis and mitigation. The section "Using the Incident ID to View Data," later in this chapter, explores this feature in more detail.
- **Event Type**—This field describes the event(s) that caused the incident. This can be a single event or a group of correlated events. To understand each event, simply click the event to see a popup window describing what the event is, Common Vulnerability and Exploit (CVE) data (if applicable), and the manufacturer's devices that can report that type of event.
- **Matched Rule**—This field reports the rule that the event data matched to create the incident. For a description of the rule, simply click the reported rule text; this brings up the Rules page, where you can read the rule details.
- **Action**—If an action is defined for a rule, such as Distributed Threat Mitigation (DTM), e-mail, or a Simple Network Management Protocol (SNMP) trap, this field shows you the type of action taken.
- **Time**—This field displays the time the incident was created. It is important to note that this time is not the actual event time; it is the time when all the events together triggered the rule.

- **Path**—This column gives you the option of viewing the incident data topographically in chronological order of occurrence or by propagation vectors from source to destination. Using these diagrams brings the entire attack or policy violation into perspective in an easy-to-understand map. To choose one of these options, simply click the applicable icon.

- **Cases**—If a case has been assigned to the incident, this column displays the respective case ID.

These functions are rather self-explanatory; however, it is important to understand in more detail the information gathered from the Event Type column and the Path column.

At times, you might be reading the Summary page and see an event or events listed and ask yourself what that means. To answer your question, all you have to do is click the event name under the Event Type column. When selected, another web browser window opens and displays some useful information:

- **Event Type Details**—This section describes in detail what the event is and provides a summary of severity and Common Vulnerability and Exploit (CVE) information, if applicable.

- **Recommended Actions**—If patches to affected platforms are needed, they are reported in this section.

- **False Positive Conditions**—If this event has any false positive conditions that could trigger it, they are explained here.

- **Affected Platforms**—This section lists the platforms this event type affects.

- **Related Information**—This section presents any extra data related to the event. It can include, but is not limited to, CVE descriptions.

- **Device Type Information**—Only certain devices can report this type of event. Regardless of their manufacturer, they are listed here.

- **Event Type Groups**—These groups are CS-MARS specific. Groups of events are a form of event type management. A single event can fall into many event type groups. An event type group is a group of specific events as reported from various devices; when all used together, they make up a certain type of attack or policy violation. In this section, you can read about what a specific group of events adds up to when combined in an attack. Figure 7-2 displays the CS-MARS Event Type Details popup window.

Now that you understand the various event types that make up a reported incident, visually familiarizing yourself with what this incident has done on your network is important—and easy to do.

Figure 7-2 *CS-MARS Event Type Details Page*

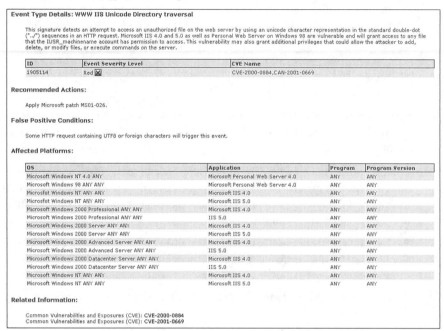

First, you must understand how the CS-MARS topologies and graphs are presented to you during your visual analysis. CS-MARS uses Adobe SVG Viewer. If this viewer is not installed as a plug-in for your web browser, you will not be able to view the graphs on CS-MARS. The following tips and tricks help you interpret the graphs and use the viewer.

- Hosts or network objects can be one of four colors:
  - **Clear**—Normal
  - **Red**—The device is under attack or is the destination of a policy violation.
  - **Brown**—The device is the attacker or the source of a policy violation.
  - **Purple**—The device has been compromised and is now attacking.
- Network paths can be one of three colors:
  - **Black**—A thin black line connecting objects denotes physical network connectivity.
  - **Orange**—The path(s) for an applicable session are displayed.
  - **Red**—This is the path of interest that you have selected for a session or incident (by moving your mouse pointer over it or by clicking it).
- Click on a device or object to view more detailed information about it.

- To zoom in on a certain area, hold down the **Crtl** key to bring up a magnifying glass. Move the mouse to the area you want amplified and left-click the mouse. To reduce the view, right-click anywhere on the topology map and select **Zoom Out**.

- To move the topology map around in your web browser window, hold down the **Alt** key until a hand appears. While holding down the **Alt** key, "grab" the graphic by clicking it with the left mouse button. You can drag it where you want and even walk the topology around your web browser window.

Now you can begin your visual analysis. CS-MARS can present the incident data to you graphically from the Summary Dashboard in two ways. By clicking the respective icons within the Path column, you can visualize the data through two perspectives:

- Path information
- Incident vector information

Path Information

The first icon under the Path column is for path analysis. To see the path for each phase of an incident, click the icon; a new web browser window appears. Figure 7-3 is an example of the path analysis for an incident.

Figure 7-3 *CS-MARS Incident Path Graph for an Incident*

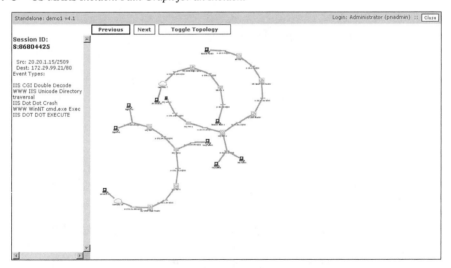

This graph gives the user a chronological view of an incident in all phases, from start to finish. It displays the network path of the incident in orange. You can choose to display only the devices in the path of the incident or the path as set against your entire network topology. These two views can be instantly toggled back and forth by clicking the Toggle Topology button.

The Previous and Next buttons walk you through each phase of the attack, as set forth by the path displayed, and highlight the applicable phase of the incident by coloring the path red and displaying its session information on the left side of the new window. If you click the session ID, located on left frame of the current window, a new window opens displaying the detailed forensic data that made up that session of the incident. Understanding the detailed forensic data is quite easy in CS-MARS; this is covered later in this chapter.

Incident Vector Information

The second icon under the Path column of the Summary Dashboard opens a window to display incident vector information. Incident vector information provides a user with information such as the direction of the flow, the number of sessions for each flow, and links to the detailed forensic data, all in chronological order. This diagram also contains the Next and Previous buttons, which can be used to step through the progression of the incident. Figure 7-4 is an example of the Vector graph for an incident.

Figure 7-4 *CS-MARS Incident Vector Graph*

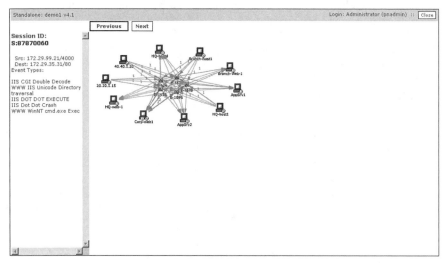

As you can see from Figure 7-4, the vectors contain arrows that denote the direction of the traffic flow from point to point. A number appears beside each of the flows. This number indicates the number of sessions that apply for this traffic flow. The center of the vector contains a colored icon, which represents the severity of the session. If you click the flow, a new window opens with a summary of the session data. Clicking the session ID in the new summary window displays session data for that flow of the attack you clicked.

Understanding the detailed forensic data is quite easy in CS-MARS; this is covered later in this chapter, in the section "Using the Incident ID to View Data."

As in the Incident Path graph, the same icons, colors, and tips and tricks apply.

Using the HotSpot Graph and Attack Diagram

Located directly underneath the Recent Incidents section of the Summary Dashboard are the HotSpot graph and the Attack diagram, as shown in Figure 7-5.

Figure 7-5   *CS-MARS HotSpot Graph and Attack Diagram*

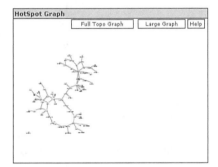 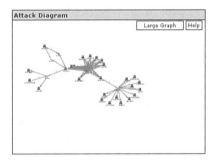

These diagrams offer a quick look into your network, displaying to the user where the most incident-related data is sourced or destined to and what the propagation path looks like. These graphs update themselves according to the Summary page refresh rate (the default is 15 minutes). This refresh rate is user configurable as low as 1 minute.

HotSpot Graph

The HotSpot graph is designed to instantly tell you where your incidents or policy violations are coming from or destined to. This graph offers two perspectives:

- **The Full Topology graph**—Displays only your network topology, including devices in your network that CS-MARS is aware of. Additionally, for areas not known by CS-MARS, it places a network cloud in your topology and identifies it as a gateway to some destination. If you click the cloud, a new window pops up giving you the option to discover or add a gateway device.

- **The Large graph**—Displays the actual HotSpot graph. In the HotSpot graph, network devices and reporting devices are displayed in the topology; all other devices are placed in a cloud.

Figure 7-6 displays the HotSpot graph in CS-MARS.

Figure 7-6 *CS-MARS HotSpot Graph—Large Graph*

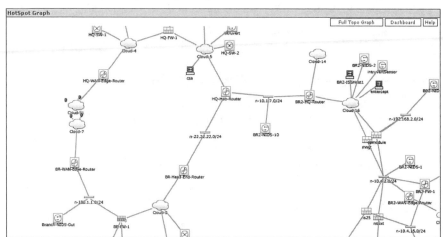

In Figure 7-6, you can see that one cloud has several dots surrounding it. On the CS-MARS interface, color is used to represent information about your network. In CS-MARS graphs, brown dots represent incidents where the attack is sourced in the topology, and red dots represent incidents where the destination of the attack is located in your network. To see the devices in that respective cloud, simply click the cloud. Devices that are deemed compromised and that are now attacking are removed from the cloud, placed in the topology diagram, and colored purple.

If the cloud represents an unknown area of the network that is logically separated by a unknown gateway device, dots might be placed around the cloud, but devices might not be shown in the cloud when you click it. Generally, if you have imported all your Layer 2 and Layer 3 devices, you won't have unknown sources; all devices will fall within your known topology.

As in other graphs, the same icons, colors, and tips and tricks apply.

Attack Diagram

The Attack diagram is a vectoring graph that is identical to the Incident Vector graph described earlier in this chapter. However, this graph includes all incidents with the Summary page and does not show the chronological flow of an attack.

Figure 7-7 is an example of an attack diagram.

Interpreting Events and NetFlow Graphs and False Positive Graphs

This section introduces you to a new type of graph, the Time vs. Rate graph. This graph displays data on an X,Y axis and uses colors to differentiate the type of data being displayed.

Figure 7-7   *CS-MARS Attack Diagram—Large Graph*

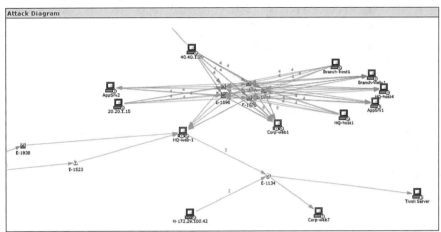

These graphs are located directly under the HotSpot and Attack diagrams on the Summary Dashboard. Four graphs are provided:

- **Events and NetFlow**—This graph displays the number of events and NetFlow records that CS-MARS received over a period of time. The default time is one day; you can change this by selecting the drop-down box provided at the top of the graph.

- **Events and Sessions**—This graph shows the delta between all received events and NetFlow records and the amount of data that has been sessionized together. This results in the graphical representation of the effective rate of data reduction.

    Figure 7-8 is an example of the graphs available on the Summary Dashboard.

Figure 7-8   *CS-MARS Events and NetFlow and Events and Sessions Graphs*

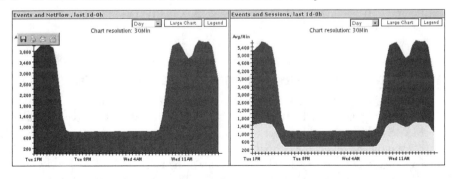

- **Activity: All Events and NetFlow—Top Destination Ports**—This graph displays the top destination ports on your network as recorded by all reporting devices over a one-day period. To view the number of events and NetFlow records associated for a particular destination port, click the **Legend** button in the top-right corner of the graph. Because this graph is also a "canned" report, you can view the actual report by clicking the **View Report** button at the top of the graph.

• **False Positive Events**—This graph displays the number of false positives the CS-MARS has generated with your data over a one-day period. This gives you a clear indication that CS-MARS is reducing your data and weeding out the false positives. By clicking the **Legend** button, you can see the number of false positives generated and which category they fall into.

Figure 7-9 displays both the All Events and NetFlow—Top Destination Ports graph and the False Positive Event Rate graph.

Figure 7-9   *CS-MARS All Events and NetFlow and False Positive Graphs*

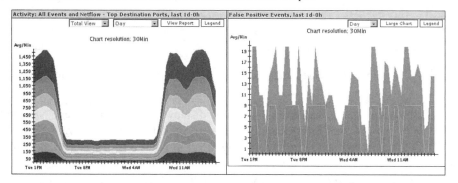

As an example, when you click the Legend button on a graph, an expanded list of data relevant to the colors and shape of the graph appear. Note the q icon after each value. By clicking this q, you can query the data it is next to, to start filtering information such as top sources, bandwidth, or raw data. Many other options for filtering are discussed later, in the "Simple Queries" section of this chapter.

Figure 7-10 displays the All Events and NetFlow—Top Destination graph, with the legend expanded.

Understanding Data on the Information Summary Column

The Information Summary column is located on the left side of the Summary Dashboard. Its primary purpose is to inform viewers how much data and what type of data the CS-MARS has been receiving over a 24-hour period. Therefore, the numbers are updated constantly and reflect the current value displayed at the latest refresh time and during the previous 24 hours. The exception to this rule is the False Positive counter and the to-do list. Figure 7-11 is an example of the Information Summary data presented on the Summary Dashboard.

Figure 7-10   *CS-MARS All Events and NetFlow—Top Destination Ports*

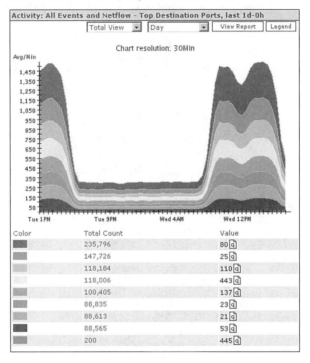

As you see in Figure 7-11, the Information Summary column displays the following data:

- Page refresh rate
- 24-hour events
- 24-hour incidents
- All false positives
- To-do list
- My Reports

Page refresh rate   This drop-down box enables the user to change the Summary page's rate of refreshing data. The default refresh period is 15 minutes. The refresh period can be changed to Never Update or to refresh to a maximum of every 30 minutes. This time period, if changed, is active only for your current viewing session. When a user ends a session, it is reset to the default.

24-hour events   This counter displays the number of NetFlows and events received over the past 24 hours. Through ContextCorrelation, sessionization of the data has occurred. The number of sessions created from this process is displayed and finalized with a percentage value that reflects the amount of data reduction that has occurred.

Figure 7-11 *CS-MARS Information Summary Column*

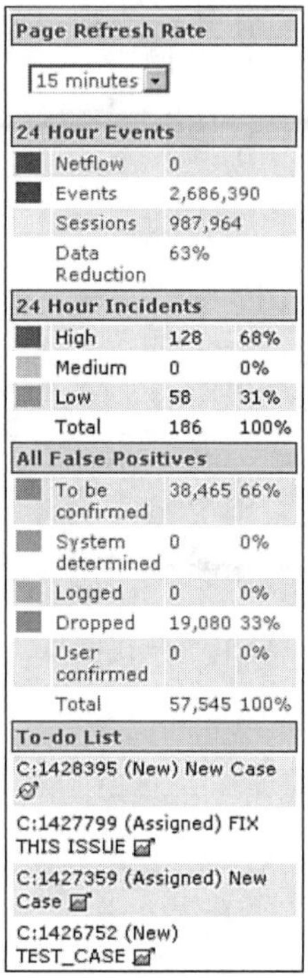

24-hour incidents   Keeping in mind that events and NetFlows received are sessionized together, the correlated session must meet a rule condition to be reported as an incident. This counter displays the number of incidents received over the past 24 hours and displays each incident severity as a percentage of the total incident data. The standard severity colors of Green=Low, Yellow=Medium, and Red=High are applied.

All false positives   Five types of false-positive indicators exist:

- To Be Confirmed
- System Determined
- Logged
- Dropped
- User Confirmed

The respective values and percentages for each of these categories are displayed along with their corresponding color indicator. This color is uniform throughout all graphs and reports in CS-MARS for each category.

To-do list   This list is based upon a user's login credentials and is specifically displayed for him or her. It displays any open cases assigned to the user or cases opened by the user that are not closed. Additionally, it provides the user with a quick link to the case details by clicking the displayed case ID.

My Reports   This section of the Information Summary column displays any reports that a user subscribed to view. It is user specific and provides a means of assigning specific reports to the My Reports tab for instant viewing of the report at its last runtime.

Interpreting the X, Y Axis Graphs

In the earlier section "Interpreting Events and NetFlow Graphs and False Positive Graphs," we discussed four X,Y axis graphs on the Summary Dashboard. Although these graphs appear on the Summary page, they can be found throughout the CS-MARS appliance in reports, queries, and the Network Status page.

At first glance, they appear to be easy to understand, but a few misinterpretations are common. To avoid this, a more in-depth explanation is necessary. Figure 7-12 uses the Activity: All Events and NetFlow—Top Destination Ports graph to aid you in reading the graph properly.

Figure 7-12   *CS-MARS X,Y Axis Graph Interpretation Model*

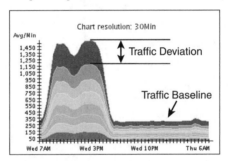

Reading the graph in Figure 7-12, it is easy to note that the average traffic flow, or baseline, is approximately 300 events per minute. However, in the graph, you see a huge spike in activity. That huge spike is where the misinterpretation occurs. Naturally, you think that because all colors increased along the X axis, there was a substantial increase in activity for all colors. This is not the case. Because the colors are layered on top of each other like lasagna noodles, if the bottom color bumps up, so do all the rest. What needs to be read is the *traffic deviation* between two colors. The increase in deviation represents the actual increase in traffic, not the corresponding value along the X axis.

One would think—and most agree—that reading the deviation using the numerical values along the X axis is problematic. The peak color could literally be off the chart. Keep in mind that your default view is a "total view." To see the peak rate, you can use the available drop-down box at the top of the graph and choose Peak View. In this view, you will see the top value for the color you are investigating. Use this number and subtract your baseline, and you will have the traffic deviation.

Using the Network Status Tab

The Network Status tab provides additional information in the form of six graphs that give a viewer a deeper look into the overall security health of the network.

Figure 7-13 displays a portion of the Network Status page.

Figure 7-13 *CS-MARS Network Status Page*

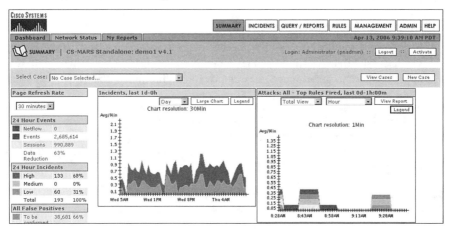

These six graphs all default to display one day's worth of data set from the last runtime of the report. Each graph can be modified to display a different amount of data:

- Specific query time
- Last runtime
- Hourly
- 1 day
- 1 week
- 1 month
- 1 quarter
- 1 year

To make this change to the frequency reported, use the drop-down box located at the top of the graph. Additionally, each graph gives you a "legend" explaining which data represents which colors and their respective values. These are the six graphs:

- Incidents
- Attacks: All—Top Rules Fired
- Activity: All—Top Event Types
- Activity: All—Top Reporting Devices

- Activity: All—Top Sources
- Activity: All—Top Destinations

Incidents   This graph displays the average number of incidents processed by CS-MARS per minute. The legend displays the All Time Total.

Attacks: All—Top Rules Fired   This graph displays the top rules that have been triggered on CS-MARS, as shown in Figure 7-14.

Figure 7-14 *CS-MARS Incidents and Top Rules Fired Graphs*

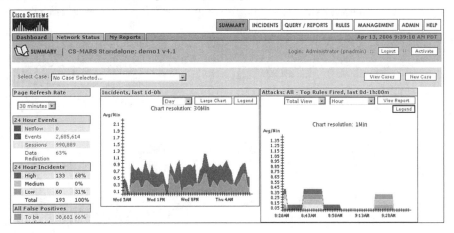

Activity: All—Top Event Types   This graph displays the top ten event types as reported by all reporting devices. The legend displays the total count for each of the top ten devices and their respective events.

Activity: All—Top Reporting Device   This graph displays the top ten reporting devices. The legend outlines the total count of events reported by each respective device.

Figure 7-15 shows sample graphs for Top Event Types and Top Reporting Devices.

Figure 7-15 *CS-MARS Top Event Types and Top Reporting Devices Graphs*

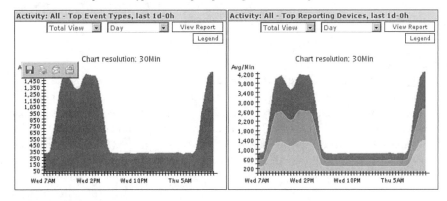

Activity: All—Top Sources This graph displays the top data transmitters, commonly referred to as top talkers, on the network, as seen through all reporting devices. This view selects the top N values for display by calculating the summed total of each value in the time range and picking those with the largest total.

Activity: All—Top Destinations This graph displays the top destinations of your network traffic, as seen through all reporting devices. This view selects the top N values for display by calculating the summed total of each value in the time range and picking those with the largest total.

Figure 7-16 shows examples of the Top Sources and Top Destination graphs.

Figure 7-16 *CS-MARS Top Sources and Top Destinations Graphs*

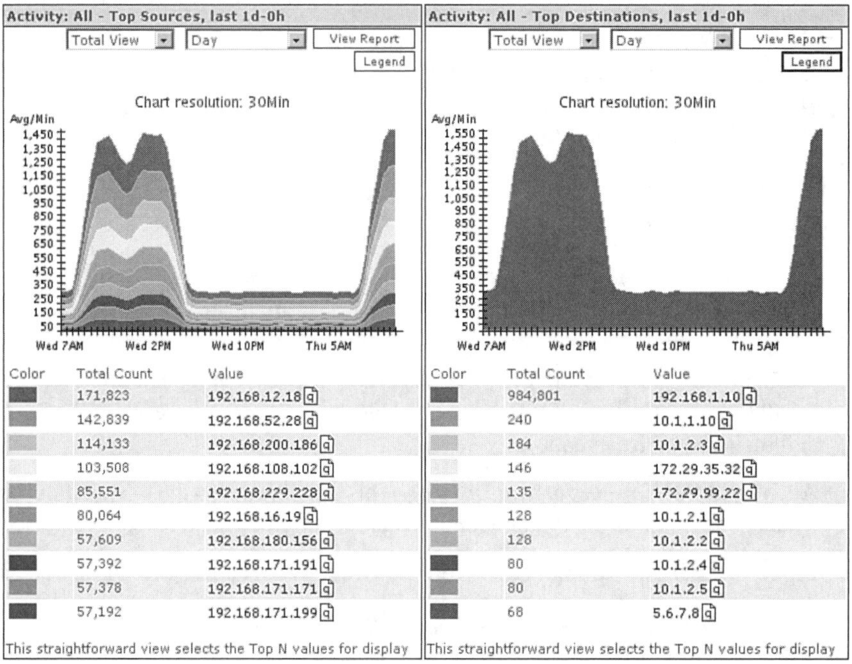

Using My Reports

My Reports is a tab located at the top-left of the Summary web page. This tab is the third one listed and offers users the capability to quickly access and read reports based upon the report's latest runtime. The selection of the reports for viewing is user specific and can be conducted on the Summary Dashboard's Information Summary column. When a user selects the Edit button, he or she is displayed a list of reports available to populate the My Reports tab. Click the reports you want to have and select the **Submit** button.

You now are redirected to the My Reports page, with your reports being displayed as in Figure 7-17.

Figure 7-17 *CS-MARS My Reports Page*

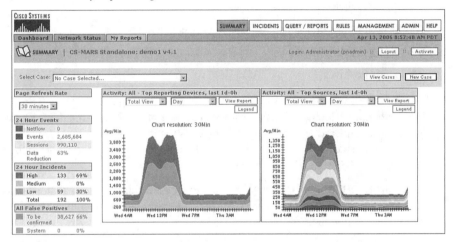

If you add a report that was just created or that has never been run, the report displayed could be blank. The report will be populated with data at its scheduled interval, or if you go to the Reports tab, select the report and run it.

Using the Incidents Page

As a security professional or an IT administrator using a SIM tool for the first time, you will be or will have been tasked with investigating incidents and conducting forensic analysis of your data. In conducting your analysis, you need to view false positives that the CS-MARS produced and be able to maintain a case history of your investigation. The Incidents page gives you the capabilities to conduct these activities and more. This section covers two tasks related to your investigations:

- Using the Incidents page
- Using the incident ID to view data

Using the Incidents Page

This section of the CS-MARS GUI is for incident analysis, false-positive analysis and acknowledgement, and case management. All three functions are based off incidents; therefore, you can investigate false-positive incidents, assign incidents a case ID and track its investigation, and investigate a reported incident and view its detailed forensic data.

You can access the Incidents page by clicking the second button in the upper-right corner of any page, labeled Incidents.

The Incidents page contains three tabs to access these functions:

- Incidents
- False Positives
- Cases

Incidents tab   The Incidents tab is a direct replica of the Recent Incidents section on the Summary Dashboard. The primary difference is that this page displays all incidents reported in the past 24 hours in increments of 25 incidents. This increment can be adjusted to as high as 10,000 incidents per page.

False Positives tab   This tab enables users to view the false positives that were created by CS-MARS or by user-defined drop rules and acknowledge the unconfirmed false-positive types by accepting them.

Cases tab   This tab grants access to the CS-MARS case-management tools. Although you can gain access to a specific case throughout many areas in the CS-MARS GUI, this particular tab leads to the management area for all cases.

Figure 7-18 displays the Incidents page and its corresponding tabs.

Figure 7-18   *CS-MARS Incidents Page*

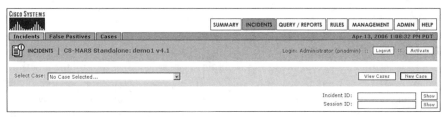

Incidents Tab

The Incidents tab is the first section you view after clicking the Incidents button. As mentioned previously, it is an exact replica of the Summary Dashboard's Recent Incidents section. You will note that Cisco decided to label this page as Recent Incidents as well; however, on this tab, *recent* means "over the past 24 hours."

In investigating incidents, you can filter your views to reduce the number of incidents shown on the page by using one or the entire group of drop-down boxes available just above the incident listings, as shown in Figure 7-19.

Figure 7-19 *CS-MARS Incidents Page Viewing Filters*

Filtering your views greatly reduces the data you are interested in seeing; however, if you are not searching for anything specific, you might just want to leave the filters off and scroll through the data manually.

By default, each page displays the most recent 25 incidents according to your filters. You can step through all 24 hours of incidents 25 at a time, or you can adjust your view for up to 10,000 per page. Additionally, you are given an option to jump to a certain number of incidents in increments according to what you set for your page view.

Figure 7-20 *CS-MARS Incidents Page Viewing Filters*

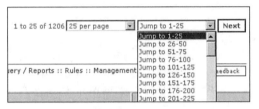

Drilling down into the Incidents details is covered in the section "Using the Incident ID to View Data."

False Positives Tab

CS-MARS determines false positives many different ways. The different types of false positives and how they are determined are discussed in Chapter 4, "CS-MARS Technologies and Theory" (see the section "Positive Alert Verification and Dynamic Vulnerability Scanning"). This section introduces you to the contents of the False Positive tab and shows you how to acknowledge unconfirmed false-positive types and turn them into user-confirmed false-positive types.

Acknowledgment is the process of validating the CS-MARS false-positive assessment of your data. It is possible, but not common, that the CS-MARS will produce a false negative—that is, incorrectly determine a false positive. This can occur if you have overlapping subnets in your network, duplicate IP addresses in your network, or improperly configured IDS/IDP sensors in your network. Nine times out of ten, this occurrence happens when something in your network is not configured properly or is not operating correctly. To date, there are no known Cisco TAC cases in which CS-MARS incorrectly identified a system-determined false positive.

When a user first opens the False Positive tab, he or she is presented with the "Unconfirmed False Positive Type" information.

In explaining the contents of the False Positive tab, Figure 7-21 is used. Note the arrows within the figure.

Figure 7-21 *CS-MARS False Positive Page with Filter Display*

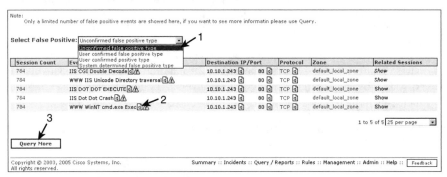

Four different views of false positives exist. In Figure 7-21, you can see the Select False Positive drop-down box, as indicated by the arrow labeled 1. This drop-down box enables you to select the type of false positives you want to view. As a basic review, these are the four types of false positive views:

- Unconfirmed false positives
- User-confirmed false positives
- User-confirmed false-positive type
- System-determined false-positive type

To acknowledge an unconfirmed false positive and turn it into a user-confirmed false positive, you must confirm the individual event. To do this, note the arrow labeled 2 in Figure 7-21. The arrow points to a triangle with a ? inside it. On the interface, yellow triangles are medium-level alerts, and the question mark denotes that the false positive event is unconfirmed. The same would be true for low-level alerts (green circles) and high-level alerts (red boxes).

When you click the yellow triangle, a new window appears. This new window provides a viewer with the reasons the event was categorized as a false positive and asks the user if this determination is correct. Figure 7-22 displays this window.

In the new window, if you select Yes and then Next to confirm the false positive, you are walked through the false-positive tuning wizard, which creates a drop rule. Simply answer the questions to create the Drop Rule.

If you select No and then Next, you are asked to confirm your decision; the event with its parameters will no longer be marked as a false positive then.

Figure 7-22 *CS-MARS Unconfirmed False Positive Acknowledgment Page*

Referring back to Figure 7-21, the arrow labeled 3 points to a button marked Query More. Only a limited number of false positive events are shown per page; if you want to see more false positives in the respective category, click the button.

Cases Tab

The ability to make case notes, assign tasks, and notify users of an action or memo allows for collaboration among CS-MARS users. The Cases tab is the third tab on the Incidents page. This page allows users to add, view, or manage cases already created. Figure 7-23 displays the Case page. Note the arrow within the figure.

Figure 7-23 *CS-MARS Case Page*

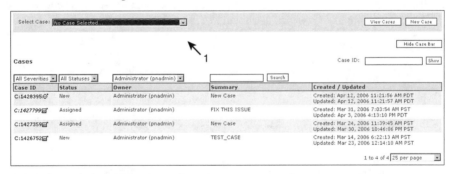

In Figure 7-23, you can see that the usual display filters are available. As in other pages, these filters help you sort out which case types you want to view.

The arrow labeled 1 points to the Case bar. The Case bar is found on every page on CS-MARS, with the exception of graphs. To hide this bar from view, click the **Hide Case Bar** button.

To select a case to view, click the **Select Case** drop-down menu on the Case bar and select the case you want to view/edit/update or, while on the Case page, click the **Case ID**.

To open a new case, click the **New Case** button; a new window opens to the Add a New Case wizard, as shown in Figure 7-24.

Figure 7-24 *CS-MARS Add a New Case Wizard*

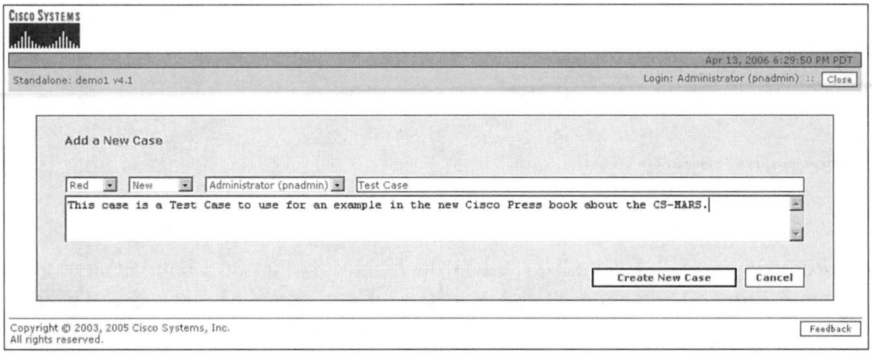

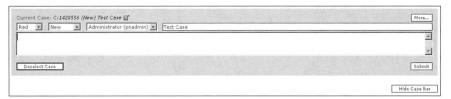

The Add a New Case wizard is rather straightforward. When you finish filling in the details, click the **Create a New Case** button; you return to the originating page.

Now that a case has been created, you are considered in case mode, and the Case bar changes to reflect the newly created case. To add incidents to this case, browse to an incident from any page that displays incidents; you will see two new buttons, Add This Incident and More, in the Case bar. Click the **Add This Incident** button to append your case with the applicable incident data.

To add new data to your open case in case mode, or to exit case mode entirely, click the **More** button on the Case bar, as shown in Figure 7-25.

Figure 7-25 *CS-MARS Case Bar—Current Case Edit Tool*

From this Current Case edit tool, you can add or modify data to your case. After you have made the applicable additions or changes, simply click the **Submit** button to apply them. To exit case mode, click the **Deselect Case** button; your Case bar returns to its original state.

To view a case's history from the Case page, click the case ID of your choice; the entire history, with appended data, is displayed. Figure 7-26 is an example of the Case History page.

As you can see in Figure 7-26, every change or addition has been recorded and tied to a user account. From this screen, you can make more changes or modify the record by clicking the Select/Edit This Case button. Note that when you select this button, the Case bar changes back into case mode.

Figure 7-26   *CS-MARS Case History Page*

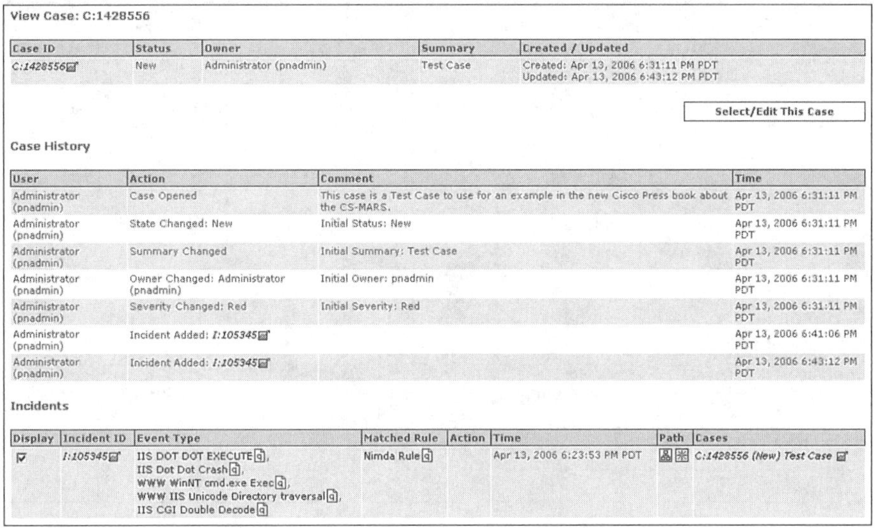

Using the Incident ID to View Data

When beginning your initial investigation into an incident, the questions come to mind of what made this occur and what it is. In the incident summary, you see the event type and the matched rule. To begin understanding the data that caused this incident to occur, you can simply click the incident ID, regardless of where that incident ID is posted. Most commonly, you will find this on the Summary Dashboard or the Incidents page; however, you will see incident IDs posted in popup windows, graphs, and cases. When you click an incident ID, you are redirected to the Incidents page, and the data shown in Figure 7-27 appears.

As you can see in Figure 7-27, the first piece of information you are presented with is the rule that was triggered to create the incident. This rule answers the question "What made this happen?" and gives the details of why the incident was triggered. Ultimately, it helps you understand the conditions that were met to create the incident. Some rules on CS-MARS are simple; others are rather complicated behavioral rules. In this example, the rule is somewhat complex. This should indicate to the user that many conditions from different reporting sources must have been met to create this rule. Thus, its legitimacy is firmer.

Just below the rule description, you will find the normalized and summarized event data, respectively, for the incident ID selected. This portion of the data presented begins to answer the question "What made this incident happen?"

In this example, a single reporting source was used; however, in many cases, you could be presented with several pages of information. Figure 7-28 displays a more complex return of data.

Figure 7-27 *CS-MARS Case History Page*

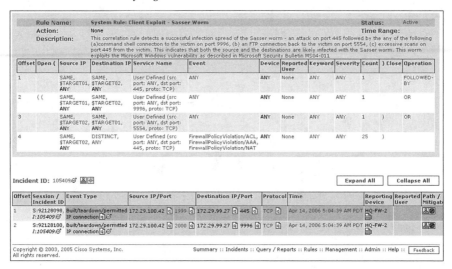

Figure 7-28 *CS-MARS Incident Investigation—Detailed Data Example*

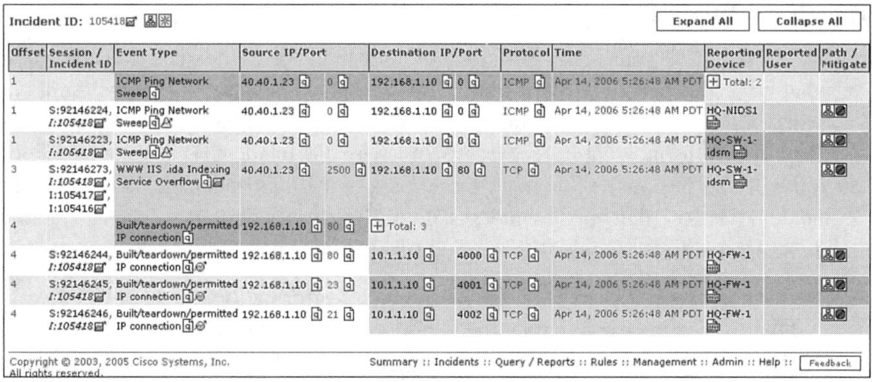

The data presented in Figure 7-28 is from three different reporting sources. You will also note that it contains much more summarized event data, with many different sessions making up a single incident ID. This is the power of sessionization, which greatly reduces the amount of data you are presented with.

Figure 7-28 is referenced for the remainder of this discussion.

CS-MARS presents normalized data during the initial incident investigation, to maintain consistency and ease in viewing data from different reporting devices. Each raw log entry is parsed and presented in an incident ID in 11 informative fields. Table 7-1 explains the 11 fields.

Table 7-1   *CS-MARS Incident ID Normalized Fields*

Field/Column Name	Description	Action
Offset	The data that matched the rule offset sequentially	None
Incident/Session ID	The unique ID CS-MARS assigned to the data	Click the ID
Event Type	Name of reported event	Click the event name for a detailed description of the event and affected platforms
Source IP/Port	Source IP and port of the event as reported by the reporting device	Click the IP or port to view detailed device/port data
Destination IP/Port	Destination IP and port of the event as reported by the reporting device	Click the IP or port to view detailed device/port data
Protocol	Type of protocol used by the event	None
Time	Time the incident or session was created	None
Reporting Device	Name of the reporting device	Click the device name to view device-configuration data
Reported User	Name of the user as reported by the reporting device	Click the name
Path/Mitigate	Opens a new window to view the path of the event and conduct mitigation	Click an icon
False Positive	Link to a false-positive tuning wizard for the event	Click the false positive

NOTE   In Figure 7-28, the False Positive column has been truncated.

NOTE   If a field is blank or contains all zeroes, the raw message field reported to CS-MARS either was blank or contained a zero value.

While viewing Figure 7-28, you might have noticed that some fields contain a q icon after its value. This q is a clickable icon, which creates an instant query using its respective value as a filter.

In the Reporting Device column, another icon appears. This icon is a small piece of paper with 1s and 0s. Clicking this icon brings up a new window displaying the "raw data" as delivered from the reporting source(s) and each event's unique event ID. Figure 7-29 is an example of this data.

Figure 7-29 *CS-MARS Raw Data Window*

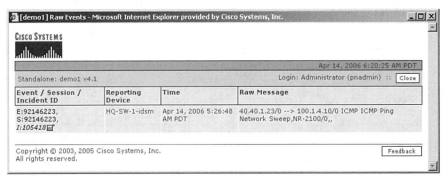

Because CS-MARS is a fully interactive device, you can view or filter any value by clicking it. You will discover that you can get to just about any section or poll any piece of information from just about any location in the GUI. While browsing through the CS-MARS GUI, take a clicking tour and walk through all the links. This is the best way to become familiar with what CS-MARS has to offer.

Simple Queries

Querying data on CS-MARS can be as simple as selecting a predefined query and submitting it, or as complex as defining behavioral variables or actions to solicit data from many sources. In this section, you are introduced to simple querying, manipulating the view of data, and being selective in what type of information you want polled.

While conducting queries on CS-MARS, it is beneficial to keep two questions in mind as they are your goals in searching for data. First, ask yourself, "How do I want to see the data?" Second, ask yourself, "What data do I want to see?" These two questions will lead you to edit the query type and populate the available filters to be more selective in the data returned from the query.

Three types of queries exist for CS-MARS, and two of the three might require changing the way you want to view the data being queried. This section prepares you to perform simple queries on CS-MARS by discussing the following topics:

- Query type
- Instant queries
- On-demand queries and manual queries

Setting the Query Type

You know that question "How do I want to see the data?" This is answered by setting the query type. At first glance, it appears that we are putting the cart before the horse by asking this first, but we are simply setting the stage for how the data we requested will be displayed over a specific timeframe.

To access the Query Type configuration tool, click the **Edit** button at the end of the Query Type field on the Query page. Figure 7-30 displays the Query Type configuration tool and the Query Type field.

Figure 7-30 *CS-MARS Query Type Configuration Tool and Query Type Field*

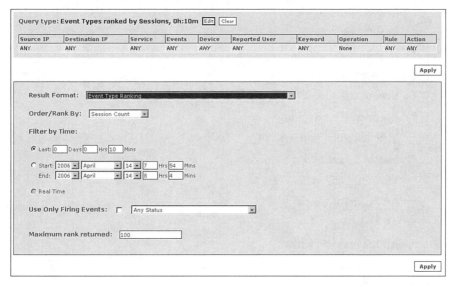

The Query Type configuration tool has five attributes that must be configured to get your expected results.

- Result Format
- Order/Rank By
- Filter by Time
- Use Only Firing Events
- Maximum Rank Returned

Result Format   This drop-down box presents the data in the format you choose. You can select the following presentation formats:

- Event Type Ranking
- Event Type Group Ranking

- Network Group Ranking
- Network Ranking
- Source Network Group Ranking
- Source Network Ranking
- Source IP Address Ranking
- Destination Network Group Ranking
- Destination Network Ranking
- Destination IP Address Ranking
- Source Port Ranking
- Destination Port Ranking
- Protocol Ranking
- Reporting Device Ranking
- Reported Device Type Ranking
- Reported User Ranking
- Matched Rule Ranking
- Matched Rule Group Ranking
- Matched Incident Ranking
- All Matching Sessions
- All Matching Sessions Custom Col.
- All Matching Events
- All Matching Events—Raw Messages
- NAT Connection Report
- MAC Address Report
- Unknown Event Report
- Blank

Order/Rank By   This selection gives you two options to sort your results by, Session Count and Bytes Transmitted. Depending on your choice of result format, Bytes Transmitted might not be available.

Filter by Time   This selection is where you tell CS-MARS what periods of time to do the query on. There are three ways to select times:

- Last number of days, hours, and minutes
- Start and end times, in military format (24:00:00)
- Real time

Use Only Firing Events   When selected, this option shows events that caused an event to be categorized as one of the following:

- Nonevaluated
- Any false positive
- Unconfirmed false positive
- Any confirmed false-positive firing events
- System-confirmed false positives
- User-confirmed false positives
- Any confirmed positive firing events
- System-confirmed positives
- User-confirmed positives

Maximum Rank Returned   This field enables a user to tell CS-MARS to return only a certain number of events. The maximum number of events CS-MARS can return in one query is 1,000. So if the number of events exceeds 1,000 in the time period you indicated, another query must be made to get the rest of the data. Cisco recognizes that 1,000 events is a low number; in CS-MARS v4.1.5, the number has been increased to 5,000.

When you have completed populating the data within the Query Type configuration tool, simply click either of the **Apply** buttons located just above or below the right side of the Query tool. The screen now should look like something like Figure 7-31.

Figure 7-31 *CS-MARS Query Type—Manually Changed*

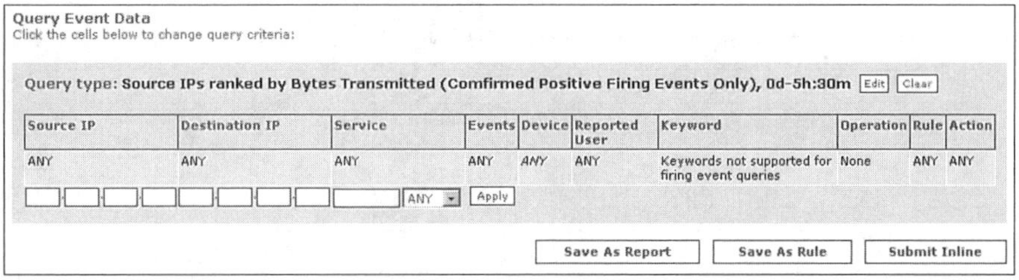

Now you are prepared to either submit your query or define additional filters to further classify the data you want to see.

Instant Queries

Remember all those little q icons after specific values displayed in CS-MARS? This powerful little icon is called an instant query. At any moment when you are viewing data, you can click this icon and query data relevant to the value the icon is next to. Figure 7-32 displays several examples of this icon as it appears on the Summary Dashboard; reference the arrow in the figure.

Figure 7-32 *CS-MARS Instant Query Icon*

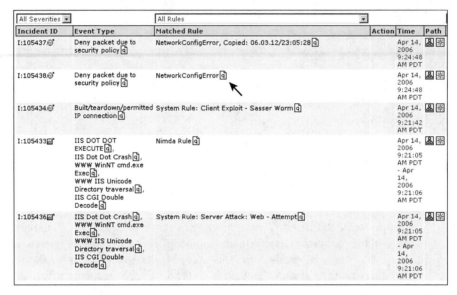

Clicking this q icon redirects you to the Query page, with the value of the q in the appropriate filter, as shown in Figure 7-33.

Figure 7-33 *CS-MARS Query Page—Populated Filter*

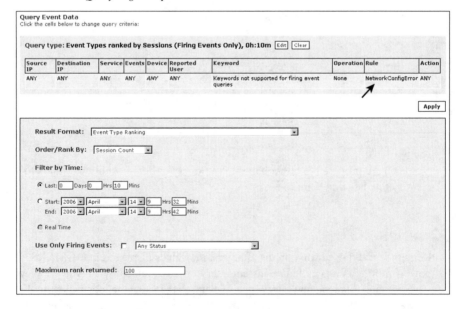

Next, you need to populate the Query Type configuration tool, apply your changes, add filters if you desire, and then submit your query.

This process is applicable across the entire CS-MARS GUI and occurs wherever you click the q icon.

NOTE   It is important to point out that if you select a q icon within the returned data from another query, your new selection will be added as another filter to the existing query.

On-Demand Queries and Manual Queries

By now, you have seen some rather sophisticated capabilities of CS-MARS and can ascertain that it is a powerful SIM. However, CS-MARS can be a quick and simple querying tool as well, with the identical functionality of an *Enterprise Class Log Aggregator*. At first glance at the Query page, it might be confusing how to query data, but just like any new product, after you do it a few times, it becomes natural. Two subjects are discussed to tune your CS-MARS querying skills.

- On-demand queries
- Manual queries

On-Demand Queries

On-demand queries are queries based on all reports that have been saved by security analysts and administrators or that were provided "canned" with the appliance. You can select on-demand queries by using the Load Report as On-Demand Query with Filter drop-down menu, located on the Query page just beneath the Case bar on the left side. Figure 7-34 displays the On-Demand query menu. Appendix D, "Command-Line Interface," defines many of the CS-MARS queries.

To view details about the available reports that can be used as an on-demand query, simply click the **Report** tab and view the list of reports.

To load the on-demand query into the Query tool, just select the query you want to use from the drop-down menu. The page automatically refreshes with the attributes necessary to run the selected query.

With the new attributes loaded into the query tool, you now have two options: submit the query or add filters. Figure 7-35 is an example of an on-demand query loaded into the Query tool.

Figure 7-34 *CS-MARS Query Page—On-Demand Query Menu*

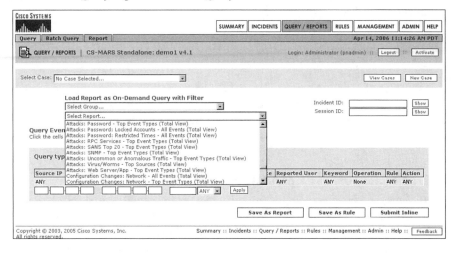

Figure 7-35 *CS-MARS On-Demand Query—Web Usage: Top Destinations by Bytes*

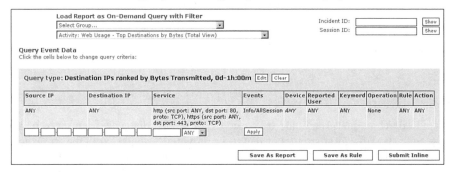

Manual Queries

Manual queries are queries initially done from scratch. Manual queries can be saved as reports so that they can be used again in the future to avoid duplicate efforts. These are some examples of manual queries that can be created:

- Real-time firewall or router logs
- IDS alarms from the DMZ sensor between 6 a.m. and 6 p.m. over the past 12 days
- Top ports used by host 192.168.1.*x* (or any IP address combination) over the past month
- Top talkers in bandwidth to the web server today
- Top destination IP address from the proxy server over the past hour
- Top sources of malware or spyware alarms within the last 12 hours

Performing a manual query involves three steps:

Step 1   Set the query type.

Step 2   Add filters, if necessary.

Step 3   Submit the query.

You were introduced to Step 1 in detail earlier, in the section "Setting the Query Type," and Step 3 is rather self-explanatory. Step 2, however, requires more explanation.

When adding filters to a query, you set them by populating the cells contained in the Query tool. Figure 7-36 displays the Query tool and its filter cells.

Figure 7-36   *CS-MARS Query Tool—Filter Cells*

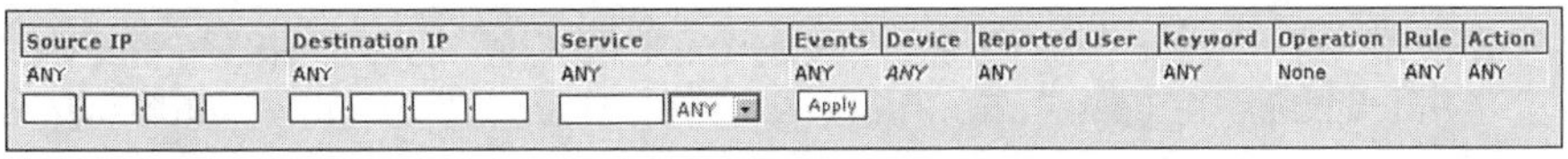

Source IP	Destination IP	Service	Events	Device	Reported User	Keyword	Operation	Rule	Action
ANY	ANY	ANY	ANY	*ANY*	ANY	ANY	None	ANY	ANY

In Figure 7-36, you can see that ten filters can be applied to a query. Each filter has a cell that is populated with the term Any, which is considered a wildcard value. To modify the filter from the wildcard, click the word **Any**; a new tool appears below the Query tool, enabling you to add data to the cell. The first three filters have additional population fields so that you can add data to these cells manually.

All cells use a similar tool to populate their respective fields, with the exceptions of the Keyword and Operation cells. Figure 7-37 displays this tool for the Reporting device filter. Note the arrows on the figure.

Figure 7-37   *CS-MARS Reporting Device—Cell-Population Tool*

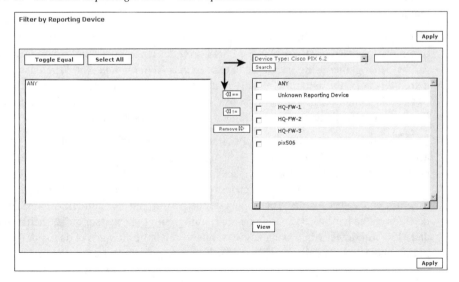

This new GUI has three common features that you should be familiar with. They each contain two information fields, a drop-down menu, and three selection buttons.

The two fields are for populating data into the cell. The field on the right provides the data for selection; the field on the left holds the data you have selected. With the default selection being any device, the word Any automatically appears in the selection field on the left.

The drop-down menu, highlighted by the top-right arrow in Figure 7-37, enables a user to select individual items, targets, devices, groups, or each. As you choose the applicable category in the drop-down box, the window on the right becomes populated with all the devices available for selection in that category.

When the right-side box is populated, you can select the devices you want to add to the cell by clicking the check box next to the desired item. You can check as many as you like.

Adding your checked selections to the left-side box is as easy as clicking the <<== button highlighted by the center arrow in Figure 7-37. The two remaining buttons beneath the <<== button are <!== and the Remove >> button.

The <!== button is an exception button. It becomes useful when adding groups of devices to the cell but excluding a few from the group. It saves time because you do not have to select many individual devices to add to the cell; you just select the entire group and then exclude one or a few that are part of that group.

The Remove >> button is for removing selected devices in the left window. To remove a device, just click the device in the left box and click the Remove >> button. It is important to note that it is not necessary to remove the Any selection in left box, because CS-MARS ignores it if any other selections follow it.

The Keyword and Operation filters are much different than all the other filters and, therefore, require further explanation.

The keyword filter enables a user to query the contents of raw messages using ASCII text or regular expressions (RegEx). CS-MARS provides ten keyword fields per query, which can be tied together using the Boolean expressions And, Or, and Not. When using ASCII text in this field, the data must exactly match the contents of the raw message. If using RegEx, the contents of the field must use RegEx guidelines. A great online tutorial for RegEx can be found at http://www.regular-expressions.info/tutorial.html.

Using the Keyword field can be a CPU-intensive process; it must search all raw data according to your search criteria. It is recommended that you use additional filters with the keyword filter, such as "reporting device" and/or "events" when searching. This restricts your search criteria and takes up much less processing power, thus reducing the time it takes to return your query results. The impact on the performance of your CS-MARS appliance depends on the hardware version you are running. Single-processor units, such as the M20 and M50, run slower when using keyword queries on large amounts of data. For the M100e, M100, and M200 models, which are dual Xeon processor appliances, the performance impact is negligible.

The Operation field enables a user to conduct multilined queries using the Boolean expressions And, Or, and/or Followed-By. When using this selection in a query, you can begin to look for the behavior of data on your network by querying data that might have relationships based upon your input. When you select one of the Boolean expressions available for this field, a new query line appears beneath the one you just populated.

Now that you understand the basics behind adding filters to your query, you should become familiar with each filter and what its purpose is.

These ten cells enable you to enter filter data:

- Source IP
- Destination IP
- Service
- Events
- Device
- Reported User
- Keyword
- Operation
- Rule
- Action

Source IP   When this filter is used, the query returns only data that has been reported to CS-MARS with this IP address as the source IP.

Destination IP   When this filter is used, the query returns only data that has been reported to CS-MARS with this IP address as the destination IP.

Service   When this filter is used, the query returns only data that has been reported to CS-MARS for the selected source and/or destination ports and protocol type. To view all the service types available in CS-MARS, using the GUI, browse to **Management > Service Management** and search for the Service type you want become familiar with.

Events   When this filter is used, the query returns only data that has been reported to CS-MARS for the selected event type. Event types are not necessarily associated with a specific reporting device and can even be behaviorally based. To view all the event types available in CS-MARS, using the GUI, browse to **Management > Event Management** and search for the event type you want become familiar with.

Device   When this filter is used, the query returns only data that has been reported to CS-MARS for the selected device(s). It ignores data from all others for this query.

Reported User   When this filter is used, the query returns only data that has been reported to CS-MARS for the selected users. It ignores data for all other reported users for this query.

Keyword When this filter is used, the query returns only data that contains the exact text entered. This text can be located anywhere within the reported message. Additionally, this filter enables you to use regular expressions to define the filter text and provides the use of Boolean expression to tie multiple text strings together.

Operation When this filter is used, the CS-MARS will conduct a single query based upon multiple query types tied together by a Boolean expression (And, Or, Followed-By).

Rule When this filter is used, the query will only return data that has been a component of a rule with CS-MARS.

Action When this filter is used, the query returns only data that has been marked with an action within CS-MARS. An example of this would be if CS-MARS forwarded a SNMP message to your HP Open View console when an incident was created. The incident would be tagged with SNMP as an action.

When populating the query with multiple filters, keep in mind that each filter is connected with the AND operation. For example, if you want to write a query for all IDS/IPS logs over the past 3 hours from IPS Senor BR-SW-1-idsm, where the sources of the IDS alarms are from the host 10.1.5.2, the query would look like Figure 7-38.

Figure 7-38 *CS-MARS—Manual Query*

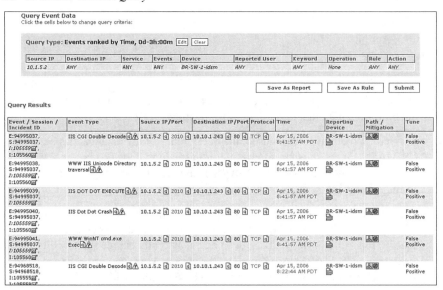

In this example the query type was All Matching Events over the past three hours. The filters used were source IP *and* device.

Summary

This chapter covered the basic operation of the CS-MARS appliance. It provided you with an understanding of how to read and interpret data, how to query to find specific information, and how to generate reports.

Understanding these tasks is valuable because doing so gives you the tools necessary to use CS-MARS data for attack investigation and attack response. The capability to gather and analyze forensic data is important; therefore, the fact that CS-MARS presents it in a way that is easy to understand puts you in a position where you can easily and quickly do incident response and stop attacks before they spread.

Now that you understand the basic operation of the CS-MARS appliance, you are ready to investigate more advanced reporting options and features, which are discussed in Chapter 8, "Advanced Operation and Security Analysis."

In this chapter, you learn about topics that are considered advanced operations:

- Creating Reports
- Creating Rules

## CHAPTER 8

Advanced Operation and Security Analysis

This chapter discusses in detail the two most advanced operations of CS-MARS: reporting and rules.

Reporting is considered an advanced operation because it is one of the more complex features available in CS-MARS. The complexity of reporting stems from the different view types, run times, report formats, and query variables of the data you want to report. You will become familiar with using the different methods in CS-MARS to create reports: using queries and creating custom reports manually. This chapter introduces you to the different types of reports and how they are sent to their recipients.

Rule creation is by far the most complex function of CS-MARS. Rules can change the behavior of CS-MARS and alter the way it processes incidents. To create a rule, one must know how querying works and how events behave; therefore, it is an advanced operation and thus the last operational subject to be covered.

Creating Reports

Using CS-MARS provides valuable insight, integration, and control of your network through correlation of data, reduction of false positives, mitigation, and visual Layer 2 and Layer 3 depiction of your network. Using this information for investigative and mitigative reasons is valuable, but it lacks substance when you do not have a means of reporting that data from many different perspectives. High-level management wants to see basic reports that are easy to read and to the point; first line managers want to see data and actions with more depth, but not actual raw data. Security analysts look for detailed raw and normalized data, in addition to topological graphs to understand what is happening and what to do about it. CS-MARS gives an organization these levels of reporting so that information can be disseminated and useful to multiple sources.

All too often, SIMs have a special feature that requires in-depth knowledge of how to create reports. In CS-MARS reporting, querying, and using rules are almost identical in design, with just different purposes and outcomes. Therefore, if you can write a query, you can write a report. By discussing the following topics, this section introduces you to report writing and the many ways to do it:

- Report formats
- Predefined reports

- Custom reports
- Methods of report delivery

Report Formats

In Chapter 7, "CS-MARS Basic Operation," you discovered that there are 26 different ways to view data by adjusting the result format on a query. Reports still use these result formats; however, in reporting, the result format can be altered by the viewing method of the report and the time range selected. Reports are formatted according to three criteria:

- Query result format and filters
- Time range of report
- View type

Query result format and filters   Using this variable for a report is exactly the same as setting up a query, as discussed in Chapter 7. In a report, this data is presented under the Query column in the report-building tool.

Time range of report   This variable (value) represents the starting and stopping points of the data that you want the report to provide. In a report, the time range is presented under the Time Range column in the report-building tool.

View type   This variable outlines the presentation format of the report. In a report, this data is presented under the Format column in the report-building tool.

Most reports contain a variable called Top N. This is simply the Top (N)umber of devices displayed in ranking for the selected report. Table 8-1 describes the four methods that you can use to view reports.

Table 3-1   *CS-MARS Report Format Types*

View Type	Description
Total view	This view selects the Top N values for display by calculating the summed total of each value in the time range and picking those with the largest total.
Peak view	This view selects the Top N values for display by examining the rate for each value in the selected time range and picking those with the highest peaks. Temporary spikes in traffic are more likely to be prominent this way than with the Total view.
Recent view	This view selects the Top N values from the past hour and displays them over the selected time range. A Recent view shows the current state and can highlight ongoing anomalous behavior. If a spike happened within the past hour, it appears in the Recent view, but the Recent view can also show more fundamental changes in the shape of the network traffic.
CSV	This view displays the summed total of the Top N results as a comma-separated values (CSV) file that can be used by other external reporting tools.

As with making a query, CS-MARS provides a tool to aid you in building reports. This topic is discussed in detail in the "Creating Custom Reports" section of this chapter.

Understanding the different report format types is essential before you write a report, which is why this topic is discussed first. Chapter 7 includes two questions about querying, one of which is, "How do I want to see the data?" This holds true for report writing as well.

Using Predefined Reports

Predefined reports are commonly called canned reports. CS-MARS contains 175 predefined reports in Release 4.1.4. This number increases with just about every new release of CS-MARS code. Cisco provides these reports, which were created from Cisco customer feedback, to every CS-MARS user.

Because there are 175 predefined reports, CS-MARS categorizes them into groups for easy access and management. Some default groups exist, and, of course, you can create your own groups. Note that while you are reviewing the different groups, some reports might appear in multiple groups. Some of these groups were created to identify which predefined reports conform to specific pieces of legislation or certain audit requirements. Cisco has promised to further expand these groups to cover other forms of legislation, such as the Gramm-Leach Bliley Act (GLBA), the Health Insurance Portability and Accountability Act (HIPAA), and the Payment Card Industry Standards (PCI). Currently, the groups focus on Control Objectives for Information and Related Technology (COBIT) and the Sarbanes-Oxley Act (SOX), among a few others. Most important, though, these forms of legislation mean different things to different organizations. CS-MARS currently supports reporting for all these; they just might not be part of a specific group. A predefined report can be easily modified to meet your specific requirements.

To view the available predefined reports, navigate to **Query/Reports > Report**. Here you will find a Grouping tool, which is the means of managing all reports. Figure 8-1 shows the CS-MARS Report page.

Figure 8-1   *CS-MARS Report Page*

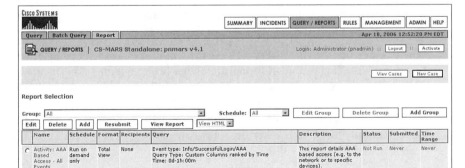

You can view predefined reports in two ways:

- Using the Report tab
- Loading reports as on-demand queries

Using the Report Tab

You use three easy steps to load the report and view it using the Report page shown in Figure 8-1.

When you first view the Report page, it lists reports in multiples of 25 by default. You can adjust this to view all the reports by using the drop-down menu at the bottom left of the viewing page; by clicking the **Next** button, you can page through the reports at a set interval, as shown in Figure 8-2.

Figure 8-2   *CS-MARS Report Page—Report View Adjustment*

To load and view a predefined report using the Report tab, follow these three steps:

Step 1   Select the radio button next to the report you want to view.

Step 2   Using the drop-down box at the top or bottom center of the page, choose either of these:

— View HTML

— View CSV

Step 3   Click the **View Report** button, located just left of the drop-down box.

When you have completed these steps, your report is presented to you in your web browser based upon your selected input, as shown in Figure 8-3.

Using this method is static. That is, you use the report as it is exactly defined, with the exception of changing the report format after it has been submitted. This method is simple and fast if the report meets all your requirements or if it is one you custom-defined to meet your needs. However, what if you want to change any of the query fields of the report or the result format? To do this, you need to return to the Query page and use the **Load Report as On-Demand Query with Filter** drop-down menu.

Figure 8-3 *CS-MARS Report—HTML View—Activity: All—Top Destinations*

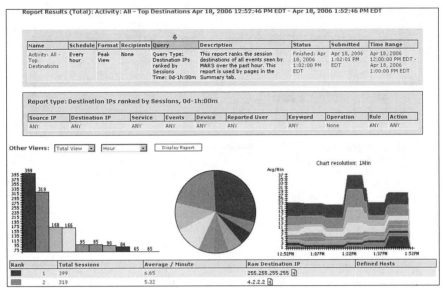

Loading Reports as an On-Demand Query

This process is rather straightforward. Simply navigate to the **Query/Reports > Query** page.

When you are first presented with this page you will notice two drop-down boxes in the upper-left corner beneath the label Load Report as On-Demand Query with Filter. The first box is for selecting a group, if you so desire. The second box contains all the reports that fall under the selected group in the first box. The default group is All, and all 175 reports in CS-MARS v4.1.4 are available for selection. Figure 8-4 shows an example of an on-demand query to show statistics for top web destinations.

When you select the report you want to view, it is automatically loaded into the Query tool.

You now have two options:

- Submit the query to view the data
- Modify the query to add filters to get your desired results

Figure 8-4 *CS-MARS On-Demand Query—Activity: Web Usage—Top Destinations*

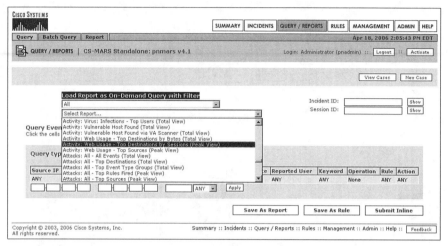

If the second option is your choice, you use the required skills that you learned in Chapter 7 to add criteria or filters. Refer back to Chapter 7 for making the additional changes you want.

When you have made your changes, or if you selected the first option, your returned results should look similar to Figure 8-5.

Figure 8-5 *CS-MARS On-Demand Query Results*

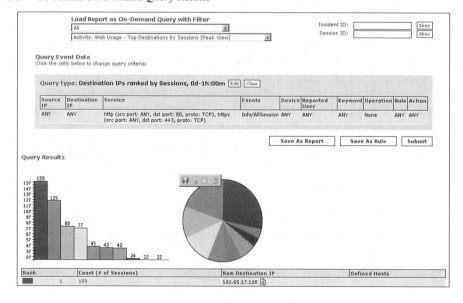

Creating Custom Reports

CS-MARS offers the capability to create reports from scratch using the Report Creation tool. Most CS-MARS customers have provided feedback that they prefer to use the Query tool to create and save a report; however, the only advantage in doing so is that you can actually see the results of a report/query before configuring the other aspects of the report. For the purposes of this section, the method using the Add button on the Reports tab is discussed. The Save as Report button on the Query page takes you to the same Report Creation tool with the query column already populated.

To create a custom report, complete the following steps:

Step 1   Browse to **Query/Reports > Report**.

Step 2   Click the **Add** button. The Report Creation tool appears, as shown in Figure 8-6.

Figure 8-6   *Naming and Describing the Report*

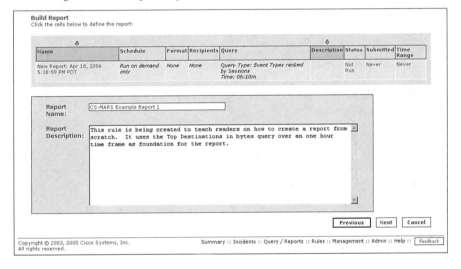

Step 3   Assign a name and description to the report and then click **Next**.

Step 4   Assign the scheduled runtime for the report and the report format, as shown in Figure 8-7. When done, click **Next**.

Figure 8-7 *Scheduling and Formatting the Report*

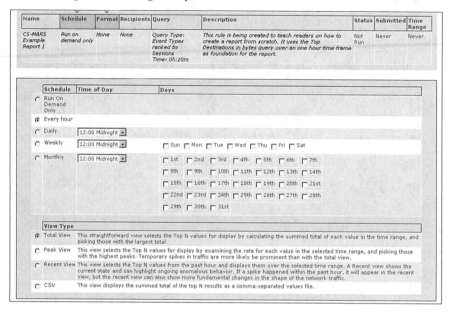

Step 5 Add the recipients of the report, as shown in Figure 8-8. When done, click **Next**.

Figure 8-8 *Adding Recipients to the Report*

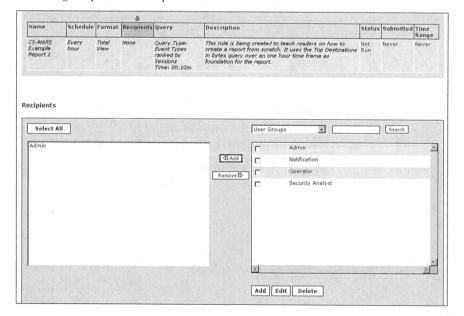

Step 6   Populate the query tool for the data you want the report to contain, as shown in Figure 8-9. You have the option to test the query for your desired results by using the **Test Query** button. Then click **Next**.

Figure 8-9   *Populating the Query Tool*

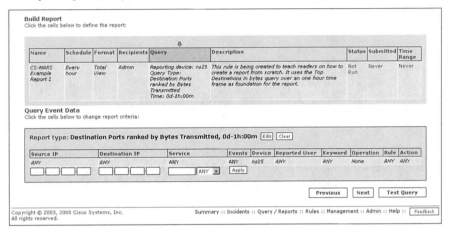

Step 7   Click **Submit** to save the report, as shown in Figure 8-10.

Figure 8-10   *Saving the Report*

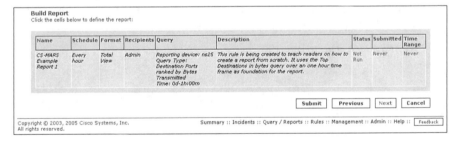

You have now successfully created a custom report.

Methods of Report Delivery

Currently in v4.1.4, CS-MARS delivers reports either locally or remotely via e-mail. Both methods use either HTML or CSV formats for the reports.

When a report is generated and viewed on CS-MARS locally, you view the report in HTML through the browser unless you select the CSV format. If you select the CSV format, a new screen appears that provides you a link to right-click and save the report locally to your workstation. After you save the file to your workstation, you can open it using an application such as Microsoft Excel. Figure 8-11 is an example of a report saved locally as a CSV file.

Figure 8-11 *CS-MARS Report Using CSV File Format*

	A	B	C	D	E	F	G	H	I	J	K	L
1	Rank	Count	Id	EventType	OwnedBy	EventPriority	Description	VulntyFlag	DenyFlag	Status	Type	
2	1	91030	1134	1302001	0	3	Built/teardown/permitted IP connection	0	0	1	0	
3	2	34	1408016	1000021	0	3	Inactive CS-MARS reporting device	0	0	1	0	
4	3	27	1523	1902100	0	2	ICMP Ping Network Sweep	0	0	1	0	
5	4	20	1053	1106001	0	3	Deny packet due to security policy	0	1	1	0	
6	5	18	1584	1903001	0	2	TCP Port Sweep	0	0	1	0	
7	6	10	1514	1902004	0	3	ICMP Echo Request	0	0	1	0	
8	7	8	1140	1304001	0	2	Accessed a specified URL or FTP site	0	0	1	0	
9	8	6	1510	1902000	0	3	ICMP Echo Reply	0	0	1	0	
10	8	6	1936	1905124	0	1	IIS CGI Double Decode	1	0	1	0	
11	8	6	1677	1903215	0	1	IIS DOT DOT EXECUTE	1	0	1	0	
12	8	6	1678	1903216	0	1	IIS Dot Dot Crash	CVE-1999-	1	0	1	0
13	8	6	1926	1905114	0	1	WWW IIS Unicode Directory traversal	CVE-2000-	1	0	1	0
14	8	6	1896	1905081	0	1	WWW WinNT cmd.exe Exec	CVE-2000-	1	0	1	0
15	14	1	1139	1303002	0	3	Stored or retrieved data from a FTP or URL	0	0	1	0	
16	14	1	1938	1905126	0	1	WWW IIS .ida Indexing Service Overflow	CAN-2001-	1	0	1	0

To send a report to a recipient through e-mail, that user must be entered into the Recipients column of the respective report. To be placed into this column, the recipient must have an account on CS-MARS. If a user does not require access to CS-MARS but will only receive reports, that user can be assigned a user account with only notification privileges.

When a report has a recipient assigned to it, it can be e-mailed to the recipient or recipient group as an HTML e-mail or as a standard text e-mail with the CSV file attached.

To assign a recipient or recipient group to an existing report, simply click **None** under the Recipients column of the respective report located within the Report tab. When you click the word None, you will see a familiar-looking screen to add users to the report column. Figure 8-12 displays this feature.

Figure 8-12 *CS-MARS Add Recipient Feature*

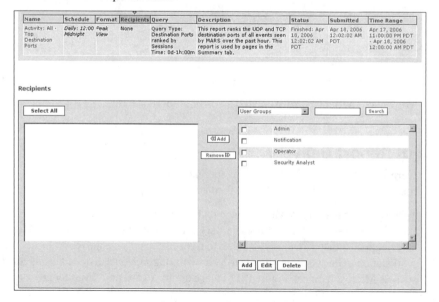

Using this tool, you can add a user or a group of users as the recipients; then click the **Submit** button (not shown on Figure 8-12) in the lower-right corner of the page. If you need to add a new user, click the **Add** button; a new window pops up, enabling you to create a new user. Figure 8-13 shows an example of this new page.

Figure 8-13 *CS-MARS Add a New User Panel*

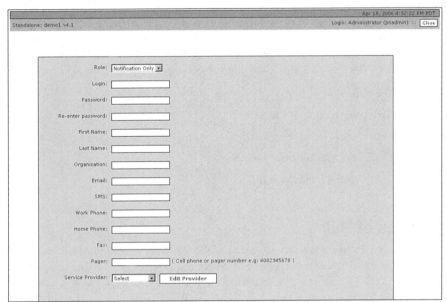

When adding a new user with only notification privileges, only the First Name, Last Name, and E-mail fields are required.

When you have finished entering the new user data, click **Submit** in the lower-right corner of the page. The new user now is available in the Recipients column.

The report will be sent to that recipient when the report is finished running at its scheduled time.

Creating Rules

Rules, rules, rules. If anything in CS-MARS needs an important emphasis placed on it, it is rules.

Rules define conditions that must be exactly met for CS-MARS to take an action. Actions vary from incident creation and false-positive creation to e-mail notification and manual sessionization. By default, when all rule conditions are met, an incident is created or data is dropped, depending on the type of rule, of course; however, you can further specify more actions. Rules can be basic, as in a single event reported by a firewall or intrusion-detection sensor (IDS), or complex, by outlining a behavior, such as a single host communicating to another host through nonstandard ports and then replicating the behavior across the network. In CS-MARS, there are more than 15,000 different known event types. As new attacks are recognized, new events are created and made available to CS-MARS through updates on the Cisco website. When you compound those numbers by placing conditions on the known events, you can begin to see that the possibilities are almost endless in defining rule conditions for your network.

The challenge is creating complex rules easily. CS-MARS is successful at this by providing a Rule Creation tool that is simple and straightforward. To understand and create rules, you need to be familiar with the following subjects:

- The two types of rules
- Active versus inactive rules
- Custom system inspection rules
- The Query tool for creating rules
- Complex and behavioral rule creation

The Two Types of Rules

In CS-MARS, rules and reports are basically the same in structure; the major difference is that they have different purposes and outcomes. Queries are the foundation for both rules and reports. Queries use filtering criteria for defining the data that you want to see in a report or for matching a rule to take an action. A default action is automatically taken when a rule condition is met. To trigger additional actions, those actions must be defined within the rule criteria. To understand default actions and how to initiate the additional actions, you must be familiar with the following two types of rules:

- Inspection rules
- Drop rules

Inspection Rules

Inspection rules are a condition or series of conditions that the data being received by CS-MARS must meet for an incident to be created and processed. The default action for an inspection rule is to create an incident ID, a unique numerical identifier for the specific data that triggered the rule. The creation of this incident ID results in further processing of this event by CS-MARS. To view the inspection rules, browse to **Rules > Inspection Rules**.

Two types of inspection rules exist: system and user defined. Figure 8-14 shows an example of a CS-MARS inspection rule.

Figure 8-14 *CS-MARS System Inspection Rule*

	Rule Name:		System Rule: Backdoor: Spyware				
	Action:		None				
	Description:		This rule detects spyware e.g. Gator, Bonzi etc. installed on hosts or requests to hosts with spyware installed. Spyware are malicious application computer without the knowledge of the user, e.g. when one visits a web site or clicks on an advertising link or installs file sharing freeware such AudioGalaxy. Once installed, the spyware automatically runs each time the host PC is started and records URLs visited, the username, password information used, and then sends this information to the spyware writers.				

Offset	Open (	Source IP	Destination IP	Service Name	Event	Device	Reported User	Keyword	Severity
1		ANY	ANY	ANY	Penetrate/Backdoor/Spyware/Request	ANY	None	ANY	ANY

System rules are rules that have been predefined in CS-MARS. System rules are easily recognized by a unique naming convention. The system rule name starts with the text "System Rule:" and is then concatenated with the rule name. More than 120 system rules are built into CS-MARS. These rules can be slightly modified by changing the following attributes:

- Action
- Source IP
- Destination IP
- Device

No other system-rule attributes can be modified.

If you want to change the other attributes, you can "duplicate" the system rule and modify all attributes in the newly copied rule. To duplicate a system rule, follow these steps:

Step 1   Check the box next to the rule name you want to duplicate.

Step 2   Click the **Duplicate** button, located at the top or bottom of the System Rules page.

Step 3   After you create any rule, regardless of the type, click the **Activate** button in the upper-right corner of the page to begin processing the rule.

The newly copied rule is located directly underneath the original rule on the System Rules page. It is labeled with the exact rule name, but with the addition of "Copied: Date/Time." It is now ready for you to modify.

User-defined rules are rules that you as a CS-MARS user create. These rules are labeled with the exact name you give them and appear in alphabetical order on the Inspection Rules page. Creating rules is discussed in the section "Creating Custom System Inspection Rules," later in this chapter.

Drop Rules

Drop rules are a condition or series of conditions that must be met for an action to be taken. The action might be for CS-MARS to drop the data from the database entirely or to log the data to the database but not allow the data to be used in an incident. A more familiar name for a drop rule is a false-positive tune—it enables you to fine-tune the rules for identifying false positives. The default action for this rule is to create a system-determined false positive. To view the drop rules, browse to **Rules > Drop Rules**.

You might want to tune out something for various reasons. Several tuning methods exist:

- Through the False Positive link
- Manually

False Positive link   When viewing events through the query tool or investigating incidents through the incident/session ID, the normalized data presented ends in a False Positive link. When clicked, this link opens a new window with the False Positive Tuning Wizard. Try clicking the False Positive link and walking through the wizard. Notice that this wizard is very straightforward and simply enables you to filter variables based upon the normalized event you selected. Figure 8-15 shows incidents that have been flagged as false positives.

Figure 8-15 *CS-MARS False Positive Tuning Link*

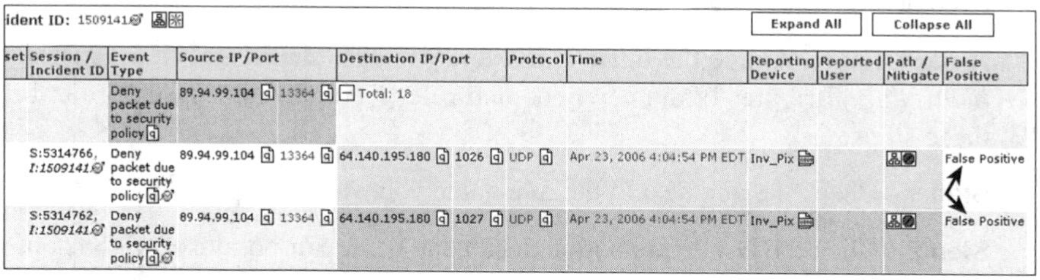

Manually   You create a drop rule manually from the Drop Rules page, located at Rules > Drop Rules. When you navigate to this page for the first time, it is blank, as in Figure 8-16.

To create a new drop rule, click the **Add** button. The drop-rule creation tool appears.

As a real-life example of how this rule can be used, consider the event Built/Teardown/ Permitted IP Connection, generated by a PIX firewall or ASA security device each time a session is opened through the firewall.

As a security or network administrator, you know that you will have thousands of these messages per day. In the following step-by-step example, you create a drop rule to completely drop this event.

Step 1   Click the **Add** button on the Drop Rules page, as shown in Figure 8-16.

Figure 8-16   *CS-MARS Drop Rules Page*

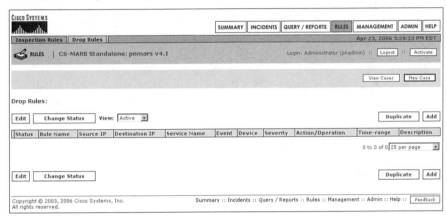

Step 2   Enter a drop rule name and description, as shown in Figure 8-17. Click **Next**.

Figure 8-17   *Naming the Rule*

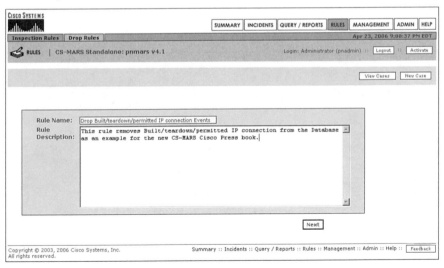

Step 3   Select **Any** as the source IP address, as shown in Figure 8-18. Click **Next**.

Figure 8-18 *Selecting the Source IP Address*

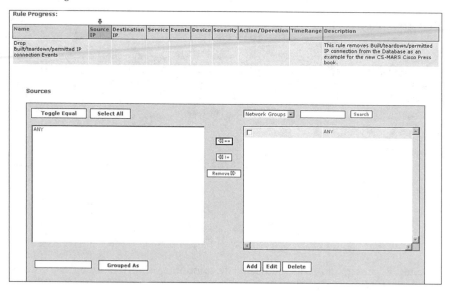

Step 4 Select **Any** as the destination IP address, as shown in Figure 8-19. Click **Next**.

Figure 8-19 *Selecting the Destination IP Address*

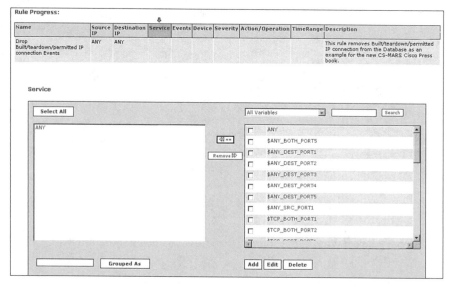

Step 5   Select **Any** as the service port and protocol, as shown in Figure 8-20. Click **Next**.

Figure 8-20   *Selecting the Service Port and Protocol*

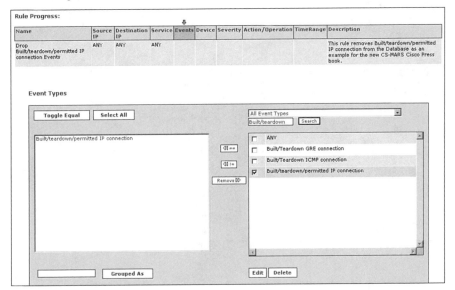

Step 6   Select **All Event Types** from the drop-down menu just above the box on the right.

Step 7   Type **Built/teardown** in the search box and click **Search**. The box on the right populates with all events that have the search text in them.

Step 8   Check **Built/Teardown/Permitted IP Connection** and click the **<<==** (Add) button. Built/Teardown/Permitted IP Connection now appears in the left box. Click **Next**.

Step 9   Select **Device Type: Cisco PIX 6.3** from the drop-down menu just above the box on the right, as shown in Figure 8-21. The box populates with all PIX firewalls added to the CS-MARS.

Step 10   Check the PIX(es) you want to have the events dropped from and click the **<<==** (Add) button. Your selection now appears in the left box. Click **Next**.

Step 11   Leave the **Any** selection populated in the Severity drop-down menu, as shown in Figure 8-22. Click **Next**.

Figure 8-21 *Selecting the Device Type*

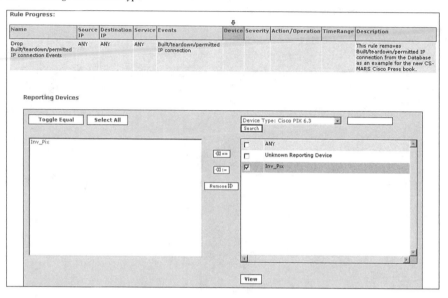

Figure 8-22 *Selecting the Severity Level*

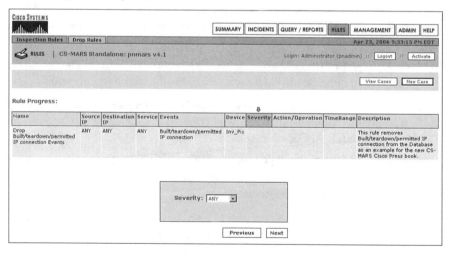

Step 12 Select the **Drop** radio button, as shown in Figure 8-23. Click **Next**.

Figure 8-23 *Selecting the Action*

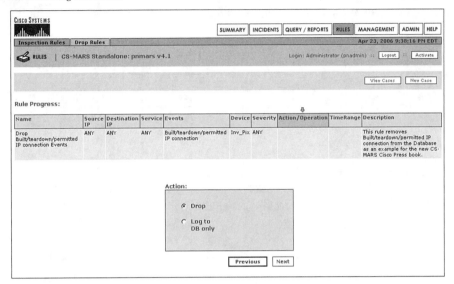

Step 13 Select the Time Range radio button **Any**, as shown in Figure 8-24.
Click **Next**.

Figure 8-24 *Selecting the Time Range*

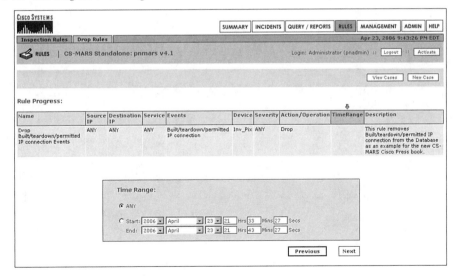

Step 14 You are now finished creating your drop rule. Review your entries in the summary, as shown in Figure 8-25, and when complete, click **Submit**.

Figure 8-25 *Reviewing the Rule Summary*

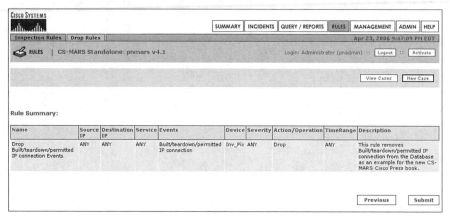

Now that you have submitted your new drop rule you will see it in the Drop Rule page. Although this new drop rule has been created and submitted, it is not being used by CS-MARS yet. You have one final step.

Step 15 Click the **Activate** button in the upper-right corner of the page, as shown in Figure 8-26.

Figure 8-26 *Activating the Rule*

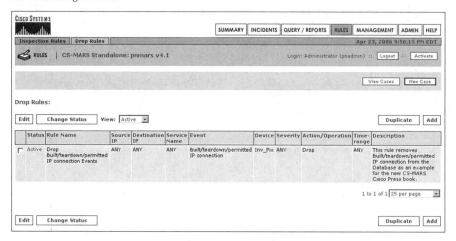

You have now successfully created and activated a new drop rule.

Active vs. Inactive Rules

All rules in CS-MARS have two states: active and inactive. Active rules are rules that are currently being used by CS-MARS with the data being received. Inactive rules are rules that are dormant—that is, currently *not* being used. While browsing through the rules pages, you might have noticed that there is no delete button or function. There is a reason for this.

CS-MARS is a SIM that maintains the integrity of the log data for the life of the data. Because theoretically you can archive data for decades, it is important to have the rules that processed the archived data available. If you decide to import archived data into CS-MARS, to maintain the integrity of that data, you should process it under the rule conditions that were available when the data was originally received by CS-MARS. Therefore, you cannot delete the rules; you can only change their states. Many a forensics investigation has been compromised because the original rules were not available to match the data.

To change active rules to inactive rules, follow these steps.

In this example, you use the recently created drop rule.

Step 1   Browse to **Rules > Drop Rules**, as shown in Figure 8-27.

Figure 8-27 *CS-MARS Drop Rules Page with One Drop Rule*

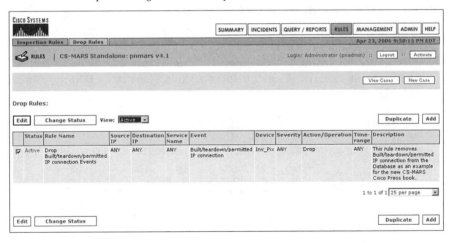

Step 2   Select the box next to the rule you want to make inactive.

Step 3   Click the **Change Status** button. The page refreshes and your drop rule disappears.

Step 4   Select **Inactive** from the **View** drop-down menu. The page refreshes, and you are now viewing your inactive drop rule, as shown in Figure 8-28. Note the status column in the rule: It now reads Inactive.

Figure 8-28 *CS-MARS Drop Rule Page—Inactive*

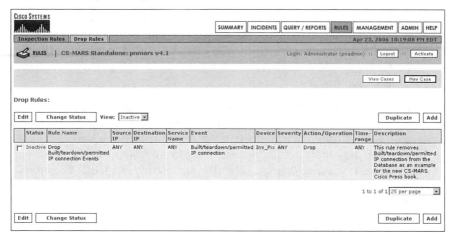

Changing the rule status from Active to Inactive applies to drop rules and inspection rules.

Creating Custom System Inspection Rules

Creating a custom system inspection rule is similar in process to creating a drop rule manually, but with much more detail, including the capability to add complexity to the rule with Boolean expressions. In this section, you will create a basic rule with a single offset. An offset is an indicator of order in rule operation. Rules using Boolean expressions have multiple offsets.

The scenario for creating this rule is that you, the administrator, want an incident to be created, and you want to be notified via e-mail when a host internally or externally makes 20 connections to any host through your NetScreen firewall in a 10-second timeframe.

Complete the following steps to create a custom system inspection rule:

Step 1 From **Rules > Inspection Rules**, click the **Add** button. You are redirected to the Rule Creation tool.

Step 2 Enter the rule name and description, as shown in Figure 8-29. Click **Next**.

Step 3 Because you are defining connections for a specific host, not any number of hosts, you must define it as a target so that CS-MARS knows these connections must be from the same unique host. In the box on the right, check **$Target01** and click the **<<==** button to add it to the left box, as shown in Figure 8-30. Click **Next**.

Figure 8-29 *Naming and Describing the Rule*

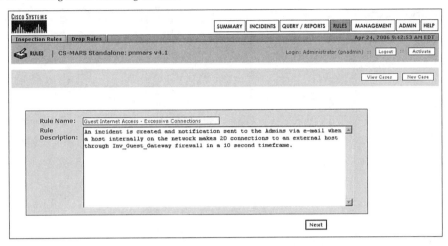

Figure 8-30 *Defining the Source*

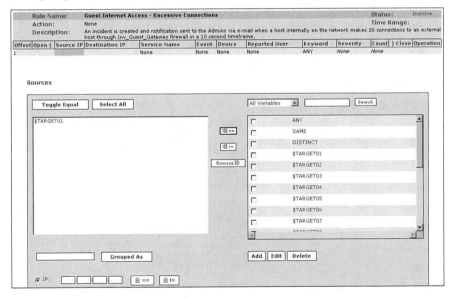

Step 4 As in the previous step, the destination is unique as well; it is not just any destination device. You want to define all connections to this unique host. To do so, you must define it as Target 2 because your source is Target 1. In the box on the right, check **$Target02** and click the **<<==** button to add it to the left box, as shown in Figure 8-31. Click **Next**.

Figure 8-31 *Defining the Destination*

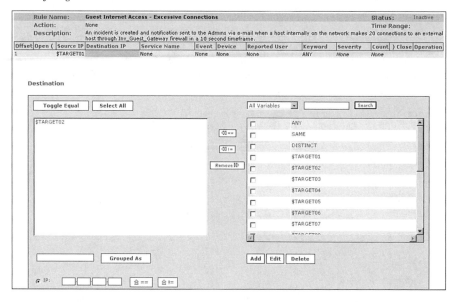

Step 5   In the box on the right, check **Any** and click the **<<==** button to add it to the left box, as shown in Figure 8-32. You are not defining a specific service, so it remains set to any service. Click **Next**.

Figure 8-32 *Defining the Service Name*

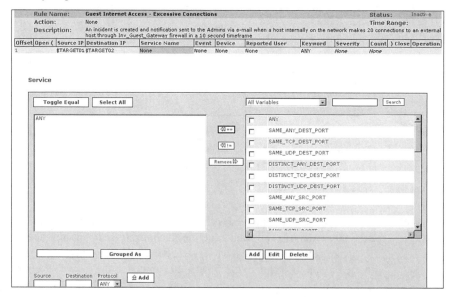

Step 6 In the box on the right, check **Any** and click the **<<==** button to add it to the left box, as shown in Figure 8-33. You are not defining any specific event, so it remains set to any event type. Click **Next**.

Figure 8-33 *Defining the Event*

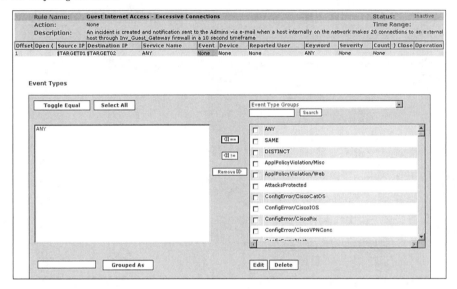

Step 7 In this step, you define the firewall that is monitoring the connections.

(a) Using the drop-down menu above the box on the right, select **Device Type: NetScreen ScreenOS 5.0**. The screen on the right populates with all applicable devices in that category, as shown in Figure 8-34.

(b) In the box on the right, check **Inv_Guest_Gateway** and click the **<<==** button to add it to the left box.

(c) Click **Next**.

Step 8 In the box on the right, check **Any** and click the **<<==** button to add it to the left box, as shown in Figure 8-35. Because you are not defining any specific user(s), it remains set to any user(s). Click **Next**.

Figure 8-34 *Defining the Reporting Device*

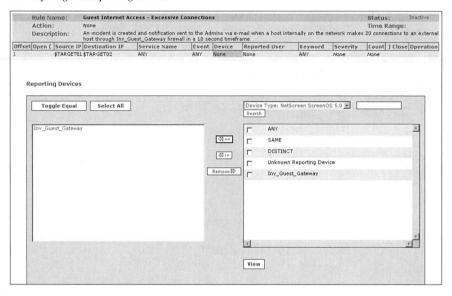

Figure 8-35 *Defining the Reported User*

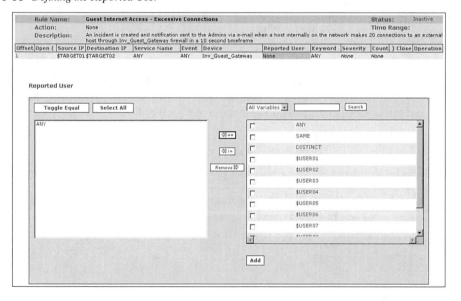

Step 9 You are not defining any keywords in the message text, so it remains set to Any. Leave the fields blank, as shown in Figure 8-36. Click **Next**.

Figure 8-36 *Defining Keywords*

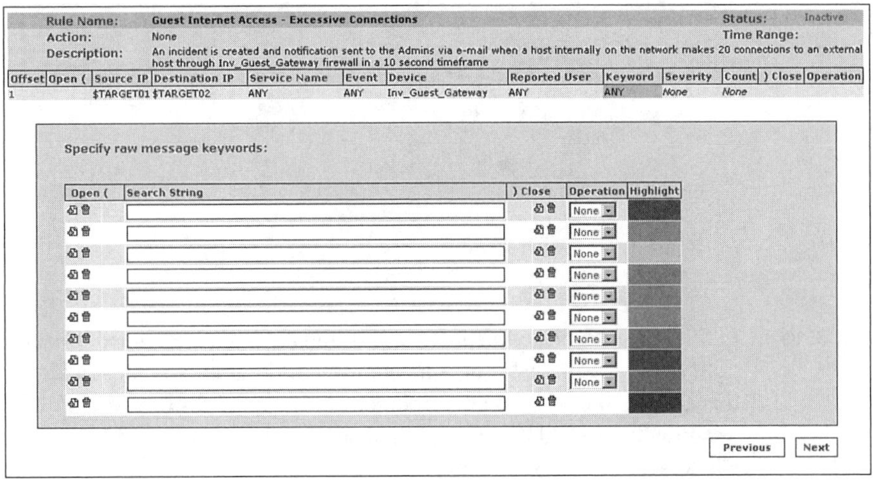

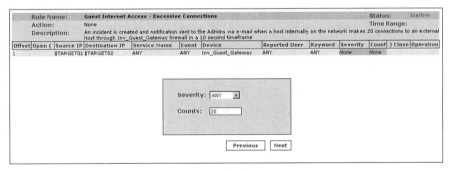

Step 10 Defining severity is not necessary, but defining the count is mandatory. The rule is being written for 20 connections; therefore, you need to enter **20** into the **Counts** field, as shown in Figure 8-37. Click **Next**.

Figure 8-37 *Defining Severity and Count*

Step 11 You are using only a single offset; therefore, you are done defining the rule conditions. Click **Yes**, as shown in Figure 8-38.

Figure 8-38 *Defining Rules Conditions*

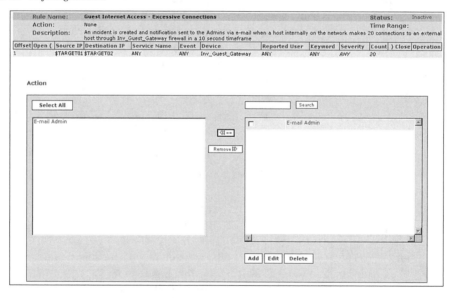

Rule Name:		Guest Internet Access - Excessive Connections								Status:	Inactive		
Action:		None								Time Range:			
Description:		An incident is created and notification sent to the Admins via e-mail when a host internally on the network makes 20 connections to an external host through Inv_Guest_Gateway firewall in a 10 second timeframe											

Offset	Open (	Source IP	Destination IP	Service Name	Event	Device	Reported User	Keyword	Severity	Count	) Close	Operation
1		$TARGET01	$TARGET02	ANY		ANY	Inv_Guest_Gateway	ANY		ANY	ANY	20	

Are you done defining the
rule conditions?

Yes No

Previous

Step 12 In this example, an action of E-mail Admin has been predefined. Because notifying the administrator is a condition of the rule, you must add this action. In the box on the right, check **E-mail Admin** and click the **<<==** button to add it to the left box, as shown in Figure 8-39. Click **Next**.

Figure 8-39 *Defining Actions*

Step 13 The criteria for this rule is that all conditions must be met over a 10-second timeframe. Enter **10** seconds in the field provided, as shown in Figure 8-40.

Figure 8-40 *Defining the Time Range*

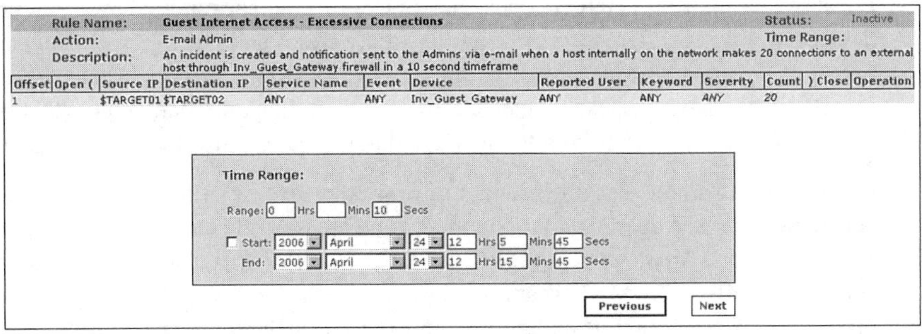

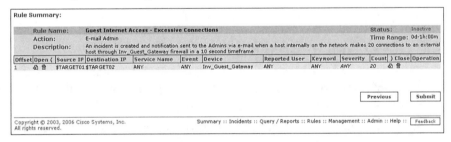

Step 14 You have now defined the rule conditions. Use the Summary page, shown in Figure 8-41, to review and modify any variables if needed. If nothing needs modification, submit the rule for processing in CS-MARS.

(a) Click **Submit**. You are redirected to the Inspection Rules page, where your newly created rule is listed at the top of the page.

(b) Click **Activate** at the top-right corner of the page.

Figure 8-41 *Reviewing and Submitting the Rule*

Your rule is now active!

Custom Rule Creation—Additional Considerations

In the previous example for creating a custom rule, several variables were simplified and require further explanation because they can affect the conditions in which a rule is triggered.

The following variables are discussed in more detail:

- Severity level
- Count
- Time range

Severity level This variable enables a user to select a reported event's severity level. Because CS-MARS is heterogeneous, the same event could be reported by different reporting device types using different severity levels—red, yellow, and green, respectively. Selecting one of these severity levels when creating a rule in CS-MARS forces the rule to use only a reported event that matches the selected severity level. It is important to note that this setting does not indicate the severity of the incident that is created when the rule is triggered.

Count This variable sets the number of times the specific offset in a rule must occur before the rule is triggered and an incident is created. A rule can contain a single offset or multiple offsets. An offset is a single line in a query or rule. Ten spaces are allowed for this variable per offset. CS-MARS cannot process more than 9,999,9999 occurrences in a single offset. Note that setting this number too high can cause the rule to never trigger because the number of occurrences might exceed the timeframe of the data local to the CS-MARS appliance.

Time range This variable sets the time that *all* offsets for a rule must occur within. Setting this variable to 1 second for a single-offset rule triggers the rule immediately when the condition of the rule is met. This variable is a maximum value; therefore, if you set your rule to 10 seconds, CS-MARS will trigger the rule if all the conditions of the rule are met in less than 10 seconds and will then reset the counter to the rule. So if you get two matches during 10 seconds, you will get two incidents. On the flip side, if the rule has multiple offsets and the rule is set for 5 minutes, it will not trigger if the events occur in 5 minutes and 5 seconds.

Using the Query Tool to Create a Rule

Using the querying tool is a much more simple method of writing a rule. Most CS-MARS users prefer this method because they can query the data first to see the results that they want to use to trigger the rule.

In this example, you create the same rule as you did in the section "Creating Custom System Inspection Rules"; however, the reporting device is changed to the PIX firewall named Inv_Pix, which controls access to the private wide-area network (WAN).

The scenario for creating this rule is that you, the administrator, want an incident to be created and you want to be notified via e-mail if within a 10-second timeframe any host attempts 20 connections to any other host through your PIX firewall. This activity could indicate excessive connection attempts.

NOTE If you are using this book with your existing CS-MARS appliance in your network, the example shown here might not return data on your appliance. Be creative and change the variables, such as the PIX firewall, to your firewall type. Other variables might need to be changed as well.

In the following example, it is assumed that you know how to use the Query tool, as you learned in Chapter 7. Query steps are not provided.

Step 1   Navigate to **Query/Reports > Query** and populate the query tool with the information that you want an incident to be created and that you want to be notified via e-mail if within a 10-second timeframe any host attempts 20 connections to any other host through your PIX firewall. Figure 8-42 shows the query page.

Figure 8-42   *CS-MARS Query Page: Write and Submit the Query*

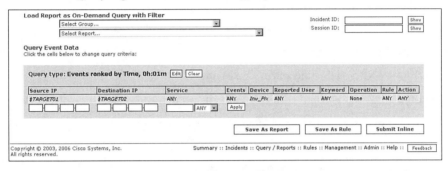

Step 2   After the query is written and returns the expected data, click the **Save as Rule** button. Figure 8-43 illustrates the Rule Creation tool that you will see after you click the Save as Rule button.

Figure 8-43   *Inspection Rule Panel: Rule Creation Tool*

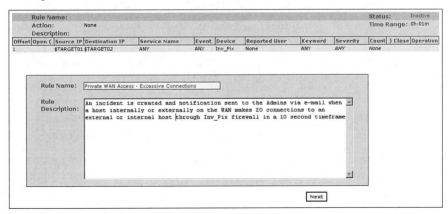

Look familiar? You learned how to use this tool in the section "Creating Custom System Inspection Rules," earlier in this chapter. The applicable data from your query in Step 1 of this example now is populated in the Rule Creation tool.

Step 3   Enter the rule name and description, as shown in Figure 8-44. Click **Next** and continue to use the tool until the rule is complete.

Figure 8-44   *Inspection Rule Panel: Completing the Rule Creation Tool*

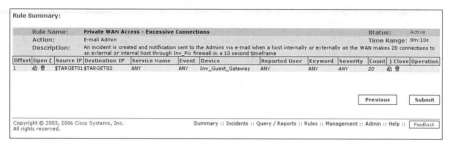

Step 4   Review the rule and click **Submit**.

Step 5   When you are redirected to the Inspection Rules page, click **Activate**.

You have now successfully created a rule using the Query tool.

Complex and Behavioral Rule Creation

Complex rules are rules that use multiple offsets tied together by Boolean expressions. Three Boolean expressions are available to use in CS-MARS rules:

- **And**—Indicates that multiple offset conditions must be met, but not in order

- **Or**—Indicates that only one of the conditions of multiple offsets must be met

- **Followed-By**—Indicates that an offset condition must follow the preceding offset condition

When writing a rule with multiple offsets, keep these expressions in mind for every offset of the rule. Depending on the one used, it might be necessary to put the offsets in a specific order.

Offsets can be grouped by placing them between parentheses to maintain the order of operation. This gives the rule more granularity in separating offsets by their expression.

Figure 8-45 is an example of a complex rule with multiple offsets placed in an order of operation. Note the arrows pointing to the offset and parentheses. In this example, the order of operation is not viewable. Offsets 1, 3, 4, and 5 are **Or**, and Offset 2 is **Followed-by**.

Earlier when you created a custom rule or used the Query tool to create a rule, you were asked, "Are you done defining the rule conditions?" For a single-offset rule, which is what you created, the answer was Yes. When defining a multiple-offset rule, you answer **No**, as in Figure 8-46.

Figure 8-45   *Inspection Rule Panel: Complex Rule—System Rule*

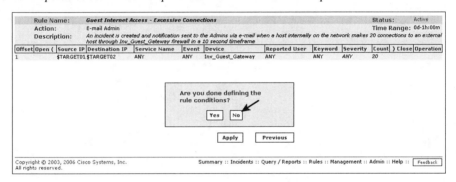

Rule Name:	System Rule: Backdoor: Active										Status:
Action:	None										Time Ra
Description:	This correlation rule detects a connection to a backdoor server or a response from a backdoor server in your network accompanied by maliciou on the server hosting the backdoor - this may indicate that a malicious backdoor service is likely running in your network. Malicious follow-up ac excessive scans, denied packets, installation of malicious services, local buffer overflow attacks etc. Backdoors such as Unix rootkits or Trojan l malicious programs that offer extensive remote control of a host and may be left by an attacker on a compromised host to maintain future rem										

Offset	Open (	Source IP	Destination IP	Service Name	Event	Device	Reported User	Keyword	Severity	Count	)
1	(	ANY	SAME, $TARGET01, ANY	ANY	Penetrate/Backdoor/Rootkit/Connect, Penetrate/Backdoor/Trojan/Connect, Penetrate/Backdoor/Trojan/SYN, Penetrate/Backdoor/CommandShell, Penetrate/Backdoor/RemoteControlApp/Connect	ANY	None	ANY	ANY	1	
2		SAME, $TARGET01, ANY	ANY	ANY	Penetrate/Backdoor/RemoteControlApp/Response, Penetrate/Backdoor/Trojan/Response, Penetrate/Backdoor/Trojan/SYN-ACK	ANY	None	ANY	ANY	1	)
3	((	SAME, $TARGET01, ANY	DISTINCT, ANY	SAME_ANY_DEST_PORT	AttacksProtected, FirewallPolicyViolation/ACL, FirewallPolicyViolation/NAT	ANY	None	ANY	ANY	25	
4		SAME, $TARGET01, ANY	ANY	ANY	DoS/Network/TCP, DoS/Network/UDP, DoS/Network/ICMP, DoS/Network/Misc, DoS/Distributed, Probe/HostInfo/All, Propagate/CopyFiles, Propagate/Worm, Penetrate/Backdoor/CovertChannel	ANY	None	ANY	ANY	1	)
5		ANY	SAME, $TARGET01, ANY	ANY	Persist/All, Penetrate/Backdoor/CovertChannel	ANY	None	ANY	ANY	1	)

Figure 8-46   *Inspection Rule Panel: Complex Rule—Rule Conditions Prompt*

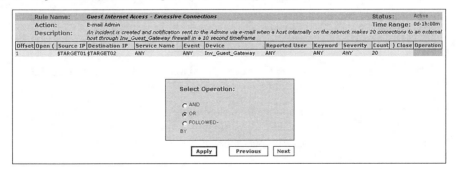

Rule Name:	*Guest Internet Access - Excessive Connections*									Status:	Active
Action:	E-mail Admin									Time Range:	0d-1h:00m
Description:	An incident is created and notification sent to the Admins via e-mail when a host internally on the network makes 20 connections to an external host through Inv_Guest_Gateway firewall in a 10 second timeframe										

Offset	Open (	Source IP	Destination IP	Service Name	Event	Device	Reported User	Keyword	Severity	Count	) Close	Operation
1		$TARGET01	$TARGET02	ANY	ANY	Inv_Guest_Gateway	ANY	ANY	ANY	20		

Are you done defining the rule conditions?

Yes   No

Apply   Previous

Summary :: Incidents :: Query / Reports :: Rules :: Management :: Admin :: Help ::   Feedback

When you select No, you are brought to the Select Operations question, as in Figure 8-47.

Figure 8-47   *Inspection Rule Panel: Complex Rule—Select Operations*

Rule Name:	*Guest Internet Access - Excessive Connections*									Status:	Active
Action:	E-mail Admin									Time Range:	0d-1h:00m
Description:	An incident is created and notification sent to the Admins via e-mail when a host internally on the network makes 20 connections to an external host through Inv_Guest_Gateway firewall in a 10 second timeframe										

Offset	Open (	Source IP	Destination IP	Service Name	Event	Device	Reported User	Keyword	Severity	Count	) Close	Operation
1		$TARGET01	$TARGET02	ANY	ANY	Inv_Guest_Gateway	ANY	ANY	ANY	20		

Select Operation:

○ AND
◉ OR
○ FOLLOWED-BY

Apply   Previous   Next

NOTE   Are your reporting devices synchronized in time? This is important in a multiple-offset rule. If the event times are seconds off between reporting devices, it could mean that your rule will never be triggered.

After you select your operation, you are ready to configure the next offset of your new rule. Figure 8-48 represents this.

Figure 8-48 *Inspection Rule Panel: Complex Rule—Begin Offset 2*

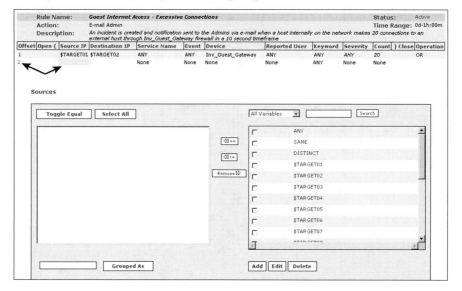

As you can see, you can create a very complex rule with different behaviors from multiple systems. The skills required to do so lie within the capability to create a rule from scratch. When you become comfortable with writing rules from scratch, you can try creating complex rules using Boolean expressions and order of operation.

Summary

This chapter covered two functions considered to be advanced operations of the CS-MARS appliance: creating reports and creating rules.

CS-MARS offers various options for customizing report content and format so that you can generate reports targeted to the needs of specific users, such as senior management, line management, network security personnel, and auditors.

The Rule Creation tool provided by CS-MARS also offers you flexibility in determining what actions you want to occur when specific conditions are met in your network. Rules can change the behavior of CS-MARS and alter the way it processes incidents. Using the information in this chapter, you can create rules to monitor specific activity on your network and create a security policy-enforcement device.

Now that you have an understanding of the advanced operations of the CS-MARS appliance, we look next at real-world examples of how you can use these tools to protect your network resources.

PART IV

CS-MARS in Action

In this chapter, you are exposed to the CS-MARS product during operation in a live environment. This chapter tells customers' stories, with details of their actions and what role CS-MARS played in protecting them. Customer examples in this chapter include the following:

- State Government
- Large University
- Hospital
- Enterprise Financial Company
- Small Business

## CHAPTER 9

CS-MARS Uncovered

In this chapter, real CS-MARS customers tell their stories. The stories are informative and paint the true picture of how CS-MARS plays a role in their networks. Although these customers have many uses for CS-MARS, these stories cover only one circumstance they wanted to share. In the interests of security and privacy, the stories have been slightly modified to protect the customers' information. All types and sizes of organizations have experienced success stories with CS-MARS; the examples in this chapter are from the following types of customers:

- State government
- Large university
- Hospital
- Enterprise financial company
- Small business

State Government

Early one morning in February, Jesse, a Cisco Security product sales specialist, woke up at 6:00 a.m. to start his usual morning routine. He poured a cup of coffee and sat down at his laptop to read the morning news. When he surfed to his local newspaper's website, he was amazed to see the headlines: "State Computer System Hacked, Personal Credit Card Data Could Have Been Exposed." As he read the story, he discovered that the state boasted that its new CS-MARS security platform had discovered that a Trojan application was installed on one of the financial database servers. The interesting part is, the CS-MARS platform that made the discovery was the evaluation unit. The state had placed a purchase order for a new CS-MARS appliance the day before going public with the "hack." Now if you ask the state, they would tell you that CS-MARS paid for itself before they even paid for CS-MARS. The following story can be broken down into three parts:

- Detection
- Action
- Resolution

Detection

State employees Ethan and Ryan were evaluating CS-MARS and had not completely integrated the evaluation unit into their network. While navigating the CS-MARS UI, they kept receiving alarms for a specific Trojan application from one of their database servers. Being curious, as a security analyst should be, Ryan began looking deeper into the data being reported and started viewing the data from multiple result formats. Within minutes, Ryan validated the primary source of the incident and contacted the department responsible for the server. While the server was being investigated, the analyst notified the appropriate individuals in the state and gave them a web-based report of the findings by posting the HTML report on one of the internal web servers.

Action

As they looked deeper into the server, they found the Trojan application that was causing the alarms. They took the server offline and contacted the FBI. The FBI confiscated the server to conduct postforensic analysis.

The state then launched an internal investigation to discover how the application had gotten on the machine. The local newspapers reported that a state employee had placed it on the server and that the employee stated it was used only for security testing purposes. It was then reported that the state employee had been placed on paid administrative leave until the investigation was complete and that the Trojan application could have been on the database server for six months. The state also released a public press release asking state residents who used certain state services to check their credit card statements for potential misuse. The investigation concluded that the state's security policies had been violated, but no theft of data had actually occurred.

Resolution

The state fully implemented a CS-MARS deployment and integrated its security and network equipment into CS-MARS. It developed policies and procedures surrounding CS-MARS capabilities, including, but not limited to, reporting, incident investigation, and notification. The current status of the employee is unknown at this time.

Large University

Janet is one woman with three jobs: She is the network engineer, the Demilitarized Zone (DMZ) administrator, and the security analyst in her IT department. She admits, "You would think that a large university would have the resources to staff my roles individually, but in reality, they do not." Janet looked to a Cisco Security Partner to solve her problem. She could not be the only solution for her numerous responsibilities, and the one she knew the least about was security. Her requirements were easy. She was looking for a product that was easy to use and could be a single repository for event data for the university's firewalls, intrusion detection, antivirus, switches, and routers. She wanted something that did not need to be monitored all the time and was proactive on her network in detecting policy violations, worms, and viruses and in monitoring network behavior—as Janet put it, "something that can bring it all together and tell me when something is wrong." Cisco introduced her to CS-MARS. Four weeks after she installed the product herself, Janet and the university learned the meaning of "return on your investment." The following story can be broken down into three parts:

- Detection
- Action
- Resolution

Detection

Janet was sitting at her desk eating a sub sandwich when the phone lines started to light up. They were not her extension, but she knew she would be getting called shortly. Minutes later, she got a call from the help desk. They told her that certain administrative servers for the staff could not be reached. People had just been kicked off them. While still on the phone, she brought up a command prompt and attempted to ping the servers. No luck on the ping. She then logged into CS-MARS and scrolled down to the Activity: All Events and NetFlow—Top Destination Ports graph. She noticed nothing but figured she would click the View Report button on the graph and change the view to Current Time. She immediately noticed a huge spike in port 53 activity. She then clicked on the q icon next to the port 53 value and queried for the results format of Source IP Address Ranking for the past 5 minutes. The results returned were clear; the primary DNS server in the DMZ had flooded the DMZ with port 53 traffic.

Action

The servers everyone was complaining about were in the same DMZ as both of the DNS servers. Knowing that she had two identical DNS servers, Janet tried to shut down the offending DNS server. She clicked the q icon next to the offending source IP and queried it for the results format of All Matching Events. The returned results provided her with the info she needed: the source IP of the DNS server and the destination IP of the data. She clicked on the Path/Mitigation icon provided by the query results and reviewed the attack path and the enforcement devices that CS-MARS suggested for stopping the attack. CS-MARS suggested disabling the switch port to the primary DNS server on the DMZ switch. Because Janet had two DNS servers, she clicked the Big Red Push button, which instructs CS-MARS to use its automated mitigation. This button disabled the port that the primary DNS server was connected to. Traffic immediately returned to normal. This entire process took Janet 5 minutes from the phone call to the mitigation, and Janet never left her desk or stopped eating her sub sandwich.

Resolution

The university has had issues with certain students playing Internet-enabled PC games. In fact, they had identified and warned several students before to stop doing so. Because the university was private, they had the luxury of controlling traffic on their network. When the problem initially came about, the university put outbound filters on the firewalls to prevent the Internet game playing and issued a new policy prohibiting this activity altogether.

When they investigated the issue, they discovered that their primary DNS server had been hacked into and that an unauthorized port and IP redirection service had been installed. The new service allowed certain ports from any IP address internally to hit it and be redirected through port 53 to a certain machine on the Internet through the firewall. Janet then used CS-MARS to find the originating IP addresses of the traffic by searching for connections to the primary DNS server using the connection ports that the redirection service allowed. She tracked down the IPs to the exact switch and got the Media Access Control (MAC) addresses.

How the rest of the investigation was conducted Janet will not speak of, but they did find the individuals responsible for the hack; not by coincidence, they were the same two individuals originally spoken to. Both students were suspended and also disclosed that more than 30 students had been playing an online game tournament against another university.

Hospital

A hospital purchased CS-MARS for HIPAA-compliant reporting and discovered during the installation how popular illegal file swapping is.

The installation of six CS-MARS M200s and a CS-MARS Global Controller was going very smoothly. The hospital had two M200s installed and reporting to the installed Global Controller. At this point, the only data being reported was NetFlow data from the main campus edge router and two of the six core Catalyst switches. They had planned to deploy the remaining M200s the next day and would schedule a change control window for configuring the rest of the reporting devices. As they were winding down for the day, the staff engineers were paid a visit by the Chief Information Security Officer (CISO). She was inquiring about the deployment and wanted to see their progress. Edmund, the hospital's senior network engineer, randomly chose one of the M200s and logged into it to show the CISO. The following story is broken down into three parts:

* Detection
* Action
* Resolution

Detection

Edmund began showing his senior manager the CS-MARS GUI and explained to her that not much data was available to see because CS-MARS had been up only a few hours. He continued explaining that they had configured a few devices to send NetFlow information to CS-MARS and had decided to store the NetFlow records just to see the box filling up. Edmund decided to show her a query using NetFlow information and randomly chose the Activity: All—Top Destinations (Peak View) report from the Load Report as On-Demand Query with Filter drop-down menu. He submitted the report, and the results appeared instantly. The very first line of results caught their eyes immediately. Edmund clicked the IP address, and CS-MARS resolved it to someothercountrynet.net (the real domain name was from a country outside the United States). The CISO immediately asked why they would be transmitting data to that country. Edmund could not answer the question and said instead, "Let's find out the source." He clicked the q icon next to the IP address in question and chose the results format Top IP Address Ranking. One result came back: the IP address of their front-end web server for their Patient Web Portal. According to Edmund, the heat was on and he needed to find out what this was all about. He quickly wrote another query, this time for the Top Destinations by Bytes Transmitted from the Web Server. Only one fact immediately caught their eyes: Every single transmission was exactly 1.65 GB.

Action

Both Edmund and his CISO were already in the data center; the web server in question was just two rows down. They grabbed one of the server guys from the floor and tried to log into the web server to see what was going on. What they soon discovered floored them both: An MPEG file located in a common Windows directory was named after a blockbuster movie that was currently in the theaters.

Resolution

They removed the file and placed an access control list (ACL) on the edge router, preventing connections that used the ports that CS-MARS reported. That evening during the change control window, the server guys installed Cisco Security Agent on the web server. Even though he went home, Edmund was a busy man that evening. His CISO required him to use a VPN tunnel from home to log in and check on the server until the CSA installation was completed.

All they had running at the time was NetFlow. The entire process of discovery took them about 15 minutes, according to Edmund. A serious amount of bandwidth was reclaimed for use by the hospital, and the threat of potential intangible costs was avoided.

Enterprise Financial Company

Financial Company X has been a CS-MARS customer for almost two years. They were looking for a SIM that had behavioral correlation, did not sit in the critical path of the data, and was an appliance. Andrew, the firm's security analyst, was tough on selecting products to review and would not budge on his criteria for selection. When a Gartner Group security analyst recommended CS-MARS, Andrew decided to take a serious look at the product. After extensive in-house product evaluation, they selected CS-MARS as their SIM. CS-MARS was capable of alerting the company to some anomalous behavior from an authorized host that gained access through the VPN gateway. Interestingly enough, they discovered an unknown virus and reported it. The following story is broken down into three parts:

- Detection
- Action
- Resolution

Detection

Andrew was on his lunch break away from the office when his cell phone went off with a funny song. He had configured his cell phone to play this song whenever he received an SMS text message. Praying that the message was not from a co-worker needing him to come back to the office, he decided to look. When he read the message, it was not from a co-worker; it was from his CS-MARS appliance. The message told him that his Worm Propagation Rule for the VPN gateway had been triggered. He immediately called his co-worker Doug and asked him to investigate while he returned to the office. Doug was already looking into the incident when Andrew called; he had been notified via e-mail at the same time as Andrew.

Action

When Andrew returned to the office, Doug was calmly waiting for him. Doug informed Andrew that one of their remote sales agents had accessed the network through their VPN gateway, and his machine had begun transmitting all kinds of ICMP packets on their network. "This is what triggered the alarm," Doug explained. Doug continued explaining to Andrew that CS-MARS reported the sales agent's username, so he disabled the account on the gateway, per procedure.

Resolution

As Doug and Andrew were discussing the next steps, a call came in from the help desk. An employee was on the road in a hotel and had gotten "kicked off the VPN" and could not log in again. They verified the VPN username and informed him that his machine had a possible worm on it. The user stated that he had updated his antivirus definition files recently and didn't think he could possibly have a virus. With the aid of the help desk, the user was sent a temporary laptop via overnight delivery, and the user immediately sent his laptop to Andrew and Doug.

CS-MARS detected and mitigated this particular threat before the worm had a chance to infect any other hosts, which would have resulted in thousands of dollars in recovery costs and perhaps a government investigation.

Using other forensic tools on the offending laptop, Andrew and Doug discovered a new virus and reported it to a leading antivirus (AV) vendor. A new definition file and CVE have been created for this day-zero worm.

Small Business

A small business outsourced most of its IT needs. An accounts-payable employee was in charge of the network and dedicated five hours per week of her time on the backups and printers.

At 4:00 p.m. every day, Kristyn would walk upstairs and load the new backup tape into the server. Occasionally, she would reboot the other server that handled the printers and file shares—for anything other than that, she called the computer company. Kristyn handled accounts payable and, according to her, if she could use a paper ledger she would! Computers were not her thing; her desktop always crashed during something important. Kristyn's manager, Alex, owned the company. She called Alex a "tech junkie." Alex handled the day-to-day business and managed the two salespeople. He had just bought two new Linksys wireless access points so the sales guys could move around the office and some new security box that told the computer company and Alex if something was going seriously wrong. Of course, the security box was a CS-MARS 20, and it e-mailed Kristyn some rather cool-looking reports that she printed for Alex once a day. These reports revealed that the company was being billed for work that was never done, and it was offering free wireless to other businesses in their building. The following story is broken down into three parts:

- Detection
- Action
- Resolution

Detection

One day when Kristyn was printing some reports for Alex, she noticed something interesting. A few defined hosts in the report came back with some rather strange names. In fact, they had the partial name and initials in them of several of the companies in their building complex. She decided to call Alex, who was in the field.

Action

Alex returned to the office when he was done in the field that day. It was after hours and no one was around, but he had the reports Kristyn had printed for him. He reviewed the reports, noted the same items that Kristyn had seen, and decided to log into his CS-MARS 20 and look around. Alex is rather comfortable with using computers and is very intuitive with technology, so looking around the CS-MARS UI was pretty straightforward to him. He began clicking on incidents and viewing his firewall logs and discovered that other people in his building were using his Internet connection. He picked up the phone and called the technical support hotline to the IT firm he had hired.

After speaking with tech support and getting some assistance filtering the queries, they determined together that the unauthorized users were coming from his wireless access points. He asked tech support if he could see what they were doing, and tech support ran some queries and e-mailed him the results. The unauthorized users were surfing the Internet recreationally and doing peer-to-peer chatting and file swapping. Additionally, Alex was able to view how much bandwidth they had used over the past week and printed that report.

Resolution

The next morning, Alex contacted his account manager from the IT firm and discussed the issues at hand. Alex gave him the reports about the unauthorized users, in addition to a statement of work outlining that the wireless access points had been secured. Alex was upset not only because his neighbors were using his wireless, but also because he had paid and trusted his IT firm to secure his network.

The net result was that Alex was credited for the work and received some free security services from his IT firm, which he diligently checked up on. Alex's business neighbors (two other companies) split the cost of his monthly Internet charge for the current month with very little discussion.

Summary

This chapter told five stories from many types of CS-MARS users with different issues and different resolutions. Taken individually, these real-world stories demonstrate how CS-MARS can address a broad range of security issues in your network—not only attacks but also inappropriate uses of your network resources. Taken together, these stories highlight the fact that all types of businesses, even those with small networks, can benefit from implementing an STM system.

Appendixes

The purpose of this appendix is to provide you with a quick reference of links to useful security websites.

APPENDIX **A**

Useful Security Websites

We spend substantial time in front of customers, and one of the questions we are frequently asked is whether we have any recommendations for security websites. This appendix is dedicated solely to our favorite websites.

This is just a sampling of sites that are available on the web. We realize that there are many, many useful security sites. It just so happens that these are our favorites. We apologize in advance if your favorite site or if a site you maintain isn't included in this list.

Security Links and Descriptions

These links are broken into four different categories to help you find what you're looking for:

- General security
- Governmental security controls and information
- Tools and testing
- Cisco security sites

General Security

Table A-1 lists links to sites that contain mostly general security information in the form of whitepapers, discussions, vulnerability information, exploit information, emerging-threat information, security training information, and some security tool downloads.

Table A-1   *General Security Websites*

Location	Description
http://securitywizardry.com/radar.htm	This site is graphical and contains late-breaking security information, such as new security threat outbreaks, the latest tool versions, and the latest security updates.
http://www.sans.org	Along with providing excellent security training, SANS is one of the original sites that tracked security trends; it provides general information on all levels of network and computer security.
http://www.cert.org	This site is maintained by the Carnegie Mellon Software Engineering Institute. It has much of the same information as SANS but focuses more on vulnerabilities and emerging threats. The security statistics provided on this site are excellent.
http://www.indiana.edu/~phishing/	This site is a security research site maintained by Indiana University. Phishing is an emerging threat, and the researchers at this site do an excellent job of raising this awareness.
http://www.slashdot.com	This site is a good location to chat with people or to read chats from people who have a good understanding of technology and who often talk about security and technology issues before they become mainstream. It's a self-proclaimed nerd site.
http://www.securityfocus.com	Security Focus is an excellent all-around security website. Among other things, it is an excellent place to sign up for various security mailing lists that match a technology that you are interested in following. This site also includes a nice tool suite for security reconnaissance to analyze the security posture of your network. It provides information and tools for almost every popular computing platform.

Governmental Security Controls and Information

Table A-2 lists links to sites that contain information pertinent to the U.S. critical security infrastructure, government surveys, cybercrime, and government recommendations for securing small businesses and enterprises.

Table A-2   *Governmental Security Controls and Information Web Sites*

Location	Description
http://www.ciac.org	This site is run by the Department of Energy and has excellent information regarding emerging vulnerabilities and security threats that pose a danger not only to the Department of Energy, but also to corporations and enterprises alike.
http://www.cybercrime.gov/ or http://www.fbi.gov; click **Cyber**	This website is linked from www.fbi.gov and has viable information on the state of criminal activities currently affecting the Internet and corporations attached to the Internet.
http://www.gocsi.com/	It is hard to classify this website as strictly governmental because it's not, but because the Computer Security Institute publishes probably the most commonly recognized yearly survey in conjunction with the FBI, which is governmental, we are listing them here. This website provides a plethora of general security information and security classes. As mentioned, they distribute a well-deployed yearly survey regarding how cybercrime has affected corporations over the year. This survey is a "must read" for any security professional or information technology officer.
http://www.cia.gov	This is not a security website, per se, but in this search box if you enter the word *cyber*, you are presented with some nice information on threats that affect national security and opinions about those threats.
http://www.dhs.gov	This is the main website for the Department of Homeland Security. You'll find some very nice resources available here, such as guides for securing small businesses and enterprises. Many of these guides are actually not painful to read and are titled appropriately, such as, "The Common Sense Guide to Cyber Security for Small Businesses." Log in and look around—you might be surprised.

Tools and Testing

Table A-3 lists links to sites that contain downloadable tools that can be used for security testing, such as network vulnerability scanning, reconnaissance scanning, penetration testing, forensics investigation, and useful system software indirectly related to security.

Table A-3   *Security Tools and Testing Websites*

Location	Description
http://www.insecure.org	This site is a must if you want to do penetration testing. It contains tools and all the information you can consume related to the topic.
http://www.metasploit.org	Metasploit is an all-inclusive exploit tool used for penetration testing. The tool is very easy to use and is gaining momentum as the free one-stop penetration tester of choice.
http://packetstorm.linuxsecurity.com	This site contains information on exploits and vulnerabilities. If you dig deep enough, you can find exploit code you can use to test possible vulnerabilities within your environment.
http://www.sysinternals.com	This is one of the best websites containing freeware utilities of system software that helps you to do forensics on running systems and to troubleshoot systems that have been potentially exploited. Look closely in here; you will find many more offerings than just described.

Cisco Security Sites

Table A-4 lists links to sites dedicated entirely to security information related to Cisco equipment and architecture.

Table A-4   *Cisco-Specific Security Websites*

Location	Description
http://www.cisco.com/go/mysdn	This site is one-stop shopping for Cisco security information. It covers signature updates for all Cisco products for new vulnerabilities and exploits and provides pertinent links to all other security-related Cisco information.
http://www.cisco.com/go/safe	This site is a "must read" for all security professionals. It contains whitepapers that outline a general architecture for securing your business. The whitepapers are product agnostic, so they are written so that the solutions aren't necessarily deployed using Cisco gear.

The purpose of this appendix is to provide you with a quick reference guide to commonly needed statistics.

APPENDIX **B**

CS-MARS Quick Data Sheets

This appendix provides you with data sheets on common technologies in CS-MARS or those used by CS-MARS v4.1. Most of these have been addressed within the previous chapters; however, a single repository of this information is presented for quick reference.

The following topics are covered:

- Quick Hardware and Protocol Specifications for CS-MARS
- NetFlow Platform Guide
- V4.1 Product Support List

Quick Hardware and Protocol Specifications for CS-MARS

This section provides information about CS-MARS hardware, protocols, and MIBs. It also includes a list of facts about CS-MARS technology. Tables B-1 and B-2 reference hardware specifications for CS-MARS Local and Global Controller-deployment modes.

Table B-1 *CS-MARS Local Controller Hardware Specifications*

LC Type	CPU	Storage	Flow/Sec	Event/Sec	RAID Level
M20	P4 3.0 GHz	120 GB	15,000	500	None
M50	P4 3.0 GHz	240 GB	25,000	1,000	Level 0
M100e	(2)Xeon 2.8 GHz	750 GB	75,000	3,000	Level 10
M100	(2)Xeon 2.8 GHz	750 GB	150,000	5,000	Level 10
M200	(2)Xeon 3.0 GHz	1 TB	300,000	10,000	Level 10

Table B-2 *CS-MARS Global Controller Specifications*

GC Type	Number of LC Supported	Storage	RAID Level
GCm	5 (M20 and M50 only)	1 TB	Level 10
GC	Unlimited	1 TB	Level 10

NOTE	All CS-MARS GCs use the same hardware as an M200 LC.

Table B-3 cross-references CS-MARS device types to Cisco part numbers and Cisco SmartNet reference numbers.

Table B-3 *CS-MARS Product Part Numbers*

Product Type	Cisco Part Number	Cisco SmartNet Level
M20	CS-MARS-20-K9	CON-SNT-MARS20
M50	CS-MARS-50-K9	CON-SNT-MARS50
M100e	CS-MARS-100e-K9	CON-SNT-MARS100E
M100	CS-MARS-100-K9	CON-SNT-MARS100
M200	CS-MARS-200-K9	CON-SNT-MARS200
GCm	CS-MARS-GCM-K9	CON-SNT-MARSGCM
GC	CS-MARS-GC-K9	CON-SNT-MARSGC

CS-MARS includes the following components:

- Steel chassis, 19-inch rack-mountable
- Motherboard
- Intel Pentium or Xeon processor(s)
- DRAM memory
- Hot-swappable RAID 10 IDE drives (most models)
- Network interface card 10/100/1000
- V.92 modem
- DVD-ROM drive
- KVM ports (USB and serial)
- Serial-management port
- Toggle switches (reboot and power on/off)
- 120 V AC, single 300 W or dual 500 W power supply
- Rack-mounting brackets
- User guides (printed Quick Start, PDF users guide)
- Proprietary software
- Oracle database (no additional licensing required)

- Linux kernel Version 4.1.2
- OpenSSL library
- Tomcat Web Server

Each appliance is UL approved and has two Ethernet interfaces. The higher-end models (M100e, M100, and M200) and both GCs have dual-redundant 500 W power supplies.

CS-MARS supports the following log-reception protocols:

- Syslog (in the clear)
- Microsoft RPC (for Windows)
- Check Point LEA (for clear or SSL encryption)
- Cisco RDEP (for SSL encryption) and Cisco POP (for IDS 3.*x*)
- SDEE
- SNMP
- HTTP or HTTPS

CS-MARS supports the following list of network-discovery protocols:

- SNMP v1 (read-only access required)
- Telnet, SSH, or FTP
- Check Point CPMI (clear or SSL encryption)
- JDBC (password protected)
- NMAP and Nessus, for active investigation

CS-MARS supports the following SNMP discovery MIBs:

- mib-2(1) .System
- mib-2(1) .Interface.iftabl
- mib-2(1) .ip.iproutetable
- mib-2(1) .ip.ipaddrTable
- mib-2(1) .ip.forwarding
- mib-2(1) .At.attable (For ARP info)
- mib-2(1) .dot1dBridge(17)
- EMIB vtpVlanState

CS-MARS uses the following protocols for mitigation or configuration discovery:

- Telnet
- FTP
- SSH

- RDEP
- HTTPS
- Check Point CPMI
- SNMP v1

CS-MARS supports the following notification protocols:

- E-mail (uses Sendmail)
- SNMP trap
- Syslog
- SMS
- ASCII text

CS-MARS has a built-in v.92 modem for SMS and ASCII text messaging.

CS-MARS Technology Facts

The following list provides facts about CS-MARS technology that users commonly need to know:

- For Secure Sockets Layer (SSL), the popular OpenSSL library is used, except for Check Point, which requires the use of Check Point's own implementation of SSL (LEA) as shipped with its Open Platform for Security (OPSEC) application programming interface (API). Currently, self-signed certificates are used, except for Check Point Management Interface (CPMI), where certificates can be imported into CS-MARS.

- The CS-MARS appliance is security hardened by the following:

  — Removing all unnecessary services.

  — Configuring firewall rules on the appliance so that ports used by internal services such as Oracle TNS listener are not accessible from the outside. Therefore, only SSH, SSL, and event-collection ports such as syslog and SNMP trap are open to the outside.

  — Providing a command shell with only a few commands. Root access to the box is not provided.

- The database inside CS-MARS is optimized for performance and designed to maintain itself without a database administrator. Data is continuously compressed and archived away to an NFS file; old logs are purged, but the statistical trending data remains inside the box.

- CS-MARS management is completely web based, so users communicate to CS-MARS using HTTPS/SSL using Internet Explorer and the Adobe VGA Viewer.

- Archiving allows the users to store the event and configuration data to a remote NAS (networked attached storage). Archiving serves two purposes:

  — To restore the CS-MARS system, in the case of hardware failure or physical damage, to its closest running state, either on the same appliance or on a brand-new appliance

  — To retrieve the historic event data in compliance with government regulation

  Data that is archived is compressed through the Ziv-Lempel algorithm (also used in GZIP) and stored in a raw ASCII format.

- Use the following formula to calculate storage for archived data:

  — By rough estimation, at 5,000 events per second with a compression ratio of 12:1 and each event having an average of 200 bytes, 1 day of storage capacity is $(5,000 \times 200 \times 86,400) / 12 = 7.2$ GB

  — To store 1 year's worth of events at 5,000 events per second, you need a NAS with a storage capacity of 7.2 GB $\times$ 365 days = 2.6 TB of storage.

- Use the following formula to calculate storage for internal data storage:

  — Use the previous formula, but remove the /12 (division by 12) for compression. Internal storage is not compressed.

- CS-MARS Local Controllers (LCs) have no licensing restrictions or per-device licensing.

NetFlow Platform Guide

Table B-4 outlines the first releases for specific NetFlow export versions per platform.

Table B-4 *First Releases for NetFlow Export Versions by Platform*

Cisco IOS Software Release Version	NetFlow Export Version(s)	Supported Cisco Hardware Platforms
11.1CA	1, 5	The Cisco 7200 and 7500 were the first platforms in 11.1CA. V5 is now available for all IOS platforms.
12.3(1), 12.0(24)S, 12.2(18)S, 12.3(2)T	9	Cisco 800, 1700, 2600, 3600, 3700, 6400, 7200, 7300, 7500, 12000
12.0(14)S	5	Cisco 12000.
12.0(6)S	8	Cisco 12000.
12.1(13)EW	5	Catalyst 4k Supervisor 4.
12.1(19)EW	8	Catalyst 4k Supervisor 4.
12.1(18)EW	5, 8	Catalyst 4k Supervisor 5.

Table B-5 outlines NetFlow support in Cisco IOS and the Catalyst 6500 Supervisory engines.

Table B-5   *Catalyst 6500/7600 NetFlow Version Support*

Supervisor	Hybrid	Native 12.1E	Native 12.2SX
MSFCx	5	5	5, 8
Sup1a	7, 8	7	—
Sup2	7, 8	5, 7	5, 7, 8
Sup720	5, 7, 8	5, 7	5, 7, 8

NetFlow Performance Information

A specific whitepaper has been written to give the details of how NetFlow implicates performance on software-based Cisco platforms. NetFlow performance impact comes mainly from the characterization of the flow information in the NetFlow cache and the formation of the NetFlow export packet and the export process.

When NetFlow is used in hardware, the main performance impact comes from exporting the flow information, but the characterization of the flows is done in hardware. In general, NetFlow is supported in hardware ASIC on many Cisco platforms, including the Catalyst 4500, 6500, 7600, 10000, and 12000 routers. The export version does not affect performance numbers for NetFlow, including versions 5, 8, or 9.

The additional CPU utilization on software platforms because of NetFlow varies based on the number of flows, as Table B-6 illustrates.

Table B-6   *Approximate CPU Use for a Number of Active Flows*

Number of Active Flows in Cache	Additional CPU Utilization
10,000	<4%
45,000	<12%
65,000	<16%

Sampled NetFlow will significantly decrease CPU utilization to the router. On average, sampled NetFlow 1:1000 packets will reduce CPU by 82%, and 1:100 sampling packets reduce CPU by 75% on software platforms. The conclusion is, sampled NetFlow is a significant factor in reducing CPU utilization.

In general, dual export has no significant CPU impact on the router, and this feature is available in IOS 12.0(19)S, 12.2(2)T, and 12.2(14)S for redundancy of the export.

Some significant factors in reducing CPU utilization from the NetFlow process include these:

- To use sampled NetFlow
- To optimize the aging timers to proper values for the amount of flows
- To leverage a distributed architecture
- To use flow masks on Catalyst 65K/7600

NetFlow Memory Allocation Information

The NetFlow cache size can vary from 1,000 to 512,000 and is configurable for software-based platforms such as 75*xx* and 72*xx*. Each cache entry consumes about 64 bytes of memory. The amount of memory on a Cisco 12K line card denotes how many flows are possible in the cache. For example, if an engine 3 line card has 256 MB of memory, NetFlow allocates 256 MB/16/64 = 256,000 entries. If NetFlow aggregation is used, depending on the user configuration, up to 512,000 entries are possible. The Cisco Catalyst 6500/7600 has different effective hardware cache sizes based on the supervisor card and PFC, as Table B-7 shows.

Table B-7 *Catalyst 6500 Hardware Cache Effective Sizes*

Catalyst 6500/7600 PFC	Effective Number of NetFlow Cache Entries Available
PFC2/DFC	32,000 entries
PFC3A/DFC3A	64,000 entries
PFC3B/DFC3B	115,000 entries
PFC3BXL/DFC3BXL	230,000 entries

V4.1 Product Support List

Table B-8 describes the products supported by CS-MARS and also identifies supported software versions, protocols, and protocol functions.

The one column in this table that might not be obvious is the CSV keyword. This is the device description that must be used in a seed file if you elect to add devices to the CS-MARS database using a CSV seed file. See Chapter 5, "CS-MARS Appliance Setup and Configuration," for a detailed description on how to use a seed file.

Table B-8 *CS-MARS V4.1 Product Support List with Additional Data*

Device Type/ Vendor	Supported Versions	Protocol: Configuration Retrieval	Protocol: Event Retrieval	Protocol: Mitigation	Device Classification	CSV Keyword
Router/Switch Devices						
Cisco router	Cisco IOS 11.x, 12.2	FTP, SNMP, SSH, Telnet	Syslog (from device); NetFlow v5, v7	—	HW	IOS
Cisco router module	Cisco IOS 12.2	FTP, SNMP, SSH, Telnet	Syslog (from device); NetFlow v5, v7	—	HW-switch	SWITCH-IOS
Cisco switch	CATOS 6.x, IOS 12.2	FTP, SNMP, SSH, Telnet	Syslog (from device); NetFlow v5, v7	SNMP	HW	SWITCH-CATOS
Extreme Extreme-Ware	6.x	SNMP	Syslog (from device)	SNMP	HW	EXTREME
Generic router	Unknown	SNMP	Syslog (from device)	—	HW	—
Firewall Devices						
Cisco PIX	6.0, 6.1, 6.2, 6.3	FTP, SSH, Telnet	Syslog (from device)	—	HW	PIX
Cisco PIX	7.0	FTP, SSH, Telnet	Syslog (from device)	—	HW	PIX7X
Cisco Adaptive Security Appliance (ASA)	7.0.1	FTP, SSH, Telnet	Syslog (from device)	—	HW	—

Table B-8 *CS-MARS V4.1 Product Support List with Additional Data (Continued)*

Device Type/ Vendor	Supported Versions	Protocol: Configuration Retrieval	Protocol: Event Retrieval	Protocol: Mitigation	Device Classification	CSV Keyword
Cisco Firewall Services Module (FWSM)	1.1, 2.2, 2.3	FTP, SSH, Telnet	Syslog (from device)	—	HW-switch (IOS 12.2 or CatOS)	FWSM
Cisco IOS Firewall Feature Set	12.2(T) and later	FTP, SNMP, SSH, Telnet	Syslog (from device)	—	—	—
Juniper NetScreen	ScreenOS 4.0, 5.0	SNMP, SSH, Telnet	Syslog (from device)	—	HW	NET-SCREEN
Check Point OPSEC NG and Firewall-1	NG FP3, NG AI (R55), NGX (R60)	SSLCA, CLEAR, ASYMSSLCA (OPSEC-CPMI)	OPSEC-LEA (from log server or management server)	—	SW-host	—
Nokia Firewall (running Check Point)	NG FP3, NG AI (R55), NGX (R60)	SSLCA, CLEAR, ASYMSSLCA (OPSEC-CPMI)	OPSEC-LEA (from log server or management server)	—	SW-host as Check Point	—
VPN Devices						
Cisco VPN 3000 concentrator	4.0.3, 4.7	SNMP	Syslog (from device)	—	HW	—
Network IDS						
Cisco network IDS	3.1	SSH, Telnet	POP (from device)	—	HW	—
Cisco IDSM	3.1	SSH, Telnet	POP (from device)	—	HW-switch	—
Cisco network IDS	4.0	SSL	RDEP (from device)	—	HW	—

continues

Table B-8 *CS-MARS V4.1 Product Support List with Additional Data (Continued)*

Device Type/ Vendor	Supported Versions	Protocol: Configuration Retrieval	Protocol: Event Retrieval	Protocol: Mitigation	Device Classification	CSV Keyword
Cisco IDSM	4.0	SSL	RDEP (from device)	—	HW-switch	—
Cisco Intrusion Prevention System (IPS), ASA module	5.0, 5.1	SSL	SDEE (from device)	—	HW	—
Cisco IPS ASA module	5.0, 5.1	—	SDEE (from device)	—	HW-ASA	—
Cisco IOS IPS (soft-ware only)	12.3(8)T or later	FTP, SNMP, SSH, Telnet	SDEE (from device)	—	HW-switch, HW-router	—
IntruVert IntruShield	1.5	—	SNMP (from management server)	—	SW-host	—
Juniper NetScreen IDP	2.1	—	SNMP (from management server)	—	SW-host	—
Symantec ManHunt	3.x	—	SNMP (from device)	—	SW-host	—
ISS RealSecure Sensor	6.5, 7.0	—	SNMP (from device)	—	SW-host	—
Snort	2.0	—	Syslog (from device)	—	SW-host	—
Enterasys Dragon	6.x	—	Syslog (from manager)	—	SW-host	—

Table B-8 *CS-MARS V4.1 Product Support List with Additional Data (Continued)*

Device Type/ Vendor	Supported Versions	Protocol: Configuration Retrieval	Protocol: Event Retrieval	Protocol: Mitigation	Device Classification	CSV Keyword
Host IDS						
Cisco Security Agent	4.0, 4.5, 5.0	—	SNMP (from CSA MC)	—	SW-host	—
McAfee Entercept	2.5, 4.0	—	SNMP (from management server)	—	SW-host	—
ISS RealSecure Host Sensor	6.5, 7.0	—	SNMP (from device)	—	SW-host	—
Antivirus						
Symantec AntiVirus	9.*x*	—	SNMP (from management server)	—	SW-host	—
Cisco Incident Control System (Cisco ICS), Trend Micro Outbreak Prevention Service (OPS)	1.0	—	Syslog (from CICC server)	—	SW-host	—
McAfee ePolicy Orchestrator	3.5	—	—	—	SW-host	—
Network Associates VirusScan	8.*x*	—	SNMP (from management server)	—	—	—

continues

Table B-8 *CS-MARS V4.1 Product Support List with Additional Data (Continued)*

Device Type/ Vendor	Supported Versions	Protocol: Configuration Retrieval	Protocol: Event Retrieval	Protocol: Mitigation	Device Classification	CSV Keyword
Vulnerability Assessment						
eEye REM	1.0	MS SQL	JDBC (from REM server)	—	SW-host	—
Qualys Qualys-Guard	3.4	—	HTTPS	—	ODS	—
Foundstone Foundscan	3.0	MS SQL	JDBC (from management sever)	—	SW-host	—
Host OS						
Windows	NT, 2000, 2003	—	Syslog (from SNARE agent) or MS-RPC event pull	—	Host	WINDOWS
Solaris	8.x, 9.x, 10.x	—	Syslog (from device)	—	Host	SOLARIS
Red Hat Linux	7.x, 8.x	—	Syslog (from device)	—	Host	LINUX
Web Servers						
Microsoft Internet Information Server	Any	—	Syslog (from SNARE agent)	—	SW-host	—
Sun iPlanet	Any	—	HTTP (from Cisco Security MARS agent)	—	SW-host	—
Apache	Any	—	HTTP (from Cisco Security MARS agent)	—	SW-host	—

Table B-8 *CS-MARS V4.1 Product Support List with Additional Data (Continued)*

Device Type/ Vendor	Supported Versions	Protocol: Configuration Retrieval	Protocol: Event Retrieval	Protocol: Mitigation	Device Classification	CSV Keyword
Web Proxy Devices						
Network Appliance NetCache	Generic	—	HTTP	—	HW	
Database Servers						
Oracle Database	9i, 10g, Generic	TCP	SQLNet (from host)	—	SW-host	
AAA Servers						
Cisco Secure Access Control Sever (ACS)	3.3	—	Syslog (from Cisco Security MARS agent)	—	SW-host	
Syslog Servers and SNMP Devices						
Generic Devices	Any		SNMP (from device), Syslog (from device)	—	—	—

The purpose of this appendix is to provide you with CS-MARS evaluation and configuration supplements. It includes the following topics:

- CS-MARS Evaluation Worksheet
- Sample Seed File
- ISS Configuration Scripts
- IOS and CATOS NetFlow Quick Configuration Guide

CS-MARS Supplements

This appendix provides you with an evaluation worksheet to aid you in a successful evaluation of CS-MARS, and supplemental CS-MARS configuration data to assist you in a quick and comprehensive deployment.

The following topics are covered:

- CS-MARS Evaluation Worksheet
- Sample Seed File
- Internet Security Systems (ISS) Configuration Scripts
- IOS and CATOS NetFlow Quick Configuration Guide

CS-MARS Evaluation Worksheet

You can use the following evaluation worksheet to set the testing criteria of a CS-MARS evaluation. It will help you to quickly recognize the value that CS-MARS can provide in your network by helping to identify the devices in your network that CS-MARS can use to analyze and correlate events, and, of course, ultimately mitigate threats.

This evaluation worksheet is designed to be used by customers, resellers, and Cisco field personnel to aid them in preparing to evaluate the CS-MARS appliance and have the data needed to configure CS-MARS ready when the evaluation begins.

Security Threat Mitigation

Technical Evaluation Worksheet

This worksheet and the information contained in Tables C-1 and C-2 are provided solely for the purpose of supporting the evaluation of a CS-MARS appliance.

Evaluation Start Date:

Evaluation End Date:

Company Information	
Contact Name	
Title	
Phone	
E-mail	

Shipping Address	
Ship-To Address	
Recipient Name	
Phone	
E-mail	
Preferred Carrier	

Network Device Information		
Firewall	Vendor	
	OS	
	Version	
	# of FW	
Router	Vendor	
	Version	
Switches	Vendor	
	Version	
VPN	Vendor	
NIDS	Vendor	
	Version	

HIDS	Vendor	
	Version	
VA	Vendor	
	Version	*e.g., Nessus/Retina*
IPS	Vendor	
	Version	
Proxy Server	Vendor	

NetFlow	
Device details	Which devices is NetFlow running on? Core routers, etc.
Usage	
Version	V5 or 7 (Circle one.)

Regulatory Compliance Requirements (If Any)	
SOX	
GLBA	
HIPAA	
Others	

Security Information Backup and Archiving Requirements
1. Is an NAS server available on the network local to the CS-MARS MARS Eval network?
2. Describe the security information backup requirement. Do you want to store old data or to purge old data and use current data?

Trending/Management Reporting Requirements
What kind of reports does your management require (e.g., Show top web users)?

Current Security Information Management Issues/Requirements
Are you able to pinpoint the source of a worm attack when it occurs? Do your sys admins have to deal with voluminous event log files?

Current Solution for Security Event Management
e.g., Syslog server . . .

SIM Solutions Evaluated/Planned

Expected Goals from This Evaluation
1.
2.
3.

Additional Inputs Required
1. Network diagram
2. Traffic statistics (e.g., MRTG graphs from core router)
3.

Sample Seed File

Reporting device data via a "seed" file is a function of CS-MARS designed to save time. Most network-management applications can generate seed files automatically; however, if you need to create one from scratch, the following steps and tables describe how to do so.

Step 1 Use an application that can save files as .csv files, such as Microsoft Excel.

Step 2 Label the columns as outlined in Table C-1, in exactly the order presented.

Step 3 Populate the rows with the applicable device information.

Step 4 Save the file with any name as a .csv file to an FTP server.

Step 5 Import the file into CS-MARS.

When you have created your seed file, every piece of information you have entered should be separated by a comma, for a total of 20 fields. The following is an example of a working seed file:

```
192.168.0.150,,,,PIX7X,ssh,sshuser,cisco123,,Cisco,,,,,,,,,
192.168.0.10,csmars,,,EXTREME,SNMP,,,,,,,,,,,,,,
```

The following tables outline the necessary fields in a seed file. Because this seed file applies to all types of reporting devices, some fields might need to be left blank. It is important to maintain the order of the fields, including the blank spaces. In Table C-1, each column is labeled with a letter. Use Table C-2 to cross-reference the letter to the required column data.

Table C-1 *Sample Seed File*

A	B	C	D	E	F	G	H	I	J	K	L	M	N	O	P	Q	R	S	T

Table C-2 *Letter-to-Column Field Cross-Reference Table and Comments*

Letter	Column Contents	Comments
A	Device name or IP address	
B	SNMP read-only community string	
C	Empty	
D	Empty	
E	Device type	Refer to Chapter 6, Table 6-2 for keyword
F	Access type	Telnet, SSH, FTP, SNMP, RPC (Windows)
G	Username	Applicable for column F, except for SNMP
H	Password	Applicable for SSH or FTP only
I	Telnet password	
J	Enable password	
K	Empty	
L	Empty	
M	Empty	
N	Empty	
O	Empty	
P	Empty	
Q	Empty	
R	Empty	
S	Empty	
T	FTP location	Example: configs/pix/abccorp_pix1.txt

ISS Configuration Scripts

ISS hosts and sensors send their data to an ISS product called SiteProtector, which is the configuration and alarm-management station for ISS products. To send the data elsewhere, ISS requires you to configure globally on every sensor or host an SNMP trap destination, and then arduously configure every signature to send its data via SNMP to that trap destination. To save time configuring ISS host and network sensors, Cisco developed the two following Perl scripts.

NOTE   Running Perl scripts on hosts or servers requires Perl to be installed. Additionally, some modifications to the script might be required, depending on how much the ISS configuration files previously have been modified.

ISS Network Sensor

The following Perl script sets SNMP traps on your ISS network sensor to be sent to your CS-MARS appliance.

```
File Name: genNewCurrentPolicy.pl.serverSensor
------------------Script Begin--------------------------------
#!/usr/bin/perl -w

# Author:  Cisco Systems
# Date:    April 2004
# Purpose: This program reads the "current.policy" file from network sensor,
#          and add "SNMP" response to each feature (signature)

use strict;

my ($filename, $line);
my ($feature);

$filename = "current.policy";
open FILE, $filename
  or die "can't open $filename";


while ($line=<FILE>) {
  print $line;
  last if ( $line =~ /template\\features\\/ );
}

while ($line=<FILE>) {
  if ($line =~ /template\\features\\([^\\]+)\\Response\\SNMP/) {
    $line = <FILE>;
    next;
  }
  print $line;
  last if ($line =~ /template\\connections\\/);
  next if ($line !~ /template\\features\\([^\\]+)\\Response\\DISPLAY\\/);
  $feature = $1;
  $line = <FILE>;
  print $line;
  $line = <FILE>;
  if ($line !~ /template\\features\\([^\\]+)\\Response\\SNMP/) {
    print "[\\\template\\features\\", $feature, "\\Response\\SNMP\\];\n";
    print "Choice  =S       Default;\n";
  }
```

continues

(Continued)

```
  print $line;


}


while ($line=<FILE>) {
  print $line;
}


close FILE;

exit 0;
------------------Script End--------------------------------
```

ISS Server Sensor

The following Perl script sets SNMP traps on your ISS server sensor to be sent to your CS-MARS appliance.

```
File name: genNewCurrentPolicy.pl.serverSensor
------------------Script Begin------------------------------
#!/usr/bin/perl -w

# Author:  Cisco Systems
# Date:    January 2004
# Purpose: This program reads the "current.policy" file from server sensor,
#          and adds "SNMP" response to each feature (signature)

use strict;

my ($filename, $line);
my ($category, $feature);

$filename = "current.policy";
open FILE, $filename
  or die "can't open $filename";


#while ($line=<FILE>) {
#  print $line;
#  last if ( $line =~ /Advanced\\Rules\\/ );
#}

while ($line=<FILE>) {
  print $line;
  #last if ($line =~ /template\\connections\\/);
  next if ($line !~ /Advanced\\Rules\\([^\\]+)\\([^\\]+)\\Response\\SUSPEND\\/);
  $category = $1;
  $feature = $2;
```

(Continued)

```
  $line = <FILE>;
  print $line;
  $line = <FILE>;
  if ($line !~ /Advanced\\Rules\\$category\\$feature\\Response\\SNMP/) {
    print "[\\Advanced\\Rules\\", $category, "\\", $feature,
      "\\Response\\SNMP\\];\n";
    print "Choice  =S      Default;\n";
  }

  print $line;

}


#while ($line=<FILE>) {
#  print $line;
#}


close FILE;

exit 0;
-----------------Script End-----------------------------
```

IOS and CATOS NetFlow Quick Configuration Guide

The following steps outline how to configure an IOS and CATOS device for NetFlow processing and how to send NetFlow data to CS-MARS.

Configuring NetFlow Export on a Cisco IOS Device

To enable NetFlow on Cisco IOS devices, please complete the following steps:

Step 1 Use either the console, Telnet, or SSH to connect to the router or the MFSC.

Step 2 In config t mode on a Cisco IOS router, issue the following to enable NetFlow export:

```
ip flow-export destination <IP address of CS- MARS> 2055
```

{2055} is a default port; you can modify this to anything you want. Just make sure you set the same port on CS-MARS for NetFlow processing.

Step 3 Set the source IP for the network interface that will send NetFlow data to the CS-MARS device.

```
ip flow-export source <interface which is facing the Protego MARS
Server>
```

Step 4 Configure the NetFlow version:

```
ip flow-export version 5
```

Step 5 Configure the flow timeout. This breaks up long-lived flows into 5-minute segments. You can choose any number of minutes between 1 and 60; if you leave the default of 30 minutes, you might get spikes in your utilization reports.

```
ip flow-cache timeout active 5
```

This ensures that flows that have finished are exported in a timely manner.

```
ip flow-cache timeout inactive 15
```

Step 6 For each interface you want NetFlow to process, do the following:

```
interface <interface>
    ip route-cache flow
```

Step 7 To test that this configuration is working, issue the following commands from an enable prompt:

```
show ip flow export
show ip cache flow
```

Step 8 Save your configuration to memory at the enable prompt.

```
write memory
```

Configuring NetFlow on a Cisco CATOS Switch

If you are running CATOS, NetFlow needs to be configured on your Layer 2 switch fabric, in addition to your Layer 3 router (also called the MSFC).

This section describes how to enable NetFlow on the Layer 2 switch fabric when using CATOS.

NOTE The MSFC running IOS is configured identically to these IOS guidelines. When a 65K switch is running in native mode, the switch is running only IOS and needs to be configured with IOS NetFlow commands.

The following commands enable NetFlow on CATOS devices such as a Catalyst 5500 or 6500 in hybrid mode:

Step 1   Use Console, Telnet, or SSH to connect to the switch, not the MFSC.

Step 2   Apply the following commands at a config t prompt:

```
set mls flow full
set mls nde version 5
set mls nde < CS-MARS IP >  2055
set mls nde enable
```

Step 3   Save your configuration to memory at the enable prompt.

```
write memory
```

The purpose of this appendix is to provide you with information about using the command-line interface (CLI) to manage and maintain CS-MARS devices.

APPENDIX D

Command-Line Interface

The main management tool for the CS-MARS device is clearly the web interface; however, some operations must be done from the CLI.

This appendix summarizes all the CLI commands and, more important, highlights the critical CS-MARS maintenance commands, such as database resets.

The appendix is divided into two sections:

- Complete Command Summary
- CS-MARS Maintenance Commands

Complete Command Summary

Table D-1 summarizes all the CS-MARS commands and their purposes.

Table D-1   *CS-MARS Commands*

Command	Function
? or Help	Displays each command and lists the purpose of the commands.
arp	Displays the current Media Access Control (MAC) and Internet Protocol (IP) address of all devices that are active in the Address Resolution Protocol (ARP) table.
date	Configures and displays the current date for the CS-MARS device.
dns	Configures the Domain Name Server (DNS) to be used by the CS-MARS device.
dnssuffix	Configures the domain name suffixes search path used by the CS-MARS device.
domainname	Configures and displays the domain name for the CS-MARS device.
exit	Enables you to switch to standard mode or log out of the CS-MARS device. This is critical if you are using CLI; when you are done, log out. Otherwise, unauthorized people can simply sit at your workstation and manipulate your CS-MARS appliance.

continues

Table D-1 *CS-MARS Commands (Continued)*

Command	Function
gateway	Configures and displays the default gateway of the CS-MARS device.
hostname	Configures and displays the device hostname of the CS-MARS device.
hotswap	Enables you to add or remove a disk in your CS-MARS device while the device is still running. This enables you to do this hardware-maintenance function with no downtime of the device.
ifconfig	This is the standard Linux-style ifconfig command. It can be used to modify network interfaces. If you lose the license for your CS-MARS box, you need to send the device model and MAC address of Eth0 to the Cisco Technical Assistance Center (TAC) for a new license key. You would use this command in conjunction with the **model** command to get the MAC address and model information of the CS-MARS device.
model	Displays the model information of CS-MARS. If you lose the license for your CS-MARS box, you need to send the device model and MAC address of Eth0 to the Cisco TAC for a new license key. You would use this command in conjunction with the **ifconfig** command to get the MAC address and model information of the CS-MARS device.
netstat	Displays the open network ports and the status of the open network ports on the CS-MARS device. This is the standard Linux-style **netstat** command; you can use a **-?** to see the options for this command.
nslookup	Displays the address resolution for a DNS name or IP address. This is the standard Linux-style **nslookup** command. It uses the DNS servers that you defined when you configured your CS-MARS device for the resolution queries.
ntp	Configures the CS-MARS to use an NTP server. When CS-MARS correlates and analyzes security alerts, it's critical that all times are synchronized because that is the purpose of NTP. Even though this section tells you the command to use for CS-MARS, all your devices should be using NTP to ensure time synchronization.
passwd	Configures the CS-MARS password database for the current logged-in user.
ping	This is the standard ping implementation used to test connectivity between devices. Enter **-?** to see the ping extended options that CS-MARS supports.
pnlog	Configures and displays system log levels. See the next section for a more in-depth discussion of this command.

Table D-1 *CS-MARS Commands (Continued)*

Command	Function
pnreset	Resets the box to factory defaults. See the next section for a more in-depth discussion of this command.
pnrestore	Restores system configuration and data from an archived file(s). See the next section for a more in-depth discussion of this command.
pnstart	Starts the CS-MARS application processes. See the next section for a more in-depth discussion of this command.
pnstatus	Shows the status of the CS-MARS application processes. See the next section for a more in-depth discussion of this command.
pnstop	Stops the CS-MARS application processes. See the next section for a more in-depth discussion of this command.
pnupgrade	Performs an operating system upgrade. See the upcoming section "CS-MARS Maintenance Commands" for a more in-depth discussion of this command.
raidstatus	Displays the status of Redundant Array of Independent Disks (RAID) configured. This command is available only in CS-MARS models that use disks that use the RAID array architecture.
reboot	Reboots the CS-MARS application. No user interaction is required to bring the box back online. This command does a clean shutdown and startup of your CS-MARS device.
route	Configures and displays routing tables for the CS-MARS device. If you are using both CS-MARS interfaces and are communicating with a device that is not local to an interface or not located in the direction of the default route, you need to add a route to let CS-MARS know where to find this device or devices.
shutdown	Gracefully shuts down your CS-MARS device.
snmpwalk	Uses read-only Simple Network Management Protocol (SNMP) queries to get information from SNMP servers on remote devices. Use the -? flag to see all the options for this command.
ssh	Secure Shell (SSH) can be used to access the CLI of a reporting device that has SSH enabled. SSH is preferred to access any device CLI through the network because it is encrypted.
sslcert	Creates a self-signed cert for your CS-MARS appliance. This cert is then used for device authentication between CS-MARS and other devices using protocols that require certificates such as SSH and Secure Socket Layer (SSL) communications.

continues

Table D-1 *CS-MARS Commands (Continued)*

Command	Function
tcpdump	Displays traffic traversing the interfaces on your CS-MARS device(s). This utility is most often used for network and device troubleshooting.
telnet	Can be used to access the CLI of reporting devices that have Telnet enabled. However Telnet is not recommended because all data is passed in clear text. SSH is preferred for accessing a device CLI through the network.
time	Displays and configures the current date and time of the CS-MARS device. NTP is recommended over this method because it can ensure that the dates and times of all your network devices are synchronized.
timezone	Displays and configures the current time zone of the CS-MARS device. NTP is recommended over this method because it can ensure that the dates and times of all your network devices are synchronized. Use the **set** command preceding the **timezone** command to start the CLI configuration wizard for setting the time zone manually.
traceroute	Displays all the routing entities between CS-MARS and a particular host. This command is normally used to vary routing or troubleshoot network problems.
sysstatus	Used to see what system resources a process on your CS-MARS device is using. It is the equivalent of the **TOP** command in many Linux and UNIX environments.
version	Displays the current operating system version and patch level running on your CS-MARS device.

CS-MARS Maintenance Commands

This section describes the commands used for the maintenance of your CS-MARS device and the CS-MARS database.

These commands are discussed:

- **hotswap**
- **pnlog**
- **pnreset**
- **pnrestore**
- **pnstart**

- **pnstatus**
- **pnstop**
- **pnupgrade**

hotswap   The **hotswap** command lets you add or delete disks in CS-MARS devices that support RAID configurations without powering down the device. This enables you to expand the CS-MARS device as desired without incurring downtime. Downtime opens possible windows when your network can be compromised without detection.

pnlog   This command displays logs on your line mode terminal indicating the status of different functions and features of CS-MARS processes and also controls the logs sent to the CS-MARS device by Check Point firewall debug logs. Using this command, you also can set the debug level that is reported in the logs. The debug levels that are set with this command determine what level of debugs is displayed with the **pnstatus** command.

pnreset   The **pnreset** command resets the CS-MARS device to factory defaults. This includes erasing the license file. You *must* write down the license file before doing a reset because when you reconfigure the device, the license key is required. When pnreset is completed, the database structures are cleared, set, and initialized.

If you have a requirement to restore the data to your sensor after a factory reset, you must first set the CS-MARS device to archive its OS and data to an NFS device. This is done through the GUI at the location **Admin > System Maintenance > Archiving**. After a pnreset is completed, you can use the pnrestore command to restore the CS-MARS device to its last-known current state.

Your sensor should be taken off the network when a pnreset is in progress to ensure that the command prompt will be returned when the reset is completed. It's important to note that a reset, which includes rebuilding and initializing the database structure, often takes an hour or more to complete. Additionally, it is recommended that when you reset the appliance to factory defaults, your interface into the unit should be locally using a monitor and keyboard.

pnrestore   The **pnrestore** command is used to send OS and data from the CS-MARS database to a network file server. You must first define the server using the GUI at the following location: **Admin > System Maintenance > Archiving**. After the data is archived, you can use the **pnrestore** command to bring the data back into the CS-MARS device. The **pnrestore** command lets you select restore options that define the type of data you want to restore. The options are as follows:

- Time and date ranges
- Operating system
- System configurations
- Dynamic database events

pnstart　The **pnstart** command enables you to manually start the CS-MARS processes from the command line.

pnstatus　The **pnstatus** command is used to view the status of each of the CS-MARS processes running on the device. The information includes the status of the process and how long the process has been active. The following is a sample of the pnstatus default output:

```
[pnadmin]$ pnstatus
Module                    State       Uptime
DbIncidentLoaderSrv       RUNNING     02:29:24
csdam                     RUNNING     02:29:24
device_monitor            RUNNING     02:29:24
discover                  RUNNING     02:29:24
graphgen                  RUNNING     02:29:24
pnarchiver                RUNNING     02:29:24
pndbpurger                RUNNING     02:29:24
pnesloader                RUNNING     02:29:24
pnids40_srv               RUNNING     02:29:24
pnids50_srv               RUNNING     02:29:24
pniosips_srv              RUNNING     02:29:24
pnmac                     RUNNING     02:29:24
pnparser                  RUNNING     02:29:25
process_event_srv         RUNNING     02:29:25
process_inlinerep_srv     RUNNING     02:29:25
process_postfire_srv      RUNNING     02:29:25
process_query_srv         RUNNING     02:29:25
superV                    RUNNING     02:29:26
```

pnstop　The **pnstop** command enables you to manually stop the CS-MARS processes from the command line. When used in conjunction with the **pnstatus** command, **pnstop** produces output showing that all processes are stopped except for a listener process that passes commands to start and stop the CS-MARS main processes, as shown in the sample here:

```
[pnadmin]$ pnstop
Please wait ...
[pnadmin]$ pnstatus
Module                    State       Uptime
DbIncidentLoaderSrv       STOPPED
csdam                     STOPPED
device_monitor            STOPPED
discover                  STOPPED
graphgen                  STOPPED
pnarchiver                STOPPED
pndbpurger                STOPPED
pnesloader                STOPPED
pnids40_srv               STOPPED
pnids50_srv               STOPPED
pniosips_srv              STOPPED
pnmac                     STOPPED
pnparser                  STOPPED
process_event_srv         STOPPED
process_inlinerep_srv     STOPPED
process_postfire_srv      STOPPED
process_query_srv         STOPPED
superV                    RUNNING     02:33:33
```

NOTE The superV process will not stop when the pnstop command is issued. This process is required to remain running at all times so that the user can access the CLI.

pnupgrade The **pnupgrade** command is used to upgrade the operating system image and data structures of the CS-MARS device. An upgrade package is first downloaded from Cisco and then one of the following methods is used to upgrade the CS-MARS device. A string is passed in the **pnupgrade** command that specifies where the upgrade image is located and also includes any usernames or passwords required to access the device containing the upgrade image. The following upgrade methods and paths are available:

- CD-ROM (includes DVD format)
- HTTPS
- HTTP
- FTP

The purpose of this appendix is to provide you with a quick reference guide to reports that are available in CS-MARS version 4.1.

CS-MARS Reporting

This appendix provides you with a description of the reports that are available in CS-MARS v4.1. This appendix simply includes a table with the report name and the report description.

You will see at a glance that these reports are not only useful for threat response, but they also meet network and host audit criteria.

CS-MARS V4.1 Reports

The following is a guide to creating CS-MARS reports. Table E-1 lists the reports in CS-MARS version 4.1.

Step 1 Click on the **Query/Reports** button, located near the top of the CS-MARS Web Management screen.

Step 2 Under the heading "Load Report as On-Demand Query with Filter," select the report that you want to run. Reports are categorized by report type, or you can select **All** to see all possible reports. Table E-1 lists the available CS-MARS reports.

Table E-1   *CS-MARS V4.1 Reports*

Report	Report Description
Activity: Authentication, Authorization, and Accounting (AAA)–Based Access—All Events	Details AAA-based access (for example, to the network or to specific devices).
Activity: AAA-Based Access Failure—All Events	Details all failed AAA (for example, RADIUS, TACACS)–based access attempts. Typically, mechanisms such as 802.1x, network device access, and Cisco NAC use AAA servers for access control.
Activity: Accounts Locked—All Events	Details events that indicate locked computer accounts because of excessive login failures.
Activity: Accounts Locked—Top Hosts	Ranks the hosts by the accounts locked.

continues

Table E-1 *CS-MARS V4.1 Reports (Continued)*

Report	Report Description
Activity: All—NAT Connections	Lists Network Address Translations (NAT) performed on nondenied sessions as reported to CS-MARS.
Activity: All—Top Destination Ports	Ranks the UDP and TCP destination ports of all events seen by CS-MARS over the past hour. This report is used by pages in the main panel's Summary tab.
Activity: All—Top Destinations	Ranks the session destinations of all events seen by CS-MARS over the past hour. This report is used by pages in the Summary tab.
Activity: All—Top Event Type Groups	Ranks event type groups by reported events that belong to each group. The event type groups give a general feeling about the type of network activity reported to CS-MARS.
Activity: All—Top Event Types	Ranks the event types of all events seen by CS-MARS over the past hour. This report is used by pages in the Summary tab.
Activity: All—Top Reporting Device Types	Ranks security device types by the number of events reported by devices of each particular type.
Activity: All—Top Reporting Devices	Ranks security devices by the total number of events reported by each device. This report is used by pages in the Summary tab.
Activity: All—Top Sources	Ranks the session sources of all events seen by CS-MARS over the past hour. This report is used by pages in the Summary tab.
Activity: All—Top Users	This report tracks the most frequent logins and other user activity by showing the most active usernames.
Activity: All Events and NetFlow—Top Destination Ports	Ranks the UDP and TCP destination ports of all events (including NetFlow events) seen by CS-MARS over the past hour. This report is used by pages in the Summary tab.
Activity: All Sessions—Top Destination Ports by Bytes	Ranks all destination ports by bytes transferred.
Activity: All Sessions—Top Destinations by Bytes	Ranks all destinations by bytes transferred.
Activity: Attacks Prevented—Top Reporting Devices	Ranks security devices by the number of attacks prevented.
Activity: Attacks Seen—Top Event Types	Ranks the top attack event types.

Table E-1   *CS-MARS V4.1 Reports (Continued)*

Report	Report Description
Activity: Attacks Seen—Top Reporting Devices	Ranks security devices by the number of attack events logged. The security devices can be firewalls, NIDS, or HIDS.
Activity: Backdoor—Top Destinations	Ranks the hosts that respond to backdoor connection attempts.
Activity: Backdoor—Top Event Types	Ranks the events that detect some form of backdoor activity. A back door could be created by an attacker on a compromised host. A backdoor event can be either an attempt to connect to a back door or a response from a server running a back door.
Activity: Backdoor—Top Hosts	Ranks the hosts that respond to backdoor connection attempts. This means that the hosts are likely infected and running back doors.
Activity: CS-MARS Host Mitigation—Failure—All Events	Lists failed CS-MARS mitigation attempts. These can result from improper network connectivity or device access credentials.
Activity: CS-MARS Host Mitigation—Success—All Events	Lists successful mitigations from CS-MARS.
Activity: Database Login Failures—All Events	Lists the event details for all database login failure events.
Activity: Database Login Failures—Top Servers	Ranks the database servers by the number of login failures.
Activity: Database Login Failures—Top Users	Ranks the users by the number of login failures.
Activity: Database Login Successes—All Events	Lists event details for all successful database login events.
Activity: Database Login Successes—Top Servers	Ranks the database server hosts by the number of successful logins.
Activity: Database Login Successes—Top Users	Ranks the database users by the number of successful logins.
Activity: Database Object Modification Failures—All Events	Lists the event details for all failed database object-modification attempts.
Activity: Database Object Modification Failures—Top Users	Ranks the users by the number of failed database object-modification attempts.
Activity: Database Object Modification Successes—All Events	Lists the event details for all successful database object-modification attempts.

continues

Table E-1 *CS-MARS V4.1 Reports (Continued)*

Report	Report Description
Activity: Database Object Modification Successes—Top Users	Ranks the number of users by the number of successful database object modifications.
Activity: Database Privileged Command Failures—All Events	Lists event details for all privileged database command-execution failures.
Activity: Database Privileged Command Failures—Top Users	Ranks the users by failed privileged database command-execution attempts.
Activity: Database Privileged Command Successes—All Events	Lists the event details for all successful privileged database commands executed.
Activity: Database Privileged Command Successes—Top Users	Ranks the users by successful privileged database commands executed.
Activity: Database Regular Command Failures—All Events	Lists the event details for all failed nonprivileged database command-execution attempts.
Activity: Database Regular Command Failures—Top Users	Ranks the users by the number of nonprivileged database command-execution attempts.
Activity: Database Regular Command Successes—All Events	Lists the event details for all successful nonprivileged database command executions.
Activity: Database Regular Command Successes—Top Users	Ranks the users by successful nonprivileged database command executions.
Activity: Database User/Group Change Failures—All Events	Lists the event details for all failed database user/group modification attempts.
Activity: Database User/Group Change Failures—Top Users	Ranks the users by the number of failed database user/group modification attempts.
Activity: Database User/Group Change Successes—All Events	Lists the event details for all successful database user/group modifications.
Activity: Database User/Group Change Successes—Top Users	Ranks the users by the successful database user/group modifications performed.
Activity: Denies—Top Destination Ports	Ranks the destination ports to which attacks have been targeted but denied.
Activity: Denies—Top Destinations	Ranks the destination hosts to which attacks have been targeted but denied.
Activity: Denies—Top Sources	Ranks attack sources by the number of denied connection attempts.
Activity: Host Admin Login Success—All Events	Details successful administrative login events to hosts.
Activity: Host Login Failures—All Events	Records all host login failure details.

Table E-1   *CS-MARS V4.1 Reports (Continued)*

Report	Report Description
Activity: Host Login Failures—Top Destinations	Ranks hosts by the number of login failures recorded.
Activity: Host Login Failures—Top Users	Ranks host users by failed login attempts.
Activity: Host Login Success—All Events	Details all host login success event details.
Activity: Host Login Success—Top Host	Ranks hosts by successful logins.
Activity: Host Object Access—All Events	Records all Microsoft Windows Object Access events from Windows Event Logs.
Activity: Host Privilege Escalation—All Events	Provides details for events that represent a user attempting to increase access rights on a particular host. Such attempts can happen remotely or from the local console and can be reported by network or host IDS devices or the hosts themselves.
Activity: Host Privilege Escalation—Top Hosts	Ranks the hosts by access-privilege escalation attempts tried against them. Such attempts can happen remotely or from the local console and can be reported by network or host IDS devices or the hosts themselves.
Activity: Host Privileged Access—All Events	Records all Microsoft Windows Host Privileged Access events from Windows Event Logs.
Activity: Host Process Tracking—All Events	Records all Microsoft Windows Detailed Process Tracking events from Windows Event Logs.
Activity: Host Registry Changes—All Events	Records the events signaling Microsoft Windows Registry changes.
Activity: Host Registry Changes—Top Host	Ranks hosts by the number of Microsoft Windows Registry changes reported.
Activity: Host Security Policy Changes—All Events	Lists all policy changes on a host affecting host security. These events are typically reported by host IDS and host agents.
Activity: Host Security Policy Changes—Top Host	Ranks hosts by the number of security policy changes on that host.
Activity: Host System Events—All Events	Records the Microsoft Windows system events—startup, shutdown, LSA registration, audit event discards, and so on.

continues

Table E-1 *CS-MARS V4.1 Reports (Continued)*

Report	Report Description
Activity: Host User/Group Management—All Events	Records user group-management events reported by hosts.
Activity: Host User/Group Management—Top hosts	Ranks hosts by user group-management events reported.
Activity: IDS Evasion—Top Event Types	Ranks the events that detect an attempt by an attacker to evade detection by network IDS systems. This may be web-based obfuscation attacks, fragmentation attacks, or TCP/IP–based attacks.
Activity: Inactive Reporting Device— Top Devices	Lists devices that are configured to be reporting to CS-MARS but that haven't reported any event in the last hour.
Activity: IOS IPS DTM Successful Signature Tuning—All Events	Lists all successful IOS IPS signature download activities, both addition and deletion. CS-MARS Distributed Threat Mitigation (DTM) turns on *active* IPS signatures on IOS routers.
Activity: Internet Relay Chat (IRC)— All Events	Lists all IRC activities. Typically, worms deposit executables on infected hosts that initiate IRC connections.
Activity: Network Usage—Top Destination Ports	Ranks destination ports by number of network sessions. This report requires that the syslog level of routers or firewalls be set to high to be able to capture session events. This report provides a general usage pattern of the network.
Activity: Network Usage—Top Destination Ports by Bytes	Ranks the top destination ports by bytes sent and transmitted.
Activity: New Malware Discovered—All Events	Lists all the new virus/worm/malware outbreaks discovered by the Cisco Incident Control Server.
Activity: New Malware Prevention Deployment Failure—All Events	Lists all devices to which ACL and signature-deployment attempts by a Cisco Incident Control Server failed, in response to a new virus/worm/ malware outbreak.
Activity: New Malware Prevention Deployment Success—All Events	Lists all destinations (Cisco IOS IPS devices and IPS appliances) to which Cisco Incident Control Server has deployed new ACLs and signatures in response to a new virus/worm/malware outbreak.
Activity: New Malware Traffic Match—All Events	Details the traffic sources and the enforcing devices that match the ACLs and signatures deployed by the Cisco Incident Control Server in response to a newly discovered malware outbreak.

Table E-1   *CS-MARS V4.1 Reports (Continued)*

Report	Report Description
Activity: New Malware Traffic Match—Top Sources	Lists the top sources that match the ACLs or signatures dynamically deployed by the Cisco Incident Control Server in response to a new virus/ worm/malware outbreak. This indicates that these sources are likely infected.
Activity: P2P Filesharing/Chat— All Events	Details all P2P file sharing or chat event details.
Activity: P2P Filesharing/Chat— Top Event Types	Ranks events detecting person-to-person file-sharing protocol and chat protocol activity. File-sharing protocols such as KaZaa, Napster, and EDonkey and chat protocols such as IRC, Hotline, and instant-messaging protocols might not be suitable in business environments.
Activity: P2P Filesharing/Chat— Top Hosts	Ranks hosts involved in P2P file sharing and chat protocol activity. Such protocols might not be suitable in business environments.
Activity: Recreational—All Events	Details all users involved in recreational activities such as games, specific websites such as gambling, and so on.
Activity: Recreational—Top Sources	Ranks the source addresses involved in recreational activities such as games, adult websites, stock sites, and so on.
Activity: Remote Access Login—All Events	Details remote access login events (IPSec, SSLVPN, PPP, L2TP, and so on).
Activity: Remote Access Login—Top User	Ranks users by remote access logins (PPP, L2TP, PPTP, IPSec).
Activity: Remote Access Login Failures—All Events	Details all failed remote access login event details.
Activity: Scans—Top Destination Ports	Ranks destination ports by the total number of events detecting scanning activity for that port. Scans involve activities such as searching for alive hosts, determining open services on such hosts, and detecting host-configuration and application settings.
Activity: Scans—Top Destinations	Ranks hosts by the total number of events detecting scanning activity directed to that host. Scans involve activities such as searching for alive hosts, determining open services on such hosts, and detecting host-configuration and application settings.

continues

Table E-1 *CS-MARS V4.1 Reports (Continued)*

Report	Report Description
Activity: Scans—Top Sources	Ranks an attack source by the total number of events detecting scanning activity for certain services. Scans involve activities such as searching for alive hosts, determining open services on such hosts, and detecting host-configuration and application settings.
Activity: Security Posture Validation Failure—Top Users	Ranks the users by security posture validation failures. Such failures are likely caused by configuration errors in posture validation rule definition.
Activity: Security Posture: Agentless—All Events	Lists hosts who are exempt from security posture validations because Cisco Trust Agent (CTA) is not running on these hosts. Examples of such hosts are print servers and non-Windows hosts.
Activity: Security Posture: Agentless—Top Hosts	Lists hosts who are exempt from security posture validations because Cisco Trust Agent (CTA) is not running on these hosts. Examples of such hosts are print servers and non-Windows hosts.
Activity: Security Posture: Healthy—All Events	Lists the detailed events for users in a *healthy* security posture state. This security posture implies that the posture of the host is up-to-date and policy compliant and does not need attention.
Activity: Security Posture: Healthy—Top Users	Lists the users in a *healthy* security posture state. This security posture implies that the posture of the host is up-to-date and policy compliant, and does not need attention.
Activity: Security Posture: Not Healthy—All Events	Lists the detailed events for users whose security posture is not up-to-date—that is, in either a *checkup*, *quarantine*, or *infected* state. The software on these hosts needs to be upgraded. The *checkup* hosts might need DAT file updates, the *quarantine* hosts must do DAT file updates before network access, and the *infected* hosts must be remediated before network access.
Activity: Security Posture: Not Healthy—Top Users	Lists the users whose security posture is not healthy—that is, in either a *checkup*, *quarantine*, or *infected* state. The software on these hosts needs to be upgraded. The *checkup* hosts might need DAT file updates, the *quarantine* hosts must do DAT file updates before network access, and the *infected* hosts must be remediated before network access.

Table E-1   *CS-MARS V4.1 Reports (Continued)*

Report	Report Description
Activity: Spyware—All Events	Details all spyware events.
Activity: Spyware—Top Hosts	Ranks the hosts running spyware applications. Spyware is malicious applications that install and run on hosts; collect the username, passwords, and credit card information; and send this information to the spyware writers.
Activity: Stealth Scans—Top Sources	Ranks attackers by the amount of stealth scanning activity. Such activities include sending crafted packets to detect host operating systems and other vulnerabilities. Vulnerability scanners can generate such events.
Activity: Sudden Traffic Increase to Port—All Destinations	Lists hosts that exhibit anomalous behavior by suddenly receiving statistically significant volume on a TCP/UDP port or ICMP traffic.
Activity: Sudden Traffic Increase to Port—All Sources	Lists hosts that exhibit anomalous behavior by suddenly sending statistically significant volume on a TCP/UDP port or ICMP traffic.
Activity: Uncommon or Anomalous Traffic—All Events	Details uncommon or anomalous traffic such as unused TCP options, uncommon ICMP traffic, nonstandard traffic on a standard port, tunneled traffic, and so on.
Activity: Unknown Events—All Events	Tracks the events that are unknown to CS-MARS.
Activity: Virus/Worms—Top Event Types	Ranks the events that detect virus or worm activity in the network.
Activity: Virus/Worms—Top Infected Hosts	Ranks hosts that are propagating a virus or worms via SMTP, POP, IMAP, network shares, and so on.
Activity: Virus: Detected—Top Users	Ranks users/workstations by viruses detected.
Activity: Virus: Infections—Top Users	Ranks users/workstations by viruses detected and not cleaned.
Activity: Vulnerable Host Found	Lists all vulnerable hosts found by IDS or VA scanners.
Activity: Vulnerable Host Found via VA Scanner	Lists vulnerable hosts and associated vulnerabilities found by importing information from vulnerability analysis (VA) scanners.
Activity: Web Usage—Top Destinations by Bytes	Ranks the web servers by bytes transferred.

continues

Table E-1   *CS-MARS V4.1 Reports (Continued)*

Report	Report Description
Activity: Web Usage—Top Destinations by Sessions	Ranks the top web destinations by session count.
Activity: Web Usage—Top Sources	Ranks source addresses based on web use.
Attacks: All—All Events	Records details (event type, destination, source) for all attack events.
Attacks: All—Top Destinations	Ranks hosts by the number of attacks targeted at each host.
Attacks: All—Top Event Type Groups	Ranks event type groups that appear in fired correlation rules. The event type groups give a general feeling about the network activity classified by CS-MARS as part of an attack.
Attacks: All—Top Rules Fired	Ranks rules fired over the past hour by a number of incidents. This provides a general feeling about the attack activity in the network. This report is used by pages in the Summary tab.
Attacks: All—Top Sources	Ranks the sources of attack events seen by CS-MARS over the past hour.
Attacks: Client Exploits—Top Sources	Ranks hosts by the number of exploits originating from each host.
Attacks: Database Server—Top Event Types	Ranks attacks on database servers such as MS SQL Server, Oracle, and Sybase.
Attacks: FTP Server—Top Event Types	Ranks attacks on FTP servers.
Attacks: Identity Spoofing—Top Event Types	Ranks events that represent attempts by an attacker to spoof his or her identity over the past hour.
Attacks: Login Services—Top Event Types	Ranks attacks on servers providing login services and remote shells. Examples include Telnet, SSH, and Berkeley r-protocols.
Attacks: Mail Server—Top Event Types	Ranks attacks on mail servers (SMTP, POP, IMAP).
Attacks: Network DoS—Top Event Types	Ranks attacks that represent network-wide denial-of-service attempts. Such attacks can include crashing or rebooting an inline network device such as a router, firewall, or switch or increasing network load by creating TCP, UDP, or ICMP traffic.
Attacks: Password—All Events	Details all password attack events.

Table E-1   *CS-MARS V4.1 Reports (Continued)*

Report	Report Description
Attacks: Password—Top Destinations	Ranks hosts by the number of password attacks attempted on them. Password attacks include attempts to (a) capture passwords, either remotely or locally, and (b) guess passwords. Password-guessing attempts are recorded as authentication failures by IDS and hosts.
Attacks: Password—Top Event Types	Ranks password-retrieving and guessing attacks. The password can be a system or application password.
Attacks: Password: Locked Accounts—All Events	Details password attacks on locked/disabled/expired accounts.
Attacks: Password: Restricted Times—All Events	Details all events that indicate login failures at restricted times; the hosts are specifically configured to disallow access at these hours.
Attacks: RPC Services—Top Event Types	Ranks attacks on RPC-based applications.
Attacks: SANS Top 20—Top Event Types	Ranks the attacks that have been included in SANS Top 20 list.
Attacks: SNMP—Top Event Types	Ranks SNMP-based attacks over the past hour.
Attacks: Uncommon or Anomalous Traffic—Top Event Types	Ranks the events that represent uncommon or anomalous traffic. Uncommon traffic involves ICMP types and TCP/IP options not in common usage or standard traffic on nonstandard ports. Anomalous traffic includes traffic that violates IETF or other well-known protocol specifications.
Attacks: Virus/Worms—Top Sources	Ranks addresses that are the source of virus/worm propagation attempts.
Attacks: Web Server/App—Top Event Types	Ranks attacks on web servers or applications built on top of web servers over the past hour.
Configuration Changes: Network—All Events	Details all the configuration changes in network devices.
Configuration Changes: Network—Top Event Types	Summarizes configuration changes to network devices such as firewalls, routers, and switches over the past hour.
Configuration Changes: Server—All Events	Details all configuration changes on hosts (reported by OS or host IDS agents).
Configuration Changes: Server—Top Event Types	Summarizes configuration changes to servers over the past hour.

continues

Table E-1 *CS-MARS V4.1 Reports (Continued)*

Report	Report Description
Configuration Changes: Server—Top Reporting Devices	Summarizes the configuration changes per server over the past hour.
Configuration Issues: Network—All Events	Lists details for events that indicate configuration error on network devices.
Configuration Issues: Network—Top Reporting Devices	Summarizes the events that may indicate certain configuration-related problems in network devices such as firewalls, routers, and switches.
Configuration Issues: Server—All Events	Lists details for all events that indicate configuration errors on hosts or host applications.
Configuration Issues: Server—Top Reporting Devices	Summarizes the events that might indicate certain configuration-related problems in servers. These are likely to be host IDS events.
Connectivity Issue: IOS IPS DTM—All Events	Lists connectivity issues between CS-MARS and IOS IPS devices. Connectivity issues might prevent CS-MARS from turning on *active* signatures on IOS IPS.
Operational Issues: Network—All Events	Lists details about all operational issues on network devices.
Operational Issues: Network—Top Reporting Devices	Summarizes the events that might indicate operational issues with network devices such as routers, firewalls, and network IDS systems.
Operational Issues: Server—All Events	Lists details about events that indicate operational errors on hosts or host applications.
Operational Issues: Server—Top Reporting Devices	Summarizes the events that could indicate operational issues with servers.
Resource Issues: IOS IPS DTM—All Events	Lists event details that indicate certain IOS IPS routers running low on memory for CS-MARS Distributed Threat Mitigation (DTM). Because of low memory, CS-MARS might not be capable of downloading and activating the complete set of *active* IPS signatures to those IOS IPS devices.
Resource Issues: IOS IPS DTM—Top Devices	Lists IOS IPS routers that are running low on memory for CS-MARS Distributed Threat Mitigation (DTM). Because of low memory, CS-MARS might not be capable of downloading and activating the complete set of *active* IPS signatures to IOS IPS devices.

Table E-1   *CS-MARS V4.1 Reports (Continued)*

Report	Report Description
Resource Issues: Network—All Events	Lists event details for all events related to resource issues on network devices such as IDS, routers, firewalls, and more.
Resource Issues: Network—Top Reporting Devices	Summarizes the events that represent resource issues with network devices such as firewalls, routers, and switches.
Resource Issues: Server—All Events	Lists event details for all resource issues on hosts. These are reported by host IDS or operating system logs.
Resource Issues: Server—Top Reporting Devices	Summarizes the events that represent resource issues with servers. These are likely to be host IDS events.
Resource Utilization: Bandwidth: Inbound—Top Interfaces	Ranks the inbound bandwidth utilization of the interfaces on the devices managed by CS-MARS.
Resource Utilization: Bandwidth: Outbound—Top Interfaces	Ranks the outbound bandwidth utilization of interfaces on devices managed by CS-MARS.
Resource Utilization: Concurrent Connections—Top Devices	Ranks the number of concurrent connections established through the devices managed by PN-MARS.
Resource Utilization: CPU—Top Devices	Ranks the CPU utilization of the devices managed by CS-MARS.
Resource Utilization: Errors: Inbound—Top Interfaces	Ranks error rates on the inbound interfaces of the devices managed by CS-MARS.
Resource Utilization: Errors: Outbound—Top Interfaces	Ranks error rates on the outbound interfaces of the devices managed by CS-MARS.
Resource Utilization: Memory—Top Devices	Ranks the memory utilization of the devices managed by CS-MARS.

The purpose of this appendix is to provide you with a quick reference guide to accessing the CS-MARS device through a serial console.

CS-MARS Console Access

This book uses the web interface as the primary mode for managing your CS-MARS device and uses the keyboard and video connector for initially setting up your CS-MARS device. But if the CS-MARS device you are managing does not have a monitor and keyboard available, you need to gain access using the CS-MARS serial console.

Console access for CS-MARS enables you to connect to the device and enter the CS-MARS command-line interface (CLI). This interface enables you to enter some, but not all, of the commands that can be done through the web interface (see Appendix D, "Command-Line Interface," for a complete list of CLI commands). This mode is mostly used for initial setup and then occasionally by Cisco Technical Assistance Center (TAC) for device troubleshooting.

Using Serial Console Access

The first thing you need to do for serial console access is to connect a serial cable between your PC and the CS-MARS device. You need the following:

- Standard Cisco rolled serial cable

- Serial connection on your PC

- Terminal-emulation software on your PC

Follow these steps to establish a serial connection to your CS-MARS device:

Step 1 Connect the serial cable to the CS-MARS serial port and connect the other end to your PC.

Step 2 The CS-MARS serial cable must be plugged into the serial port shown in Figure F-1 and labeled as #1.

Figure F-1 *CS-MARS Backplane*

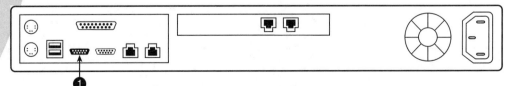

Step 3   Set the terminal emulator on your PC with the following values:

  — Baud = 19200

  — Databits = 8

  — Parity = None

  — Stops = 1

  — Flow control = None

Step 4   After these steps have been completed, you should be able to just press
Return to display the login prompt.

If this is a new installation, the default username and password will both be pnadmin.
Starting with Version 4.1 of the CS-MARS operating system, the first time you log in, you
will be prompted to change your default password.

This is for your own protection. If the default username and password were allowed to
remain the same, it would be a trivial task for an attacker who had access to your network
to gain administrative access to your CS-MARS device. You should use a hard-to-guess
password that contains special characters and has a length greater than eight characters.

See Chapter 5, "CS-MARS Appliance Setup and Configuration" for information on
initially configuring your CS-MARS device.

Note that because valuable startup information is displayed when CS-MARS is starting, it
is recommended that you use the keyboard and monitor because these messages will not be
displayed when you connect to the serial port. The serial port does not become active until
the appliance is fully booted. The first text you will see is the login prompt sequence.

The purpose of this appendix is to provide you with a quick reference guide to configuring CS-MARS to accept logs and events from the Check Point Customer Management Add-On (CMA) or Check Point SmartCenter. This appendix contains the following topics:

- Configuring Check Point NG FP3/AI and CS-MARS
- Configuring Check Point Provider-1 R60

CS-MARS Check Point Configuration

This appendix provides detailed step-by-step instructions on how to configure CS-MARS to accept events from Check Point security appliances.

Configuring Check Point NG FP3/AI and CS-MARS

This section consists of two parts. The first part explains how to configure the Check Point devices; the second part explains how to configure CS-MARS.

The following prerequisites must be met before you begin these configurations:

- The CS-MARS user must have administrative privileges.

- CS-MARS requires a Check Point management server with a username and password that has read access to perform discovery.

- Check Point user credentials with the administrative privilege are required to create an OPSEC application in the Check Point management server.

Check Point–Side Configuration

This section describes how to configure the Check Point NG FP3/AI modules to communicate with CS-MARS.

Step 1 You must first log into Check Point SmartDashboard. If you are using Provider-1, log into the SmartDashboard of the CMA.

Step 2 CS-MARS must be created as a host through the **Manage > Network Objects** menu.

You must create an OPSEC application that enables CS-MARS to use CPMI and LEA communication methods.

Step 3 Click the **Communication** button to initialize the certificate.

The "activation key" used in this process will be entered in CS-MARS in a later step.

Step 4 After the certificate is initialized, copy the SIC name. You will need this name when configuring the client SIC in the CS-MARS management interface.

Step 5 From the SmartDashboard main menu, select **Policy** and **Install Database**.

Step 6 Create firewall policies to allow CS-MARS to access the Check Point management services (default ports used: 18210, 18190, 18184) to the management/log servers.

Step 7 Install the firewall policies to all applicable targets.

Step 8 Copy the server SIC name from the management server. This will be used in the CS-MARS GUI and will be used for discovery using CPMI and for retrieving logs using LEA.

Step 9 For each additional log server managed by this SmartCenter, from **Network Objects**, double-click to view the properties. Copy the server SIC name for each additional log server to retrieve logs securely with CS-MARS using LEA.

CS-MARS Configuration

This section defines the steps necessary to configure CS-MARS so that it can communicate with the Check Point device.

Step 1 Log into CS-MARS CLI and use Telnet over the following ports to verify access to the SmartCenter and log server(s): default ports (18210-Certificate, 18190-CPMI, 18184-LEA) and the telnet a.b.c.d port.

Step 2 Log into the CS-MARS management interface.

Step 3 Navigate to **Admin > Security & Monitor Device** and create a new host (or, if it already has been created, select the existing SmartCenter host). The hostname must be exactly the same as the one used in the SmartDashboard.

Step 4 Add the Check Point management console as a reporting application.

Step 5 Configure the parameters for discovery, retrieving logs, and SIC communication.

Step 6 To enable SIC communication, a certificate needs to be retrieved from the Check Point CA:

(a) Enter the IP address of the CA; in most cases, this is the SmartCenter IP address.

(b) Copy the client SIC name from the OPSEC application created for CS-MARS.

(c) Enter the activation key that you used to initialize the certificate.

(d) Click the **Pull Certificate** button.

The certificate can be pulled only once for an OPSEC application. If you need to retrieve the certificate a second time, the certificate must be reset from the Check Point SmartDashboard.

Step 7   After providing all required fields in the Setting page of the management console of the CS-MARS UI, click the **Discover** button. If it comes back with a success message, proceed with the rest of the settings.

If it fails, click the **View Error** button to get a more detailed error message.

The following are the most common errors you might encounter during a discovery of your Check Point device:

— "Client SIC name or Server SIC name is wrong." The best way to avoid this is to use the copy and paste function from the Dashboard; this should ensure that the name is correct.

— "Invalid certificate used."

— "Invalid username or password was configured on your CS-MARS device."

— "Unsupported version of Check Point." Discovery works only with NG FP3 and above.

— "Invalid authentication method used." The default method is SSLCA. Check the fwopsec.conf file on your Check Point device and ensure that the configuration methods are correct. CS-MARS currently supports three authentication methods for CPMI communication: SSLCA, ASYM_SSLCA, and CLEAR.

— "Invalid access port." The default port of secured communication is 18180. Again using the fwopsec.conf, verify that this is the port your Check Point device is configured to use.

— "CS-MARS does not have access to port 18190 (or the one specified in fwopsec.conf) for CPMI." Try using the **telnet** command from the CS-MARS CLI to the access port.

— "Policy database was not installed after creating OPSEC application in the SmartDashboard."

— "Firewall policies were not installed permitting CS-MARS to connect to the SmartCenter."

For additional Check Point discovery-related debug information, use the CS-MARS CLI **pnlog** command. Use the **cpdebug** attribute to specify the appropriate debug level. Level 9 flushes out all debug messages. You can view the message using the **pnlog showlog cpdebug** command from the CLI.

Step 8   After successful discovery, the CS-MARS management interface displays all the modules that were discovered from the SmartCenter. This includes all standalone log servers that are managed by the SmartCenter.

Step 9   The next step is to configure all standalone log servers that were discovered:

(a)   From the discovered modules, identify all the log servers. Configure these log servers before setting the log server for firewalls.

(b)   Select the check box for the log server.

(c)   Click the **LogInfo** button.

(d)   Select the radio button **Self**. This makes the module a log server so that other firewalls can refer to it.

(e)   Type in the IP address of the log server that is reachable from CS-MARS as the reporting IP. If NAT is used between your CS-MARS device and your Check Point device, you must use the "NATted" address.

(f)   Select the certificate from the drop-down list or click the **Add** button to add a new certificate.

(g)   When you select the certificate, it automatically fills in the client SIC name. Copy and paste the client SIC name from the OPSEC application if this is different.

(h)   Copy and paste the server SIC name from the log server device in the SmartCenter. Refer to the earlier section.

(i)   Select the log authentication method: SSLCA (default), ASYM_SSLCA, or CLEAR.

(j)   Enter the log access port (default: 18184).

(k)   Click the **Submit** button.

Presently, no "test LEA" functionality is available, so the only way to verify the configuration is to "activate" it using the CS-MARS management interface and verify the connection using **netstat –an** from the CS-MARS CLI or to do a query against the device.

Step 10 Add log servers that are not managed by SmartCenter:

    (a) If any log server is missing in the discovered module, you must add it manually by clicking the **Add** button.

    (b) Select the check box for the newly created module and click the **LogInfo** button.

    (c) In the popup window, select the radio button next to Self.

Note   Refer to your Check Point log server settings to populate the applicable fields in CS-MARS.

Step 11 All firewall modules that are discovered or manually added must be associated with at least one log server in the CS-MARS UI. Configure the log info for all FW modules:

    (a) Select the check box next to Firewall Module and click the **LogInfo** button.

    (b) If the selected firewall is sending logs to the management server, select the radio button next to Management.

    (c) If the selected firewall is sending logs to a different log server, select the radio button next to Log Server.

    (d) From the drop-down list, select the log server. If this log server is not listed, select the **Add** button to define the log server, and then proceed.

Step 12 For the path and mitigation feature to work, all the modules, including the management server, and the routes need to be entered manually into the CS-MARS UI.

    (a) Click the **Route** button on the Setting page to enter routes for the management server.

    (b) Select the check box next to each of the modules and click the **Route Info** button to enter routes for the firewall/log server modules.

    (c) The SNMP Read Only community string is optional for resource utilization monitoring. Currently, it is not used for discovery and log support.

Step 13 Submit and activate:

    (a) The CS-MARS UI warns you if a module is not associated with the log server.

(b) CS-MARS UI does not warn you for routes.

(c) After a successful submit, click the **Activate** button.

Step 14 Verify the CS-MARS log server connectivity by using **netstat –an** from the CS-MARS CLI.

Step 15 Perform a query from the CS-MARS UI to view the logs.

Modifying the Communications to the SmartDashboard/CMA

If standard communications are not used in your Check Point deployment, use the following methods to discover or edit the communication parameters.

- For modifying default access types for CPMI and LEA, edit **fwopsec.conf** on the OS via administrative root access on the server that SmartCenter is installed on.

- In a Provider-1 environment, the fwopsec.conf file under **customers** needs to be edited. For example, for MLM use **fwopsec.conf** in the following directory:

  ```
  /var/opt/CPmds-R55/customers/MLM15/CPfw1-R55/conf/fwopsec.conf
  ```

  In Linux and other operating systems, the location of the file might vary.

- For either method, restart the SmartCenter/log server after modifying the fwopsec.conf file.

These points are true for customer management add-ons (CMAs), which are the SmartDashboards and customer log modules (CLMs) in a Check Point Provider-1 environment. CS-MARS does not support discovering CMAs, MLMs, and firewalls automatically from the Provider-1/MDS (multidomain server). Instead, CS-MARS users must discover each CMA, which will discover all the modules managed by that CMA.

Cisco has internally tested Provider-1 R55 with HotFix13, without changing the default parameters defined in fwopsec.conf for both discovery (CPMI) and log support (LEA).

After the CS-MARS box is "activated" with the changes, it connects to the log servers and pulls traffic logs and audit logs. The user can verify the connections by doing an ad hoc query for event types/sessions for those Check Point devices or by logging into the CS-MARS CLI and doing a **netstat –an**. The **netstat** command should display two connections per log server.

Known Open and Closed Issues

Testing with Provider-1 Version R55, Check Point Solution ID: sk14637 requires the log server to be configured to use ASYM_SSL. So in the CS-MARS UI, the log access type needs to be ASYM_SSLCA, and the fwopsec.conf file needs to be edited to have the following:

```
Edit: /var/opt/CPmds-R55/customers/MLM15/CPfw1-R55/conf/fwopsec.conf
LEA_SERVER    auth_port    18184
LEA_SERVER    auth_type    asym_sslca
LEA_SERVER    port         0
```

This file location is for the Linux OS. For another OS, refer to the Check Point manual. The port = 0 means that the log server is not listening in *clear* mode.

After editing the fwopsec.conf, restart the log server.

If discovery using CPMI requires ASYM_SSLCA, the fwopsec.conf after editing will be as follows:

```
CPMI_SERVER       auth_port       18190
CPMI_SERVER       auth_type       asym_sslca
CPMI_SERVER       port            0
```

Configuring Check Point Provider-1 R60

In Version R60 of Check Point, CS-MARS can use the same Open Platform for Security (OPSEC) application across all customer management add-ons (CMAs) and customer log modules (CLMs), by creating the OPSEC application on the Provider-1 itself. This eliminates the need for creating an OPSEC application on each CMA. This section lists the use case to create an OPSEC application from the Provider-1/SiteManager global dashboard and get the server SIC names for CMA and CLM.

To perform this procedure, you must have administrative privilege on Provider-1/ SiteManager-1.

Step 1 Log into the Provider-1/SiteManager-1 UI.

Step 2 Create CS-MARS as a Provider-1 GUI client by selecting the **GUI-Client** tab and adding a new GUI client. Make sure that you have selected the check box next to **Provider-1 GUI client**.

Step 3 Create an OPSEC application in the global dashboard of Provider-1 permitting CPMI and LEA.

Step 4 Initialize the certificate by clicking the **Communication** button on the OPSEC property page. Copy the SIC name. This will be the client SIC name used for CMA/CLM and for creating a certificate in CS-MARS.

Step 5 Save the changes made in the global dashboard. Follow the instructions on the popup message to install the policy from SiteManager-1.

Install the policy from SiteManager-1. Install additional policies to permit CS-MARS to access CMA and CLM.

Step 6 Copy the server SIC for the CMA from the SiteManager. This will be used in CS-MARS UI for discovery using CPMI.

NOTE If you have multiple CMAs, in CS-MARS you can use the same Server SIC name. For each CMA, there needs to be a Check Point management console device in CS-MARS. CS-MARS *will not* discover modules if you create a Provider-1 device and use the IP address of Provider-1 as the access IP. CS-MARS will have to use the IP address of the CMA.

INDEX

Numerics

C

H

hardware specifications for CS-MARS, 73, 301, 303–304
HIPAA (Health Insurance Portability and Accountability Act), 10
host intrusion-prevention layer (defense-in-depth), 32–33
HotSpot graph (Summary Dashboard), 213–214
hotswap command, 331

I

ICS (Cisco Incident Control Server), 31
IDSs (intrusion detection systems)
  CS-MARS communication, configuring, 170–171
  Juniper NetScreen IDP, configuring CS-MARS communication, 180
importing device information into CS-MARS, 120–121
inactive rules, 77, 265–266
in-band incident notification, 16
Incident ID field (Summary Dashboard), 208
incident ID, viewing, 229–232
incident notification, 16
incidents, 76
  path vectors, displaying, 83
  vector information, viewing in Summary Dashboard, 212–213
  viewing in Summary Dashboard, 208–211
Incidents page, 223
  Cases tab, 227–228
  False Positives tab, 225–227
  Incidents tab, 224–225
Information Summary column (Summary Dashboard), 216, 219
initial CS-MARS configuration, 108–111
  system parameters, entering, 111–113
inspection rules, 76, 256–257
  customizing, 266–270, 273
  viewing, 256

installing CS-MARS, 108
instant queries, 235
intangible costs of cyberattacks, 58–59
interaction between reporting devices and CS-MARS, 93
  agents, 95–96
  case-management tools, 97
  notification methods, 96–98
interpreting X, Y axis graphs, 219
IntruVert IntruShield v1.8
  adding to CS-MARS database, 178–180
  communication with CS-MARS, configuring, 177–178
IPSs (intrustion prevention systems)
  Cisco IPS appliance
    adding to CS-MARS database, 174–175
    configuring CS-MARS communication,171–174
  Cisco IPS Catalyst switch modules, configuring CS-MARS communication, 176
  Cisco ISR, configuring CS-MARS communication, 176–177
  Cisco SSM configuring CS-MARS communication, 177
  Enterasys Dragon, configuring CS-MARS communication, 188
  IntruVert IntruShield v1.8, configuring CS-MARS communication, 177–178
  ISS RealSecure Sensor, configuring CS-MARS communication, 183–185
  Snort IPS Sensor, configuring CS-MARS communication, 187
  Symantec ManHunt, configuring CS-MARS communication, 181
ISS (Internet Security Systems)
  network sensors, configuration scripts, 321–322
  RealSecure Sensor
    adding to CS-MARS database, 185–186
    configuring communication with CS-MARS, 183–185
  server sensors, configuration scripts, 322–323
  SiteProtector, 320

CISCO SYSTEMS

Cisco Press

3 STEPS TO LEARNING

STEP 1

First-Step

STEP 2

IP Routing
Fundamentals

A comprehensive introduction to routing
concepts and protocols in IP networks

Mark A. Sportack

Fundamentals

STEP 3

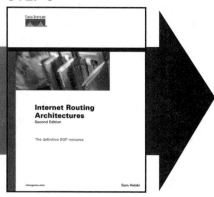

Internet Routing
Architectures
Second Edition

The definitive BGP resource

Sam Halabi

**Networking
Technology Guides**

STEP 1 **First-Step**—Benefit from easy-to-grasp explanations.
No experience required!

STEP 2 **Fundamentals**—Understand the purpose, application,
and management of technology.

STEP 3 **Networking Technology Guides**—Gain the knowledge
to master the challenge of the network.

NETWORK BUSINESS SERIES

The Network Business series helps professionals tackle the
business issues surrounding the network. Whether you are a
seasoned IT professional or a business manager with minimal
technical expertise, this series will help you understand the
business case for technologies.

Justify Your Network Investment.

Look for Cisco Press titles at your favorite bookseller today.

Visit **www.ciscopress.com/series** for details on each of these book series.

CISCO SYSTEMS

Cisco Press

CCIE PROFESSIONAL DEVELOPMENT
RESOURCES FROM EXPERTS IN THE FIELD

CCIE Professional Development books are the **ultimate resource for advanced networking professionals**, providing practical insights for effective network design, deployment, and management. **Expert perspectives, in-depth technology discussions, and real-world implementation advice** also make these titles essential for anyone preparing for a CCIE® exam.

CISCO SYSTEMS

CCIE® Professional Development
Routing TCP/IP
Volume I

A detailed examination of interior routing protocols

ciscopress.com

Jeff Doyle, CCIE No. 1919

1-57870-041-8

Look for CCIE Professional Development titles at your favorite bookseller

Cisco BGP-4 Command and Configuration Handbook
ISBN: 1-58705-017-X

Cisco OSPF Command and Configuration Handbook
ISBN: 1-58705-071-4

Inside Cisco IOS® Software Architecture
ISBN: 1-57870-181-3

Network Security Principles and Practices
ISBN: 1-58705-025-0

Routing TCP/IP, Volume I
ISBN: 1-57870-041-8

Troubleshooting IP Routing Protocols
ISBN: 1-58705-019-6

Troubleshooting Remote Access Networks
ISBN: 1-58705-076-5

Coming in Fall 2005
Cisco LAN Switching, Volume I, Second Edition
ISBN: 1-58705-216-4

Routing TCP/IP, Volume I, Second Edition
ISBN: 1-58705-202-4

Visit **www.ciscopress.com/series** for details about the CCIE Professional Development series and a complete list of titles.

Learning is serious business.
Invest wisely.

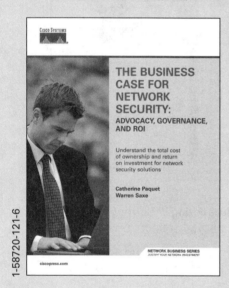

BOOKS ONLINE

ENABLED

THIS BOOK IS SAFARI ENABLED

INCLUDES FREE 45-DAY ACCESS TO THE ONLINE EDITION

The Safari® Enabled icon on the cover of your favorite technology book means the book is available through Safari Bookshelf. When you buy this book, you get free access to the online edition for 45 days.

Safari Bookshelf is an electronic reference library that lets you easily search thousands of technical books, find code samples, download chapters, and access technical information whenever and wherever you need it.

TO GAIN 45-DAY SAFARI ENABLED ACCESS TO THIS BOOK:

- Go to **http://www.ciscopress.com/safarienabled**

- Complete the brief registration form

- Enter the coupon code found in the front of this book before the "Contents at a Glance" page

If you have difficulty registering on Safari Bookshelf or accessing the online edition, please e-mail customer-service@safaribooksonline.com.